DIVE
NORTH-WEST
SCOTLAND

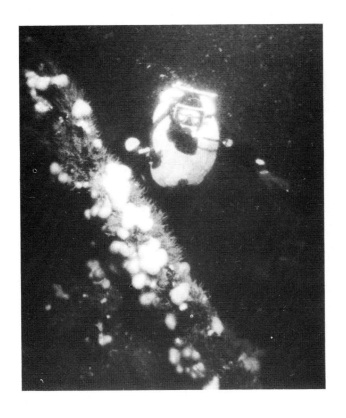

by GORDON RIDLEY

© Copyright 1985   Revised 1990
by Underwater World Publications Ltd
40 Grays Inn Road, London WC1X 8LR

Book designed and produced by Nigel Eaton

Main maps by George Lanham, Robin Gray
Photographs by Gordon Ridley
Other main illustrations by Maurice Davidson and Gordon Ridley

Typeset in Helvetica – by Inhit Ltd, 16b High St, Godalming,
and printed by The Southampton Book Company, 151 Albert Road
South, Southampton.

ISBN: 0 946020 04 3

In the same series:

This volume is dedicated
to my wife, Kathleen,
without whose total support
I would have been unable to
explore the remote
North West coast as
thoroughly.

– Gordon Ridley

CONTENTS

Area maps accompany Chapters 3-15. Smaller maps, photographs, and drawings, showing locations of particular interest are included as relevant.

Advertisers' announcements appear on pages 4, 12, 27, 41, 51, 159, 170, 183, and 197-200.

NOTE: The site numbers in this volume run on from those in Volume I, *Dive West Scotland*, which covers the area from Solway to Fort William. This numbering system will continue in Volume III for sites in the Western Isles and their outliers, the Northern Isles, and the East Coast. *See "How to use this book".*

dive  Spiro

where-ever you go!

Spiro dive shops
in Scotland:

EDINBURGH
Edinburgh Diving Centre
30 West Preston Street
Edinburgh

GLASGOW
GMT Diving Co. Ltd
520 St. Vincent Street
Glasgow

GLASGOW
Sub-C Services
16 Gardner Street
Glasgow

OBAN
Oban Divers
Laggan
Oban
Argyllshire

STORNOWAY
Engebret Ltd
Sandwick Road
Stornoway
Isle of Lewis

ABERDEEN
S.S.S. Marine
631-633 George Street
Aberdeen

Spirotechnique [UK] Ltd

Silverdale Road, Hayes, Middlesex UB3 3BE Telephone: 01-573 7615 Telex: 23247 Spiro G

Preface

Diving in Scottish waters

In Volume I of this four-part work I suggested that if you were to sample the delights of Scotland's diving, then you too would fall under its captivating spell. From the demand for the first volume and from the numerous requests for Volume II it would appear that many British divers have done just that.

It is an honour to be invited to produce a divers' guide to that immense section of coastline – the remote North-west of Scotland. It would be very easy to eulogise at length this coastline of superlatives and its diving. However, I simply make you this promise – you will never forget your best dives here in one of the last of Europe's wilderness areas. I have little doubt that I have failed to do the area justice. . . . But a start has to be made somewhere.

The opinions expressed in this volume are my own and they do not necessarily reflect on any BS-AC position I hold or have held in the past. The views that I have set out have been arrived at as the result of much thought and after many discussions with other practising, experienced, exploratory divers.

Acknowledgements

In Volume I I thanked many people for their help. As the work on the four volumes is really just one long, continuous process, those thanks are still applicable here.

So many people have helped me in gathering the information for this book that it is almost invidious to pick out anyone.

This book would not have been written without the help of two very important groups of people – my family, and my diving friends. My debt to them is enormous, and I thank them all.

I again thank my friend Dr Graham Durant for his patient advice on geology and his tolerance of my geological misconceptions. He has helped me considerably with Chapter 2.

Finally, I must thank those who have helped unstintingly with diving information. In all, about 60 people have contributed, and in Volume III I intend to list them all. However, I cannot fail to mention four friends who have each contributed information on over 100 dive sites. They are Maurice Davidson, Crawford Grier, Nick Tapp, and George Brown. George, in particular, is developing an outstanding knowledge of the sites of the North-west. Maurice supplied some of the line drawings scattered throughout the text.

Appeal for information

By the end of the third volume of this work I shall have described well over 2,000 dive sites. This represents about one dive for every three miles of the Scottish coastline! It must therefore be obvious that there are huge numbers of dive sites just waiting to be discovered. It should also be borne in mind that most of the dive sites are described from the information resulting from one visit by one diver under one specific set of conditions; caution should therefore be exercised in their interpretation and application.

The author and publisher would be very grateful, therefore, to receive any information on extra sites and conditions and for information that updates and extends those already described.

How to use this book

This work is divided into four separately-published volumes.

Each volume is divided into two parts – a detailed listing of dive sites, and a number of general sections. I must emphasise here that the general chapters at the start of each volume (Scottish Geology and Scottish Marine Life in this volume), and the appendices of each volume, are intended to be complementary. Only when the four volumes are viewed as a whole does the full pattern emerge.

Because this work covers such a large area, I have been obliged to considerably condense the information. In many cases, I possess extra information on sites (especially on some of the wreckings), and I will be pleased to correspond, via the publisher, on specific points.

Each of the chapters describing a specific diving area starts with general information on that area, and ends with details of relevant local facilities and emergency services. Note that I have not quoted details of the secretaries of local diving clubs, as these are changed frequently. The headquarters of the parent organisations (addresses in Appendix 1) can supply current lists on request.

Accommodation of various types is widely available in most of the areas covered, and it is only mentioned when there are specific reasons for this. The Scottish Tourist Board publish excellent annual booklets covering accommodation to suit all tastes. There are also accommodation guides produced by the local tourist offices.

Access to dive sites is only mentioned where it is not obvious. Generally, access is by means of a small boat; the exceptions are where there is access to shore dives from a road along the shore. Because of the complexity of the coastline and the fact that many sites are accessible by several routes, I have integrated the descriptions of small-boat, hired-MFV, shore, and wreck dives.

Sites are described in an approximately clockwise fashion from the Sound of Mull and the Isle of Mull, to Duncansby Head at the East of the North coast. Again, because of the convoluted nature of part of the coast, this has not always been applied rigorously. A number of sites which have not yet been dived have also been indicated where it is felt that they have importance. This is made clear in the text, and further information would be

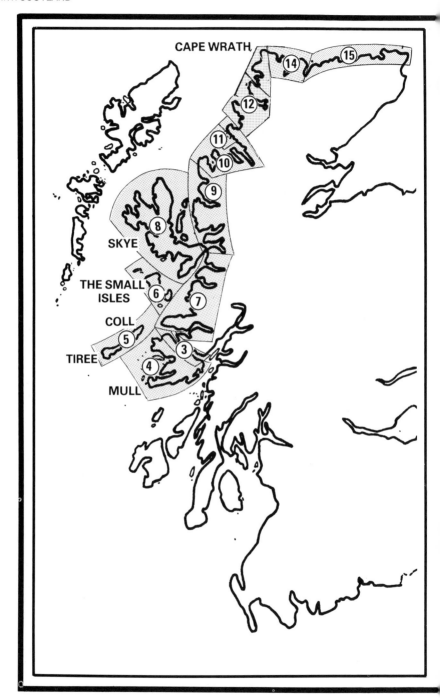

Chapter areas

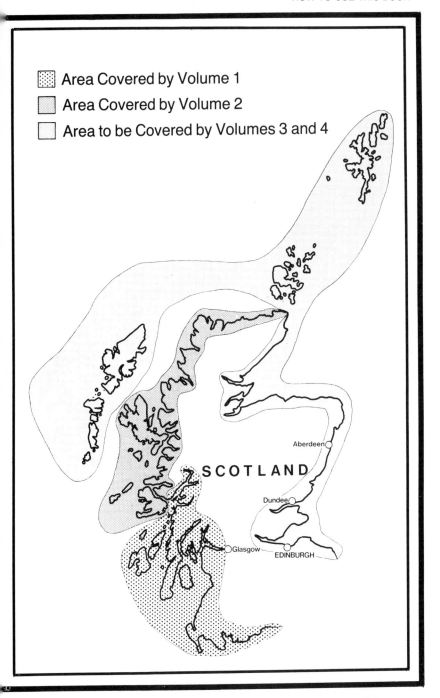

Area Covered by Volume 1
Area Covered by Volume 2
Area to be Covered by Volumes 3 and 4

SCOTLAND

Aberdeen

Dundee

Glasgow
EDINBURGH

Areas covered in Volumes I, II, III and IV

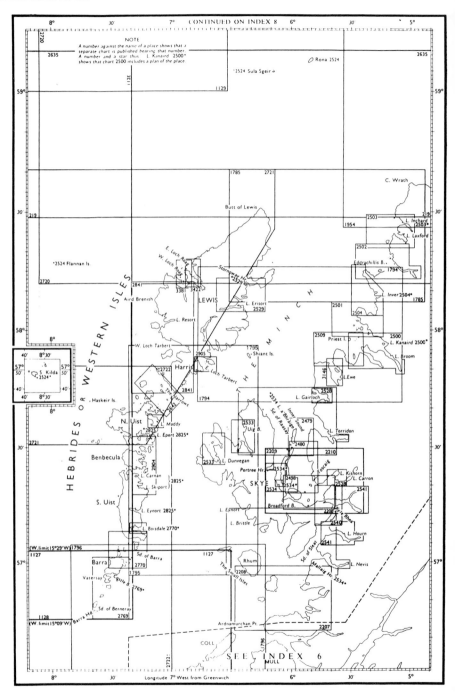

Admiralty charts for the West coast. Useful charts for sites on the North coast include 2076, 2162, 1954 and 2162.

welcome. Similarly, quite a number of wrecks are mentioned when their position may only be known approximately. These points of general information are still given site numbers for reference purposes.

Usually each numbered site refers to a specific point on the chart, but sometimes a whole area of coastline is described under one site. Each site is described in terms of access (where this is not obvious), tidal stream data (if relevant), depth and bottom profile, unusual dangers, and any special precautions that may be necessary. Attention is drawn to interesting underwater features, such as rock scenery, the marine life, and the visibility. Wrecks are briefly described, together with how to find them. There is obviously not the space to describe all the wrecks fully; however, I have included sets of transits where these are known to me and when they are appropriate. As I stated in Volume I, there is still some furtiveness in this area!

Reference is often made in this guide to Admiralty charts and Ordnance Survey maps. The information contained in these complements much of the information given in this guide, and it is *essential* that you refer to them (along with other sources of information) as frequently as possible. I have assumed, in fact, that you will use this guide in conjunction with the appropriate OS 1:50,000 map and Admiralty chart.

Six-figure national grid references are given for almost all sites, except those few that are well out to sea. Considerable care has been taken over the accuracy of their details. They are taken mainly from the OS 1:25 000 maps where these are available.

Additionally, latitudes and longitudes are given for most wrecks and offshore sites. The grid references given for wrecks are often approximate, and are (mainly) only intended to enable divers to find the general area on the map. Note that a six-figure grid reference specifies a square of side 100m, whereas latitude and longitude to seconds specifies a 31m square. (If quoted only to minutes then a 1852m square is specified.)

Bear in mind that many of the areas, especially on the West coast, do not lend themselves to ready division into chapters. It would be well to check chapters describing adjacent areas to find extra sites available from any particular base. The best way to do this is to examine the site maps for each chapter; these have all the sites numbered on them, and should give a rapid cross-check on the content of the relevant chapters.

Divers should also be reminded of my comments in Volume I about Gaelic names. Most of the sites are given the title of the land features nearest to them. These names are usually Gaelic, and I have included a short glossary in Appendix 4 so that you can check the meanings (which are often very illuminating). Grid references assume fresh importance because many of the Gaelic names are for small geographical features that may not appear on small-scale maps, and because there is also considerable duplication of some names.

CHAPTER 1

Marine life in Scottish waters

Marine life groups

The marine life of Scotland is much like that of the rest of Britain, except that some southern species are replaced by northern ones. Overall, there is a wide range of marine life groups in Scottish waters. Among those commonly encountered by divers are:

Mammals. Lots of grey seals (up to 8 ft long) are seen, and they often accompany divers at many sites. The common seal (up to 5 ft long) inhabits Scottish waters, but it breeds at sea and is seen less frequently on the remote islands than the grey seal. Dolphins and whales (including killer whales) are quite frequently sighted. Field identification of whales is notoriously difficult, and their markings never seem to match those in the keys!

Fish. Pelagic fish, by their nature, are not often seen by divers, and it is mainly the bottom-living fish that appear the commonest. The main fish of note are wrasse (ballan, cuckoo, etc), dogfish, rays, flatfish, anglerfish, lumpsuckers, conger eels, ling, cod, pollack, gobies, and blennies. Basking sharks are also common in the right places. One would expect to see the occasional large visitor from deeper waters, and in fact a sunfish has been recorded. No really large sharks have yet been seen, though medium and smaller varieties have been noted!

Crustaceans. Lobsters are found in the areas of appropriate boulder bottom, and crawfish can be common. There are both spider and hermit crabs, and edible and other crabs are common and can grow to a large size. Squat lobsters hide in cracks. Norway lobsters occur on deep muddy bottoms.

Molluscs. Topshells, limpets, and cowries, are all common. Octopus and cuttlefish are often seen. Seahares and many species of nudibranchs are very common in the right habitats.

Echinoderms. Sea urchins are common (and grow very large!) Sea cucumbers, too, are well recorded. Starfish are plentiful, with the common, purple, spiny, cushion, sun, feather, and brittle, stars all being regularly encountered.

Worms. Peacock fan worms are found in sheltered waters and at the back of the deeper sea caves. Serpulid tubeworms are found on many of the rocky surfaces.

Anthozoa. Huge numbers of anemones occur in Scottish waters, and their colonies can create quite striking underwater landscapes. Among the most notable are *Sagartia, Bolocera, Cerianthus* (burrowing), *Corynactis* (jewel), *Metridium* (plumose), *Actinia* (beadlet), and *Urticina* (dahlia). Cup coral *(Carophyllia)* is common as is soft coral *(Alcyonium)*.

Other encrusting life. Sponges (especially *Myxilla, Hymeniacidon, Ircinia,* and *Halichondria*)) are very common. *Tunicates* (especially *Dendrodoa, Clavelina,* and *Ciona*) abound. Hydroids (especially *Tubularia*) are well represented, particularly in surge gullies.

Drifting life. *Aurelia, Cyanea,* and *Rhizostoma* jellyfish are common, as are sea gooseberries and comb jellies. Long strings of salps are also common at the right time of the year. By-the-wind-sailors sometimes occur in large shoals.

Habitats

The habitats for marine life in Scottish waters are rather more varied than might at first be imagined.

The dominant species in bays with sandy bottoms are burrowing anemones, flatfish, rays, anglerfish, and crabs.

Mud slopes and bottoms are often inhabited by burrowing anemones, worms, and, (where the bottom is flat) Norway lobsters. This habitat is what most divers end up on (particularly in the firths and lochs) so you should become well used to it!

Kelp forests provide a magnificent habitat for marine life. They can be both shallow and deep, horizontal and vertical. This habitat is met on virtually all shore dives, and burrowing through the kelp can be quite rewarding in the absence of better things to do underwater. All manner of crustaceans, small fish, sponges, anemones, and nudibranchs can be seen here.

Mud and silt often cover sheltered rocks, and here the marine life is poor. The sheltered waters of dead-end caves may also offer little life, though burrowing enemones have been recorded.

The sheltered areas of deep, overhanging cliffs are a favourite haunt of tube worms, ascidians, and some anemones. Often these are dark, and a torch will be useful.

Deep bedrock seabed is often coated with *Lithothamnion* and its relatives – the encrusting purple algae. Crustaceans and fish are also common. In good visibility, this habitat can provide memorable diving.

Submarine shoals provide a magnificent oasis for life (and diving), especially when they have considerable depth around them. Encrusting life such as soft corals, anemones, sponges, and hydroids, is common, and both large shoals and solitary fish can usually be seen.

Exposed vertical walls are usually inhabited by sponges, anemones

Lobsters are common in Scotland in areas with boulder bottoms.

(especially jewel anemones), soft coral, hydroids, and nudibranchs. This habitat offers excellent potential for macro photography, and is usually enjoyed by all divers.

Exposed surge gullies and tunnels are inhabited by similar species to exposed vertical walls, though the strong surges of water make it more likely that robust species will colonise successfully. They are also favourite haunts for seals.

Among the best habitats for marine life are areas with strong tidal streams. Both fish life and encrusting life are particularly rich. The rocks are often solidly colonised by soft corals.

Wrecks provide an interesting habitat, too. In rocky areas they are inhabited by the same species that live in the nearby rocks. Their nooks and crannies are also a favourite haunt for conger eels and fish. In muddy areas such as the Firth of Clyde they provide an oasis of firm substrate for life to colonise. As such they can be very rewarding.

Areas with heavy freshwater run-off are found near the heads of a number of sea-lochs with shallow sills. The water will actually stay in two layers if undisturbed, though usually it mixes to become brackish. Most sea life cannot tolerate such conditions, though flounders seem very happy!

There are occasional sites where fresh-water springs emerge underwater in the sea. The life here can be quite unusual, with strange sponges and hydroids often present.

Vertical zonation

When steep rocks drop into deep water there is a characteristic zonation of life as the depth increases.

Typically, there is an extended upper zone of black lichen and dark-green seaweed which is often fertilised by bird droppings. This is followed by a wide band of dulse and sometimes limpets, and on sheltered shores there are fucoid seaweeds. Then there is a deep zone of barnacles.

Moving down to the zones that are completely underwater at all times, the first band is the alaria zone, composed largely of oarweeds and coralline algae. The kelp zone then usually forms an extensive forest from 6-30m, and can even be found deeper than 30m, indicating the extent of the water clarity. The kelp forest may be absent at very exposed sites, and it is then replaced with the characteristic carpet of anemones, tunicates, tubularia and sponges. Below this zone is an area of soft coral and some cup coral. Deep rocks and the seabed do not have as much life, though the deep shoals are often covered with coralline algae. Very deep sites often have a brittlestar carpet.

Zonation around the coast

The Solway is very sandy and muddy with strong tides and poor visibilty. The West Coast and Inner and Outer Hebrides are all substantially affected by the Gulf Stream, and their life is Atlantic in character, with habitats ranging over the full spectrum. The Hebridean Outliers are oceanic islands, with wave-washed rocky habitats. The Northern Isles are similar to the West Coast, though a little cooler.

The North Sea tends to be sandy and muddy. It is also considerably colder in winter, and its marine life is therefore rather more restricted than in the other areas.

Other wildlife

The interface of land and sea provides a rich habitat for many species. These include seals and several other marine creatures as well as the many seabirds which help make Scotland a paradise for bird enthusiasts.

The auks (puffin, guillemot, razorbill, black guillemot) abound on the ledges of the sea cliffs of North-west Scotland and the islands, and can make a visit to the areas in the late spring particularly memorable. The gannet is the Scottish seabird par excellence; the massive colonies at St Kilda are the biggest in the world. Of the petrels, the fulmar is now ubiquitous, but the Manx shearwater is restricted to the islands, and the storm and Leach's petrels are only found breeding on the Hebridean Outliers. The arctic and great skuas are birds of the northern moors and islands; they feed by harrying other seabirds in flight and seizing their catch.

Of the inland water birds, one of the first species to colonise the northern lochs after the last glaciation was the black-throated diver, which is able to swim 400m underwater. This was followed by the red-throated diver, the ptarmigan, the whimbrel (a small, northern curlew), the dotterel, the golden plover, and the tiny red-necked phalarope. The great northern diver now breeds at higher latitudes, though it is still seen in Scotland in winter.

CHAPTER 2

The Geology of Scotland

The Scottish coast

One of the most striking features of the Scottish coastline is the difference between the West and East coasts. The West is higher, much indented by narrow sea-lochs, and fringed for much of its length by two lines of islands. In contrast, the East is lower, though often cliff-lined, and has only five main inlets.

The North coast is similar to the West coast, though on a smaller scale. The South-west coast, between Clyde and Solway, is often fringed with moderate cliffs. To the South there are several wide bays.

From Cape Wrath to Loch Broom, the coast is rugged and intensely glaciated. Further inland there are high mountains. North of Gairloch and the Applecross peninsula, the hinterland is a high plateau. South of Loch Alsh, the mountains almost reach the coast, making Lochs Hourn and Nevis into the finest sea-lochs in Scotland.

The proximity of Skye and Mull to this section of coast emphasises the mountainous scenery. The coast South of Oban is ruggedly indented, though heights now begin to fall. By the time that Knapdale and Kintyre are reached, the hinterland is generally about 300m high, though the Mull of Kintyre is higher. Arran is mountainous, but the coastal fringe is low, though backed by high ground.

There are also extensive flat areas along the coast. These are much commoner on the East coast, though there are some superb little beaches along the North coast, and also a surprising number on the West coast, too. Between the flat and sandy areas there are many cliffs – some of them reaching 120m in height. On the East coast these are of sedimentary origin; and although this is also the case on the West coast, North of Skye (where the cliffs are of Torridonian sandstone) large areas of intensely glaciated gneiss and great sheets of basalt give the West coast cliffs a different appearance.

The Outer Hebrides almost mirror the mainland by having a flat and largely-sandy West coast, and a very glaciated, rugged, and cliffed, East coast.

Where sea-lochs meet the sea it is very difficult to distinguish between

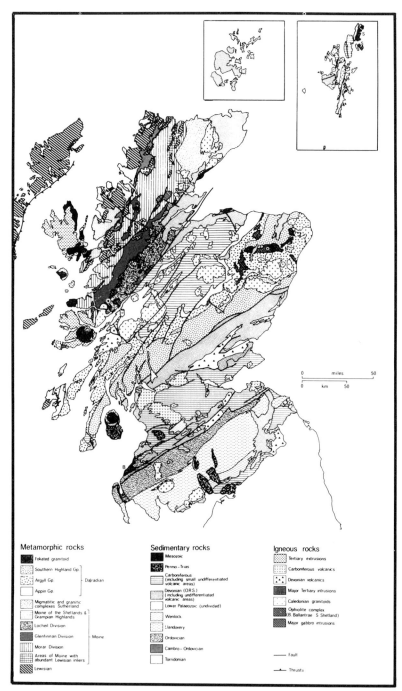

Metamorphic rocks

- Foliated granitoid
- Southern Highland Gp.
- Argyll Gp. } Dalradian
- Appin Gp.
- Migmatitic and granitic complexes Sutherland
- Moine of the Shetlands & Grampian Highlands
- Lochiel Division
- Glenfinnan Division } Moine
- Morar Division
- Areas of Moine with abundant Lewisian inliers
- Lewisian

Sedimentary rocks

- Mesozoic
- Permo-Trias
- Carboniferous (including small undifferentiated volcanic areas)
- Devonian (O.R.S.) (including undifferentiated volcanic areas)
- Lower Palaeozoic (undivided)
- Wenlock
- Llandovery
- Ordovician
- Cambro-Ordovician
- Torridonian

Igneous rocks

- Tertiary extrusions
- Carboniferous volcanics
- Devonian volcanics
- Major Tertiary intrusions
- Caledonian granitoids
- Ophiolite complex (B. Ballantrae S Shetland)
- Major gabbro intrusions

- —— Fault
- ▲—▲ Thrusts

Geological map of Scotland

true sea cliffs and a steep slope caused by ice action on the sides of the fiord. Additionally, very little of the coast of Scotland is directly the work of waves on the modern shore. It is a 'secondhand' coast, whose cliffs and other features were formed at least 5,000 years ago.

The geology of Scotland

The coastal scenery of the islands and mainland of Scotland is extremely variable. Steep cliffs characterise many parts of the coastline, whereas elsewhere the topography is much more subdued. Such differences, noticeable to any visitor to the Scottish coastline, reflect Scotland's rich geological heritage.

A glance at the geological map of Scotland shows that there are many different rock types forming the part of the Earth's crust which is now Scotland. In fact, the diversity of rock types of different ages within Scotland makes it one of the most complex geological regions in Europe, if not the world.

Scotland has a long and complex geological history, with the oldest rocks dating back some 3,000 million years. These rocks form part of the mainland in North-west Scotland and the Outer Hebridean islands (from where they derive their name of Lewisian). They are crystalline gneisses derived from pre-existing rocks by metamorphism at high temperatures and pressures. They characteristically form low, undulating scenery.

On the mainland to the North of Skye the Lewisian gneisses are overlain *unconformably* (ie, involving a break in the sedimentary process) by horizontally-bedded, brownish-red sandstones of Torridonian age. These 900-million-year-old rocks, and the underlying Lewisian gneiss, form the coastal scenery from Kyle to Cape Wrath.

The Inner Hebridean islands are principally the product of a much more recent geological event. Fifty-five million years ago, in the Tertiary period, a chain of volcanoes stretched from St Kilda southwards through the present-day islands of Skye, Rum, Mull, and Arran, into the Northern Ireland area. The result of this volcanic episode was the eruption of a series of lava flows which now form the terraced scenery which characterises northern Skye and western Mull. The rocks of many of the smaller islands such as Canna, Sanday, Muck, and Staffa, also formed in this way. The molten rock which did not erupt as lava flows cooled slowly within the Earth's crust to form coarsely crystalline rocks which have now been revealed at the surface by erosion and which form the rugged hills of Skye, Rum, Ardnamurchan, central Mull, and northern Arran. One other product of this Tertiary volcanic activity was the emplacement of some molten rock into linear fissures, and this is now preserved as dykes which are conspicuous along the coastline of much of the Inner Hebridean islands.

From the Oban area southwards, the coastal scenery is the result of the differential erosion of the harder (quartzite, metabasalt), and softer (slates, schists) rocks of Dalradian age. These 600-million-year-old rocks form the characteristic scenery of Lorne, the Kintyre area, and into the Firth of Clyde. Near to Oban itself, the Dalradian rocks are overlain by sedimentary rocks, and lavas of Old Red Sandstone aged about 350 million years. These are conspicuous South of Oban on Kerrera and the mainland.

In the South of Scotland, the coastline from Girvan southwards is formed

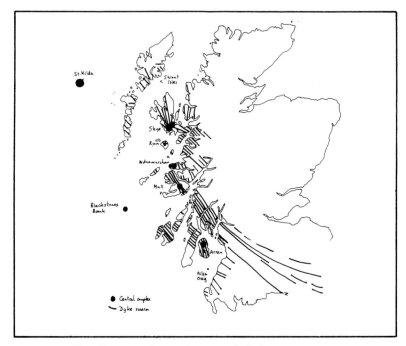

Tertiary volcanoes and dyke swarms

of Ordovician and Silurian sedimentary rocks (460-410 millon years old). North of Girvan into the Clyde estuary, the coastline is formed of sedimentary Carboniferous rocks (360-285 million years old), and these reappear along the eastern Scottish coastline from St Andrews southwards.

North of St Andrews, Old Red Sandstone sediments and lavas crop out along the shore as far as Stonehaven, and these reappear in the Moray Firth, around the Caithness coast, and in the Orkney Islands.

The Banffshire coast is formed of Dalradian rocks similar to those seen in the West of Scotland, although the rocks in the East have been affected by greater amounts of metamorphism than those in the West.

The relationship of all these various geological units to one other is not simple. Some rock units have been juxtaposed by faulting; other contacts are conformable, unconformable, or intrusive (ie, where molten magma has forced its way into gaps and solidified into igneous rock). The geology of the individual areas is usually the product of smaller-scale local features, and it is these which can control the nature of individual dive sites.

The coastal scenery is primarily influenced by the rock types exposed, but it is also the result of the more recent geological history of Scotland. In the Quaternary period (ie, the last 2 million years) Scotland was subjected to several periods of glaciation. The ice sheets and glaciers caused great erosion, and sculptured the Scottish scenery into its present form. Deposits from the retreating ice sheets blanket many of the rock areas of Scotland, and cover large areas of the continental shelf.

The structure of Scotland

The well-known division of Scotland into Northern Highlands, Central Highlands, Midland Valley, and Southern Uplands, is easily justified in terms of faults. The Great Glen Fault (running from Loch Linnhe, to the Moray Firth) divides the Northern and Central Highlands; the Midland Valley is separated from the Central Highlands by the Highland Boundary Fault (from the Clyde to Stonehaven), and from the Southern Uplands by the Southern Uplands Fault (from Dunbar to Loch Ryan).

There is a further important break in the North-west – the so-called Moine Thrust. The rocks here were thrust in a West-north-west direction over the underlying ground, on a line from the Sound of Sleat to Loch Eriboll.

The Great Glen is thought to have been subject to a shear when the North-west of Scotland moved to the South-west. This is justified by similar masses of granite being found 65 miles apart at Strontian and Foyers. The Great Glen Fault itself extends northwards to the Black Isle and Tarbat Ness, and then right up to the eastern side of the Orkney Isles (where it joins the Walls Boundary Fault) passing through the Shetland Isles. To the South, it runs as far as Colonsay, having passed through South-east Mull.

The origins of the Minch are somewhat obscure. The collapse of a lava plateau may be associated with the eastern submarine cliff, but the whole of the Long Island seems to have been subject to shearing along the Minch Fault because there are similar areas of Lewisian gneiss between Loch Laxford and Little Loch Broom on the mainland, and the area from the Sound of Harris to Loch Eynort in the Outer Hebrides.

Faulting and thrusting plays a quite important part in accounting for the Scottish coastline, though many of the features were superimposed on the faults after their formation.

As mentioned earlier, a belt of Lewisian and Torridonian rocks run from Loch Eriboll to the Sound of Sleat. The gneiss forms a characteristic glaciated, hummocky coastline, with many rounded, low islands lying off the shore. It also forms dramatic cliffs, such as those at Cape Wrath. The gneiss in the Outer Hebrides forms good cliffs between Gallan Head and Husinish Point, on the East coast, and at the Butt of Lewis. Sandstones also form excellent cliffs if the bedding is horizontal or inclined landwards. If it dips to the sea, the slope to the sea is gentle, and it may be ledged.

Moinian rocks make up the coast on the West from Loch Hourn to Loch Linnhe, and on the North from Whiten Head to Strathy Bay. Dalradian rocks make up the Banff coast, the coast from MacDuff to Aberdeen, and also the West coast from Loch Linnhe to Kintyre. However, in Banff the rocks are highly folded and form 30m-high cliffs. The North-eastern corner of Aberdeenshire consists of fine, sandy bays between low headlands of metamorphic rocks. There is a granite mass around Peterhead.

The Old Red Sandstone forms some of the most spectacular cliffs in Britain. They are often well jointed, and impressive *geos* are cut into the lines of weakness. These can be clearly seen at Dunnet and Duncansby Heads. They reappear at Tarbat.

As previously noted, the Tertiary volcanic area of the West includes Skye, the Small Isles, the western end of the Ardnamurchan peninsula, Mull and the Treshnish Isles, Staffa, Arran, the Blackstones Igneous Centre, and St Kilda. There are no other comparable areas in Britain, and the cliff scenery is magnificent.

The eastern coast of the Midland Valley is much longer than the western coast. The rocks are almost wholly Old Red Sandstone and Carboniferous. On both sides of the Firth of Forth there are numerous plugs and vents of former volcanoes. The Clyde coast is similar, but more sheltered. Arran is a separate entity.

The Southern Uplands are mainly closely folded Ordovician and Silurian sediments. On the East, around Burnmouth and Fast Castle, the coastal scenery is spectacular, including the igneous mass of St Abb's Head. In the South-west, the coast from Girvan to Balcary Point is composed of the same sediments, though the most characteristic feature is the succession of raised beaches.

The major inlets on the Scottish coast

The river system of Scotland. First, we must examine how the river system of Scotland came into being. This is usually explained in terms of Scotland being part of a continental land-mass which stretched from Ireland to Scandinavia in the early Tertiary period. Most rivers flowed from the main watershed (created by uplift) near the present West coast in a South-easterly direction to a Miocene sea (about 25 million years ago). But as a result of river capture and glaciation, the West-East courses are now much broken up.

The subsequent rise in sea-level caused the lower parts of the valleys cut by these rivers to be converted into sea-lochs. Much more ice came from the Scandinavian glaciers than from those of eastern Scotland; consequently the eastern valleys were not as long, and only some of their upper portions resemble the the western sea-lochs.

The major sea-lochs of Scotland. There is some disagreement as to the relative importance of rift valleys associated with faults as opposed to the work of ice during periods of glaciation in the formation of the sea-lochs.

In North-west Scotland, the sea-lochs run South-east to North-west; in the middle of the West coast they run East-West; and further south they run North-east and South-west. In many cases, a fault created a line of weakness for a stream, and later glacial ice, to follow.

It is convenient to classify sea-lochs into types 'A', 'B', and 'C'. Type 'A' sea-lochs have deep-water entrances and no sills; consequently, they are easily penetrated by sea water, and might be thought of as estuarine sea-lochs. Types 'B' and 'C' are fiordic sea lochs, and are partially separated from the main coastal waters by relatively shallow submarine barriers or sills which create inner basins. Type 'B' sea-lochs have a single sill, while type 'C' have two or more sills.

Fiordic sea-lochs experience more extreme conditions than the nearby open sea. They are hotter in summer, and colder and less saline in winter. In summer, there is also less oxygen in the water of the deeper basin. The severity of these effects depends on relative sill depth and width, tidal range, freshwater inflow, and wind.

The sea-lochs table (which includes selected sea straits and fiordic freshwater lochs) emphasises their differences as well as their similarities (the East coast inlets are included mainly for comparison). Undoubtedly, ice has played a prominent part in shaping pre-existing valleys, some of which have been associated with faulting. An examination of the charts covering the West of Scotland show that the valleys of the sea-lochs were at one time the headwaters of a major system of Hebridean rivers, which extended as far seawards as the edge of the continental shelf. The sea-floor over which these rivers were to flow consisted of thick flows of basalt with dykes of dolerite; that this was then subject to extensive collapse is shown by the way that many of the volcanic Inner Hebrides end in abrupt cliffs.

The origins of the Firth of Clyde, the North Channel, and the Solway Firth, are difficult to explain. The general view is that the whole area has become submerged, having in the past been part of a large land-mass stretching right to Ireland, with rivers draining to the South-west. The Clyde flowed in the opposite direction to its present course. The Solway was much as at present, and most of the rivers were tributaries of a river flowing South through the North Channel. The Firth of Clyde was the southward extension of the Loch Long river.

Recent movements of the Scottish coast

Although this complex subject has been the target of much learned investigation, there are still large areas that are not adequately documented or explained.

The levels of both the land and the sea have altered considerably in geologically-recent times. It is estimated that, at maximum glaciation, sea level may have fallen by up to 120m. The ice thus formed weighed heavily upon the land and depressed it considerably. As the ice melted, the sea-level rose, and the land, released from the weight of the ice, also rose. The level of the sea relative to the land of Scotland therefore depends on the relative magnitudes of these two factors.

Additionally, the block that makes up Scotland is very slowly tilting – falling in the West, and rising in the East. The *eustatic* water movement (worldwide change in sea-level due to ice sheet growth/decay, sediment deposition, and volume changes in ocean basins) is measured in millimetres per century at the present time. But the *isostatic* recovery of the land (slow crustal movements) has varied from about 8.5m per 1,000 years 12,000 years ago, to 0.7m per 1,000 years in the last 4,000 years.

The remains of raised beaches in Scotland have been recognised for some considerable time. But it is now realised that the concept of '100ft' '50ft', '25ft', and '15ft', levels is rather too simple. Levels centred around 100ft and 25ft are now considered more important, though even these represent a simplification because of the balancing of movements. It was merely fortuitous when an old shore-level remained constant over some distance at, say, a height of 30m, and it is much more normal for features from the same ancient sea level to be found at many different levels. Nevertheless, it is helpful to think of the '30m' and '8m' levels.

The mechanism of their formation is essentially this:
1. The '30m', or Late-glacial, beach was formed at the time of large glaciers. The land was depressed by the weight of ice resting upon it.
2. Much later sea-level continued to fall until it reached a level of about 60m below its present one about 11,000 years ago. About seven or eight different raised beaches were formed in the period 13,000-12,000 years ago. During this time, sea-level actually fell by some 30m in 2,000 years.

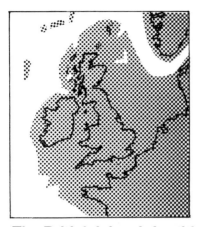

The British Isles: left, with maximum ice-caps; right, if all the ice had melted

3. The ice melted, and sea-level rose above that of the present. The '8m', or Post-glacial, level was thus formed about 6,900-6,600 years ago.

4. Since then, there have been further fluctuations, but sea-level has generally fallen relative to the land of Scotland. This is corroborated by the fact that Loch Lomond (present elevation +8.5m) became a freshwater loch about 5,500 years ago, and Loch Shiel (+3.5m) about 4,200 years ago. However, another raised beach was formed in the Solway about 2,000 years ago.

Shorelines cut in rock occur at heights of up to 51m. The associated rock platforms can be over half-a-mile wide, though they are often much narrower. The backing cliffs can be up to 90m high. Shore platforms are absent from much of the mainland coast mainly because glacier ice covered these areas when the platforms were being cut. Other raised shorelines were formed, then glaciated, and may now be overlain by till (deposits from receding glaciers).

On the central section of the West coast the Late-glacial beach declines steadily in height in all directions away from Callander in Stirlingshire. The Post-glacial beach shows a tilt that varies with direction from Callander. The rate of these declines is measured in terms of fractions of a foot per mile. Both groups of beaches are tilted, so what is regarded as the same beach may be at very different heights in different places.

The finest examples of raised beaches in Scotland occur in western Jura and North-east Islay. They are older than other raised beaches, and may actually be Inter-glacial.

On the North coast four main types of features are recognised:

☐ Rock shelves or platforms backed by cliffs, usually much degraded.

☐ Flat, usually irregular, features produced by wave action, but not backed by cliffs.

☐ Deposition features found mainly in more sheltered places.

☐ Terraces cut in glacial drifts, often close to the mouths of large rivers.

Cliffs in northern Scotland normally descend far below the present sea level. At their bases there is an often-considerable gradient to the 'final break of slope', beyond which lies the gently-undulating seabed. This final break is about −90m in Shetland, −60-65m around Orkney and the adjacent mainland, and about −55m at Peterhead.

East coast raised beaches have been studied in detail, and four types of shorelines have been identified:

☐ Late-glacial (formed before the Perth re-advance, which occured about 9,500 years ago).

☐ Raised shorelines associated with the Perth re-advance.

☐ Buried shorelines.

☐ Visible Post-glacial shorelines.

There is a scarcity of raised beaches in both Orkney and Shetland. This may be explained by suggesting that the Northern Isles are descending relative to Caithness, and therefore the beaches have been submerged. There is also plenty of evidence of submergence in the Outer Hebrides, but little sign of raised beaches.

The underwater geology of Scotland

Evolution of the North Atlantic Ocean. Two hundred million years ago the North Atlantic did not exist as an ocean; the continental plates of North America, Greenland, and Western Europe, were joined in one huge land-mass. Then, about 170 million years ago, a split began to form between America and Europe – the Atlantic Ocean was born!

The split continued to widen as new crust erupted from the mid-Atlantic Ridge. About 100 million years ago the split started to move northwards as the Greenland and European plates moved apart – first along the Porcupine Seabight, then along the Rockall Trough. This movement of Greenland and Rockall away from Europe stopped about 75 million years ago, when the spreading zone moved 900 miles to form the current spreading axis between Greenland and the Rockall Plateau. The rate of spreading was originally 1.7cm/year; this fell to 0.7cm/year during the Lower Tertiary, then rose to the present rate of 1.18cm/year.

Active sea-floor spreading around the Reykjanes Ridge (South-west of Iceland) has been taking place since the beginning of the Tertiary period, 60 million years ago. The initial break-up of the Greenland-Rockall Plate was accompanied by an outburst of volcanic activity – covering vast areas of South-east Greenland, Iceland, the Faeroe Islands, Rockall Plateau, Northern Ireland the Inner Hebrides, and western Scotland with lava – which has continued to the present day in Iceland, which actually lies across the mid-Atlantic Ridge.

Basins off Scotland. A chain of several deep basins extends northwards across the continental shelf West of Britain. These are thought to represent abortive attempts in the separation of the Greenland – Rockall Plate. The structure of the shelf of western Scotland is controlled by the four main faults – the Minch Fault, the Camasunary-Skerryvore Fault, the Great Glen Fault, and the Outer Hebrides Fault. These faults form the margins of a number of deep, sediment-filled troughs whose depths were gradually increased by tensional stresses during the Tertiary and Mesozoic periods.

Two troughs – the Sule Sgeir and West Shetland basins – lie to the North of Scotland. But, in contrast with the West of Scotland, there is only one major basin lying off eastern Scotland in the North Sea.

Seabed characteristics. The waters of Scotland are bounded by the mid-Atlantic Ridge in the West; by the European continental shelf to the East; and to the North by a smooth, relatively-shallow area between Scotland and Greenland. The shelf margin (variously defined as the 100-fathom or 200-metre isobath) varies in width and gradient and has a sedimentary cover mainly derived from erosion of the land.

The shelf runs about 60-70 miles West of the Outer Hebrides, and located on it are a number of shoals, the most important being the 80 square miles of the Stanton Banks about 40 miles South of Barra Head. West of the Outer Hebrides, the seabed consists of coarse sand, stone, and shell, though near to the shore sand predominates. In the Minch, the seabed is hard and stony, with isolated patches of sand and mud. Off the mainland coast, sand and shell dominate, though these are replaced by mud in the lochs and bays. Within the 40m isobath, the whole Scottish coast (except the East) abounds with rocks, islets, and reefs, though again in the lochs these are covered by sedimentary mud.

Further information

The geological history of Scotland is an exceedingly complex and many-threaded story stretching over 3,000 million years! That the story is very complicated is demonstrated by the number of specialist publications on the subject (though there are fewer on the underwater geology). Divers can learn more by consulting the following works:

The Coastline of Scotland, Steers, 1973.
Geology and Scenery in Scotland, Whittow, 1977.
Highland Landforms, Price, 1976.
Admiralty Underwater Handbook to the Western Approaches to the British Isles, 1970.
Geology of the North west European Continental Shelf, Naylor & Mounteney, 1975 (Vols. I & II).
Evolution of Scotland's Scenery, Sissons, 1967.
Hydrography of Scottish West Coast Sea-lochs, Milne, 1972.
Geology of Scotland, Craig, 1983 (2nd edition).
Britain Before Man, Geological Museum, 1979.
On the Rocks, Wood, 1978
British Regional Geology – 1. *Grampian Highlands,* Johnstone, 1966; 2. *Northern Highlands,* Phemister, 1960; 3. *South of Scotland,* Greig, 1971; 4. *Midland Valley of Scotland,* Pringle, 1948; 5. *Tertiary Volcanic Districts* Richey, 1961; 6. *Orkney & Shetland,* Mykura, 1976.
Geology of the Sea of the Hebrides, Binns, McQuillin, Kenolty, 1974.
Geology of the Malin Sea, Evans, Kenolty, Dobson, Whittington, 1982.

THE BALANCED SYSTEM
WITH PRECISION INSTRUMENTS

◉Tabata

DIVING SUPPLIES INTERNATIONAL LTD.
UNIT 2 FACTORY ESTATE, ENGLISH STREET
HULL HU3 2BE NORTH HUMBERSIDE
Telephone (0482) 25772

For diver's kit send £1.50 —
includes catalogue and decals.

Diving the Hispania, one of the top Scottish wrecks outside Scapa Flow.

CHAPTER 3

The Sound of Mull

Dividing Mull into two chapters may seem a little strange, but the diving in the Sound of Mull is, in fact, of a quite different calibre to that of most of the rest of Mull. The area is also more accessible.

The diving in the Sound of Mull is of a very high order. There are several excellent wrecks including the *Hispania*, which many divers consider the best-preserved large wreck in Scottish waters. There are sensational underwater cliffs and drop-offs at Lochaline, Pennygown Quarry, Calve Island, Auliston Point, which are among the best 'wall' dives in Scotland. In addition, there are also some excellent rocky islets.

Returning to the wrecks, there is the added flavour of at least two old wrecks; the Spanish galleon of Tobermory, which is supposed to contain a treasure of 30 million ducats; and the wreck of the *Dartmouth*. What may not be so well known is that Bloody Bay at the North of the Sound was the scene of a sea battle between John, last Lord of the Isles, and his son Angus. Nothing more is known, but it is interesting to speculate on what might have happened to any vessels lost.

The Sound of Mull separates Mull from the mainland by a distance of 1-2 miles. Depths in the main part of the Sound range from 37-91m. Near Auliston there is a deep channel at 59-110m leading to Loch Sunart. At the East side of the South end of the Sound the depths are 91-128m.

The Sound of Mull is accessible in a number of ways. A long boat journey from Oban is undertaken by some groups with inflatables. The road round Morven can also be taken, and this is probably the cheapest way. A third way is via the ferry to Mull (from Oban or Lochaline). And finally, the most luxurious way is to hire a charter boat.

Lochaline Dive Centre is an excellent new centre run by Douglas and Jayne Lamont. It provides first class facilities for the visiting diver. Self-catering accommodation is available in 12 twin rooms, each with private facilities. Catering is in a large kitchen with an adjacent dining room. There is also an old church which has been converted into a centrally-heated bunkhouse for 10 in 4 rooms. There is a dining room and a fully-equipped kitchen. Accommodation can also be provided in a residential 6-berth caravan and in local B&B establishments. Diving out of Lochaline Dive Centre is via a hard boat (with 2 dives per day including hot drinks) or with assault craft. Compressed air facilities are very efficient by virtue of a 24 cu ft/min compressor and 4000psi air bank. There are good launching facilities, free moorings and spacious parking.

Mull is serviced by Mull Diving Centre on Salen Pier. The centre offers the

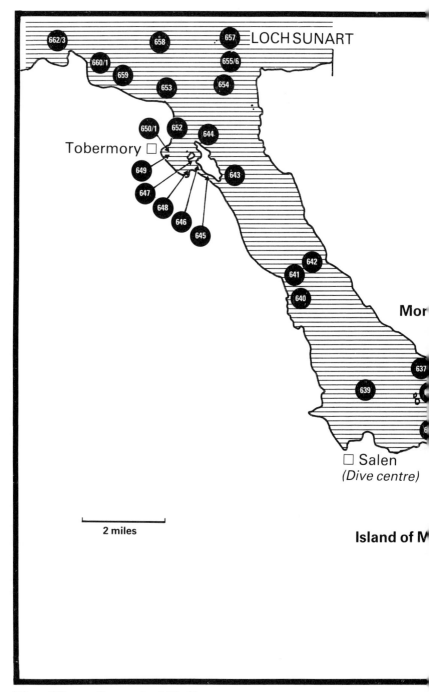

Dive Sites : Sound of Mull

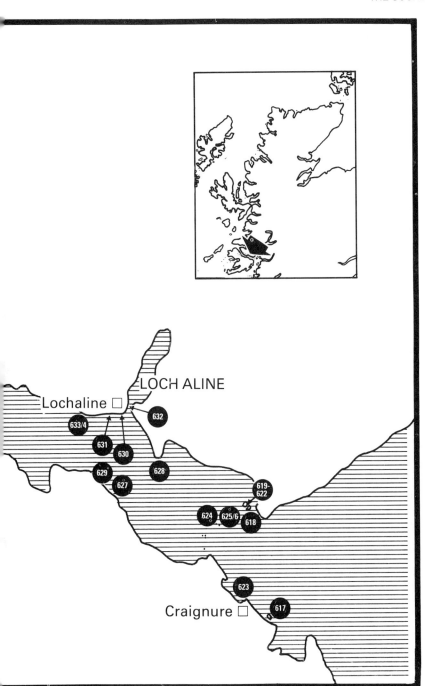

LOCH ALINE

Lochaline

632

633/4

631

630

629

627

628

619-
622

624 625/6 618

623

Craignure

617

normal range of facilities to divers, and, although I have never stopped there, divers speak highly of the facilities and the staff.

Dive sites

The dives in this chapter are described from the South-east of the Sound of Mull, to the North-west.

The Sound of Mull is accessible from Mull diving centre, at Salen, though divers have taken inflatables as far as the wreck of the *Rondo,* which is a 38-mile round-trip from Oban. In fact, a 6m rigid-keel inflatable has been taken right round Mull from Oban, a distance of almost 90 miles, in 3 hours!

Sites 617-624 can be approached from Salen, Lochaline, Craignure, or Oban, depending on your base.

617 Sgeir Ruadh. NM732363.* A muddy slope falling steadily to 20m, then more steeply to beyond 40m. Not particularly recommended.

618 Wreck of the Thesis. NM729404. This wreck lies 350m North-west of the South tip of Morvern and about 50m from the shore. It is quite easy to locate with an echo-sounder. The wreck is lying at right angles to the shore, with the bows at 12m and the stern at 30m. The boat was lost in 1891, and has been substantially salvaged by Richard Grieve of Salen Diving Centre. She is 50m long, and many of the plates have been blown off, especially those around the bows. The vessel is, however, still basically intact. Encrusted with life, with plentiful fish life, and with crockery still to be found, the wreck makes an excellent dive. Tidal streams run at up to 2 knots. LW slack +0055 Dover.

619 Wreck of the Girl Sandra. NM726404. This is the wreck of a 10m tug lying in depths of 2-4m with a 45 degree list to starboard at the South of Eilean Rubha an Ridire. She was lost in 1981, and the prop and all the portholes have already gone.

620 Wreck of the Ballista. NM723406. This is the wreck of a fishing boat lost in 1975. She lies at the North-east tip of Eilean Rubha an Ridire. Her masts show above the water, so she is easily located. The toilet on the *Ballista* is still in working order and has a plumose anemone living in it. The iron prop is accessible.

621 Wreck of a salvage barge. NM723406. This lies directly underneath the *Ballista* and was lost in about 1940.

622 Wreck of HMS Dartmouth. NM724407. Lost in 1690, the Royal Navy frigate *HMS Dartmouth* was 25m long and carried 32 guns. She was found in 1973 by Bristol Undersea Archaeology Group, and was a protected historic wreck site for several years. Substantial surveying and salvage has now been completed, and the artefacts are in the Scottish Museum. Now

* Reminder: Site numbers in this volume of The Diver Guide to Scotland run on from those in Volume 1.

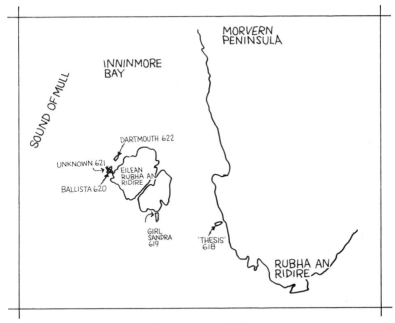

Sites 618-623

that the group has stopped working on the vessel the site is completely kelp-covered. The depth is 10m.

623 Craignure Bay. NM722370. A rather uninteresting dive at 10m over a bottom of flat rocks, silt, and sand.

624 Glas Eilean. NM715399. On the South side of the group of islets the cliffs drop to 16m and open out into a field of soft corals which cover everything. An excellent dive, but beware of strong tidal streams (see Site 618).

625 Wreck of the River Tay. NM723399. This wreck lies at approximately 56 30 00N 05 42 00W. The depth here is 30m.

626 Wreck of the Aleksander. NM723399. This lies in the same position as the *River Tay*.

627 Avon Rock. NM673421. This rock reaches to within 2m of chart datum and is marked with a buoy. On the North-east side there is a steep rock-and-boulder slope to over 50m. Watch the tides; slack water at low water at +0055 Dover.

628 Wreck of the Evelyn Rose, Ardtornish Point. NM692425. This trawler of 327 tons was lost in 1954. A rocky boulder-slope leads to sand and shingle at 28m, where the boat lies. Scallops on the bottom, and good fish life.

628a Ardtornish Point. NM692425. An excellent scenic dive down sheer drop-offs to 50m+. A good area for lobster and crays. Best at slack water.

629 Rubha Leth Thorcaill. NM667423. A stepped cliff-face to 25m with a 0.5-knot tide. Quite a pleasant dive, with sea pens and the unusual soft coral *Alcyonium glomeratum*. Shore access from plantation track.

630 Wreck of the Johanna. This was a 10m wooden fishing boat lost in 1968, 200m South-south-east of Lochaline Pier. The depth appears to be 100m, putting the vessel well out of reach of sports divers.

631 Lochaline Pier. NM673442. This site gives a stunning dive down a drop-off to 90m-plus. The pier is cantilevered out over the cliff, and the cliff runs vertically to 71m where a steep mud slope runs on into the depths. There are tangles of virtually-invisible, monofilament fishing line at 71m. Curious tidal streams are created as the Sound of Mull and Lochaline meet: dive at neaps as the water 'boils' with fast and dangerous down-eddies. The top 7m of the cliff is kelp-covered. Further down it is full of gullies.

632 Lochaline Pier to Caolas na h-Airde. NM673442 – NM681446. When the tide is flooding into the channel leading to Lochaline it is possible to drop down the cliff at Lochaline Pier and drift along the cliff and through the channel. The in-going stream begins at +0135 Dover, and runs at up to 2.5 knots on springs. The bottom of the channel is of white sand which continues to a depth of only 2m. A careful shore dive.

633 Slate wreck, Rubha Dearg. NM663444. An old fence comes down to the water at Rubha Dearg, just past a small stone cottage. The 18th-Century wreck lies on a ledge at 14m immediately out from the fence. It is thought to be a Welsh smack. A shore dive is possible, though strenuous.

634 Rubha Dearg. NM663444. Beyond the slate wreck there is a good drop-off to 32m and beyond. Wrasse, squat lobsters, dogfish, and crayfish, are found here. Beware of vertical down-eddies.

634a Fishnish Bay. NM643423. A Cessna 150 plane (lost some years ago in mysterious circumstances) has recently been located in this bay by a local scallop diver. No further details of the location, but depths range to 30m in the outer bay.

634b Fuinary Rocks. NM618461. An excellent scenic dive. Descend to about 20m on the inside of the buoy and swim inshore following the ledges toward Lochaline. Plenty of life among the rocks.

635 Sgeir Ghlas. NM623434. The cliff on the seaward side extends to around 20m. Probably a boat dive, but can be done from the shore.

636 Pennygown Quarry. NM607437. An amazing cliff dive. The chart shows the 50m submarine contour becoming coincident with the 30m one. From the shore there is a sand slope to 20m, then the vertical cliff to 70m! Lots of crevices for marine creatures. Highly recommended. Launch at Salen.

637 Wishing Stone. NM604466. A shore dive down a gently-sloping mud bottom covered with scallops, brittle stars, sea pens, etc. Not too exciting.

638 Wreck of the Rondo, Dearg Sgeir. NM595453. This important wreck

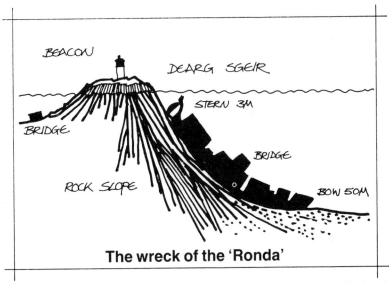

The wreck of the 'Ronda'

lies North-east of Salen Bay on the islet of Dearg Sgeir. It is easy to find as it is situated just a few metres offshore at the North-west of the islet, and immediately East of the light tower. Its stern is in 9m, but the bows are at 51m because the vessel is lying very steeply down a nearly-vertical cliff, with the deck at an angle of 70 degrees. The craft is 80m long and had a gross tonnage of 2363 tons. The stern is solidly encrusted with plumose anemones, and a swim down to the bows and back makes a most impressive dive. At about 27m there is a route between the keel and the rock slope. Tidal streams up to 0.7 knots; LW slack at +0030 Dover.

639 Unknown wreck. NM573456. This wreck lies in 32m of water about 1 mile North-north-east of Salen Pier at 56 32 22N 05 56 50W. It was located in 1947. Boat access from Salen.

640 Rubh' a' Ghlaisich. NM554494. A sloping muddy bottom to 30m. Lots of scallops, but otherwise rather boring.

641 Wreck of the Hispania. NM552504. Another most impressive wreck, considered by many to be the finest wreck in Scotland apart from those in Scapa Flow. The wreck lies 20m South-east of a buoy which is positioned in a direct line between Rubh' ant-Sean Chaisteal and Glenmorven Cottage. She is often marked with a small buoy. The 1340-ton (81m-long) vessel was carrying a cargo of asbestos mats when she was lost in the 1950s. The wreck sits upright in about 25-30m of water, with the deck at 15-20m. The whole wreck is encrusted with plumose anemones and tube worms. A highly recommended site. Both this dive and that on the *Rondo* are made much easier by diving at slack water, as tides approaching 2-3 knots run locally in the Sound of Mull. LW slack at −0030 Dover.

642 Dun Ban. Two wrecks on the chart here. One lies at the South end of Dun Ban (NM570505) and has got just 1m of water over her. The other lies at the North end (NM569503) where she went aground. Shore access.

The wreck of the 'Hispania'

643 Rubh' an Iasgaich, Calve Island. NM529541. A boulder slope running to at least 30m. Octopus have been seen here.

644 Calve Island, North-west side. NM521555. The whole North-west of Calve Island from Rubh' an Righ (NM518556) to Sgeir Calve (NM527548) gives exciting cliff-face diving, with the point NM521555 being the best. Here, the cliff runs to 46m in places to give magnificent diving down chimneys, cracks, and crannies. These contain much life, including sponges and cup corals, and the wall is heavily encrusted with a carpet of sea squirts. Orange sea pens occur on the mud-slope below the cliff. This dive is considered by many to be one of the finest cliff faces short of the Hebridean Outliers, though I find that those of the Small Isles are better. Boat access is from Tobermory.

645 Wreck of the SS Pelican. NM522544. This wreck (which was finally used as a coal hulk by Caledonian MacBrayne) lies upright in Calve Sound immediately offshore in 20m of water off the slip serving a white cottage. The hull is intact and the clipper bows are the most notable sight. A good second dive. Boat access is from Tobermory.

646 Unknown wreck, Calve Sound. NM520545. This is a dried-out wreck perched on rocks just North-west of the *Pelican.* In the channel round the

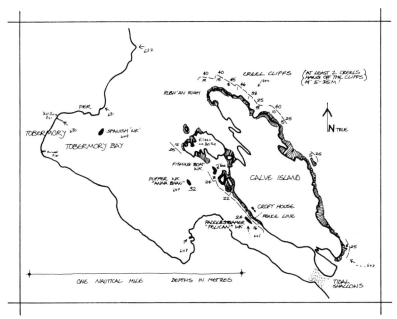

Diver's panoramic view of North Calve

back of the island is another wreck which is totally broken up. This group of islands gives good snorkelling, or a second dive to a maximum depth of 7m. There are many seals about.

647 Wreck of the Anna Bhan, Tobermory Bay. NM517546. This wreck can be found by locating the low rocks between Eilean na Beithe and Calve Island, then swimming South-west down the cliff and out on mud to 34m where the vessel is lying on its side. She has nets over her bows and was lost when her moorings dragged in a gale. *Please note that this is the 'new' position for the* Anna Bhan *and that information published in the past by myself and others was incorrect.*

648 Aros Pier, Tobermory Bay. NM515543. A poor shore dive on to flat mud at 18m. Lots of holes with Norway lobsters.

649 Wreck of the Armada Treasure Ship Almirante de Florencia. NM508552. This fabled wreck lies in Tobermory Bay, and its position is known accurately (it lies about 80m off the jetty). Unfortunately, it lies under several metres of mud! The vessel may also have been the *San Juan de Sicilia*. Though the treasure may well have been recovered at the time of its loss during the flight of the Spanish Armada, a number of efforts have been made over the years to salvage this wreck. These attempts have, however, always been defeated by the quantity of mud to be moved. The wreck belongs to the Duke of Argyll, and a salvaged bronze cannon can be seen at his seat at Inverary Castle on Loch Fyne.

North Calve

650 Off Tobermory Pier. NM506554. A shore dive on to soft mud and mooring tangles. Dive at night or on Sunday, and beware of fishing boats. Lobster, pipe fish, and octopus, galore, with lots of junk and debris.

651 North-west of Tobermory Pier. NM509554. Further on from Tobermory Pier to the North there is a steep boulder slope at 24m on to mud. Prawns and Norway lobsters are a feature of this site.

652 Rubha na Leip. NM513558. An average dive down a sandy slope to about 25m.

653 Rubha nam Gall lighthouse. NM508570. A rocky/sandy/muddy slope to 25m-plus. Squat lobsters, plumose anemones, and sea squirts, have been seen here.

654 Little Stirk Rock. NM533575. A superb dive down the kelp-covered walls of this 3m-high rock. There is sand slope with scallops, then a cliff-face to huge, gloomy boulders that take you to 41m. Recommended. Tidal streams of up to 1 knot are noted; LW slack −0030 Dover.

655 Big Stirk Rock. NM534578. Very similar to Site 654.

656 Wreck of the SS Crane. This wreck is of a 209-ton puffer lost in 1908 somewhere around Big Stirk.

657 Red Rocks. NM529511. A recommended dive over a very rocky seabed at 15m. The kelp-covered gullies are full of life because of the tidal stream. Tidal streams as Site 654.

658 New Rocks. Very similar to site 657.

659 Bloody Bay, South end. NM487576. A good cliff-face from the surface to 30m, with lots of nooks and crannies. The huge boulders on the bottom

Looking towards Ardnamurchan from the Sound of Mull

are covered with corals including the soft coral *Alcyonium glomeratum* which here reaches over half-a-metre long.

660 Unknown wreck, Bloody Bay. NM478588. This 80-year-old wreck of a ferry lies on a ledge at 18m close to the shore.

661 Ancient wrecks in Bloody Bay. Although there was a sea battle here in 1493 between the last Lord of the Isles and his son, it is highly unlikely that anything remains (or was even sunk). But you may stumble across something!

662 Ardmore Point. NM470593. An interesting site with craggy rocks and a cliff reaching down to over 20m. An exposed site with lots of fish life. Tides run at up to 2 knots. Slacks at +0455 and −0230 Dover.

663 Wrecks of French crawfish boats. Two of these vessels were wrecked near Ardmore Point (NM470593). Half of one is on the shore, and half of the other is at 10m. Boat access is from Tobermory.

Area information and services

Hydrographic charts: 2390 Sound of Mull (1:25,000).
Ordnance Survey 1:50,000 maps: 47 Tobermory; 49 Oban & East Mull.
Ordnance Survey 1:25,000 maps: NM44/54-Salen (Mull); NM45/55-Tobermory; NM63/73-Duart Point (Mull); NM64/74-Loch Aline.
Local BS-AC branches: Dunstaffnage Marine Laboratory Special, Oban (1055); Fort William (1148).
Local SS-AC branch: Oban; Western Isles (Mull).
Air supplies: Mull Diving Centre, The Pier, Salen, Aros, Isle of Mull (068 03) 411; Seafare, Portmore Place, Tobermory (0688) 2277; Oban Divers, Laggan, Glenshalloch, Oban (0631) 62755; Fort William BSAC.
Outboard motor sales and service: Seafare (0688) 2277; Nancy Black, 24 Argyll Square, Oban (0631) 62550.
Boat charter: Seafare (0688) 277; Mull Diving Centre (068 03) 411; Ian

Slade, Beadun, Eas Brae, Tobermory, Isle of Mull; Jim Kilcullen, 3 Dal-an-Aiseig, North Connel (0631 71) 454; Oban Divers (0631) 62755.

Harbourmaster: Tobermory (0688) 2131.

Local weather: Glasgow Weather Centre 041 248 3451; Oban Coastguard (0631) 63720.

Sea area: Malin (but these are very sheltered waters).

Tidal constants:

	DOVER	OBAN
Tobermory	−0500	+0020
Salen	−0455	+0025
Loch Aline	−0508	+0012
Craignure	−0505	+0015

Coastguard: Oban MRSC (0631) 63720; Tobermory (0688) 2200.

Lifeboat: Islay (Port Askaig). (*Inshore lifeboat:* Oban).

Police stations: Tobermory: (0688) 2016; Salen (068 03) 322; Craignure (068 02) 322.

Hospitals: Oban County Hospital (0631) 63636; West Highland Hospital, Oban (0631) 63727.

Recompression chambers: Dunstaffnage Marine Laboratory, Oban (0631) 62244; Underwater Training Centre, Fort William (0397) 3786/3136.

Vehicle recovery (AA): Glasgow 041 812 0101; Oban (0631) 62852 (office hours only).

Ferry operators: Oban-Craignure – Caledonian MacBrayne (0631) 62285 and (06882) 343; Lochaline-Fishnish – Caledonian MacBrayne (096 784) 237.

Local tourist information: Tobermory (0688) 2182; Oban (0631) 63122/63551.

Places of local marine interest: Dunstaffnage Marine Research Laboratory, Oban (0631) 62244; Sea Life Centre (Loch Creran), Ledaig (063 172) 386.

Accommodation: Lochaline Dive Centre (0967) 84662; Mull Diving Centre (068 03) 411; Oban Divers (0631) 62755; B & B and guest-house accommodation is plentiful.

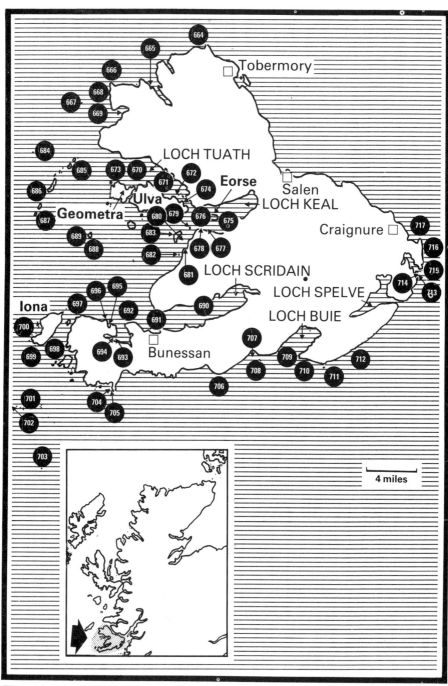

Dive Sites : Mull

CHAPTER 4

Mull

Mull is the third largest island in the Hebrides (after Lewis/Harris and Skye), and is probably also the wettest. It is a mountainous island, and all the coastal views are dominated by the high ground. It is also a hauntingly beautiful, empty island, full of surprises for the explorer. The coastline is over 300 miles long, with three large sea lochs (Lochs Tuath, na Keal, and Scridain).

Mull was probably an island long before the recent series of Ice Ages, and Late-glacial and Post-glacial marine erosion has had little effect on the coast. There have been considerable variations in sea-level over the last 50 million years, and on Mull there is evidence of marine features at altitudes of 250-300m. There are also numerous traces of raised beaches from more recent geological times, especially on the East coast.

Mull's first inhabitants left stones and cairns scattered over the island and crannogs (wooden lake dwellings supported on stilts on artificial islands) in several of the lochs. The Irish Celts arrived in the 2nd Century, and over the next 1600 years Mull was settled by newcomers from many different parts of Europe.

In the 18th Century the population of the island reached 10,600, though in the latter part of that century people began to be moved off the land in order to make way for sheep farming. When the grazings were ruined, the Victorians turned the island into a shooting estate by introducing red deer. The population is now 1600.

This story is a typical one along the West Coast, and through the Hebrides. The area is, in fact, an artificially-created wilderness.

There are many interesting dive sites on Mull, but the Ardmeanach peninsula between Loch na Keal and Loch Scridain is rather special. One mile South of Balmeanach is Mackinnon's Cave. This is 30m high and 180m deep, with stalactites at the deepest part. It has to be entered at low tide, so be careful with your timing. A further couple of miles South-west is MacCulloch's Tree, which was engulfed by lava and fossilised. It is 12m high and nearly 1m in diameter, and between the 'tree' and Mackinnon's Cave lies the Wilderness, a rugged coast of great beauty. A little further South is the Burgh, an NTS reserve for red deer, wild goats, otter, eagle, peregrine, sparrow hawk, and buzzard.

Staffa is a flat-topped island three-quarters-of-a-mile long. It contains three caves – Goat Cave, Clamshell Cave, and the world-famous Fingal's Cave (which allegedly inspired Mendelssohn to pen his Hebridean

Overture). Of the three lava zones around the cave it is the lower zone which is made of the impressive basalt columns.

The Treshnish Isles are an interesting group of islands and skerries, some of which are tied together in pairs by reefs (called *tombolos*). Lunga is the highest, at 103m. The Dutchman's Cap is 87m high.

They are well worth a visit, both to dive, and to explore the islands above the surface. Predictably, the farthest island – Dutchman's Cap – is the best, and demonstrates the raised beach phenomenon to perfection. Boat access is from Calgary Bay, or Ulva Ferry, each being about 12 miles away. Maximum spring tidal rates are only half a knot.

The diving around Mull can be rather good, with a number of sites, such as Torran Rocks and the South coast, still to be fully explored. Tides are not too strong, but the West and South sides of the island are exposed to the prevailing weather from the West and South-west.

There is a dive centre at Salen pier. Air, accommodation, boat hire, and equipment facilities, are available. Contact Richard Grieve at Aros (068 03) 411.

The main ferry terminal is at Craignure, to which the ferry from Oban runs. There is also a small vehicle ferry connecting Fishnish on Mull with Lochaline on Morvern. There is an airstrip near Salen, but only private charter flights are available.

Tobermory, a wonderfully picturesque village with a superb harbour, is the capital of Mull, with a population of about 650. It is a popular port of call for divers, and boats may be hired for diving excursions. Robin Turner of Seafare (a shop on the seafront) offers diving and boating equipment, together with air fills, boat charters, and repair facilities.

Dive sites

The sites in this chapter are described anti-clockwise around Mull, starting from the North entrance to the Sound of Mull, then going down the West coast and back along the South and East coasts.

664 Wreck of the trawler Robert Limbrick, Ardmore Bay. NM466590. The exact position of this vessel (which was lost in 1957) is not known exactly. The whole bay is shallower than 30m.

665 Croig, North Mull. NM401543. Shallow and sandy off the pier, with some scallops.

666 Caliach Point, West Mull. NM348545. A dive to 18m on to sandy shingle. There is tidal action off the point; LW slack +0145 Dover, HW slack −0415 Dover. Launch at Port na Caillich (NM356538).

667 Wreck of the MV Teunika, West Mull. NM319531. This 199-ton (34m-long) vessel was lost in 1969 at 56 35 40N 06 23 36W, about 3 miles South-west of Caliach Point. The wreck is in 30m of water with a chartered clearance of at least 18m.

668 Wreck of the Aurania, West Mull. NM345538. This wreck is of a 13,936-ton (158m-long) liner lost in 1918 to a U-boat torpedo. The exact position is 56 36 00N 06 19 36W, 500m South of Caliach Point, and 40m out from the cliff-face, running North from a conspicuous flat-topped rock

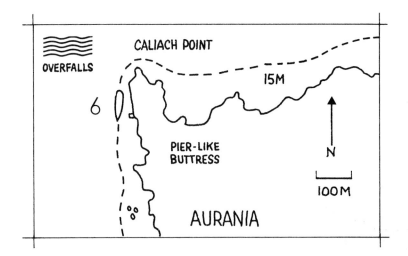

outcrop. The wreck lies in a North-South direction at 15-20m. She is well broken up, but large pieces still stand 7m above the seabed.

669 Calgary Bay, West Mull. NM367508. Pleasant diving along the underwater cliffs falling to 15m. Boat access is from the bay itself.

670 Sgeir na Cille, Loch Tuath. NM395454. A pleasant shore dive to a rocky reef at 12m, with gullies and skerries. The bottom is purple coralline algae, and the fish life is good.

671 Sgeir Dubhail, Loch Tuath. NM429417. Rather shallow and muddy, with scallops, crabs, tube worms, and plumose anemones. Depth: 8-10m. Launch at Laggan Bay (NM452407).

672 Sgeir Ruadh, Loch Tuath. NM434312. As Site 671.

673 Tigh na Caillich, Geometra Island. NM358422. A rather disappointing dive. A weedy bottom leading down gently to 15m, then a mud slope with scallops. Visibility: up to 6m. Launch at Laggan Bay.

674 Sound of Ulva. NM445398. Rather similar to Site 671. There is not much tidal action. A ferry crosses to the private island of Ulva.

675 Eorsa Island, South east corner, Loch na Keal. NM 488376. A gentle pebble slope on to sand at 20m. Life as at Site 671. Launch at Ulva Ferry, Laggan Bay, or Clachandhu (NM454353).

676 Eorsa Island, South-west corner. NM476377. A very steep mud-and-boulder slope to 40m-plus. An interesting dive, with much encrusting life at 30-35m. Crabs, wrasse and brittle stars have been seen here.

677 Loch na Keal, South shore. NM475363. A shore dive straight from the road. A slope to 10m, then a vertical rock-face which plummets to the 35m level. Cup corals, gorgonians, soft coral (*Alcyonium glomeratum*), plus a *washing machine*, are all to be seen.

678 Aoineadh Mor, Loch na Keal. NM463364. There is shore access to this site, which features a steep sand slope with rock outcrops to beyond 30m. There are seapens in the sand.

679 Samalan Island. NM453364. A disappointing dive over rocks thickly covered in kelp at depths of about 15m.

680 Sgeir nan Damh, West Mull. NM443353. A shallow dive to a maximum of 10m. Large scallops at 5m on sand, and many seals, are to be seen. A great variety of life around the shallow rocks. Shore access.

681 Gribun Rocks, West Mull. NM443338. Another nice dive with lots of life to look at. Shore access.

682 Eilean Dubh Cruinn, West Mull. NM442334. Very thick kelp over a bottom of broken boulders to a depth of 15m. All the life normally expected of such an area. Shore access.

683 Inchkenneth, West Mull. NM433356. Sand at first, then a steep mud-and-boulder slope to 30m-plus. Dogfish, crawfish, anemones, and sea cucumbers. The visibility is typically around 15m, but this is an exposed site. More possibilities of exploration exist here, and some submarine caves may well be found when the shoreline is fully examined. Launch at Clachandhu.

684 Wreck of HMS Jason, West Mull. This is the wreck of an 810-ton (70m-long) gunboat sunk by a mine in 1817. The position is 56 33N 06 28W, which is about 4 miles North-west of Lunga in the Treshnish Isles. The depth is 42m.

685 Fladda, Treshnish Isles. NM300442. The North-east side of the island has a steep incline of small boulders leading down on to a sand slope at 15m which runs down to 30m. Visibility is typically around 12m.

686 An Calbh, Lunga. NM271410. A steep boulder bottom gives way to coarse white sand at this site. Depths reach about 20m.

687 Bac Beag, Dutchman's Cap. NM241380. This site features a bouldery bottom at about 25m, with lots of life in the nooks and crannies. Good fish life generally.

688 Fingal's Cave, Staffa, NM324350. Access is by boat from Ulva Ferry. Depths in the cave are only 6m. There are a number of freshly-fallen boulders to concentrate the mind while finning the 75m into the head of the cave! For this reason the tourist boats no longer allow their passengers to enter the cave, so for safety's sake perhaps we should follow their example. Also of danger is the swell which occurs in the cave on all but perfectly-calm days. Outside, the bottom drops away and there are interesting gullies and sunken boulders to explore in the shallows. The amazing geological formations (a continuation of the Giant's Causeway in Antrim, Northern Ireland) at Fingal's cave make this site difficult to resist.

689 Staffa, West coast. NM322355. This is a very exposed site which is shallow for some distance from the shore. The kelp forest on top of the boulders gives good diving if your interest is the small forms of marine life.

The amazing geological formations at Fingal's Cave on Staffa make it difficult to resist as a dive site

690 Scobull Point, Loch Scridain. NM468270. Shore access is possible by following the rough track beyond Tioran (NM479279) for about 1 mile, then taking a left turn just before the site. A gentle rock-and-sand slope changes to a vertical cliff at 20m. The cliff drops to 35m.

691 Sgeirean Mor, Loch Scridain. NM407242. The North side of this site has a cliff dropping to at least 20m. Boat access (with difficulty) is from Knockan (NM404237).

692 Biod an Sgairbh, Ardtun Head. NM376249. This is an exposed site with clear water. There is a boulder bottom at 30m and deeper. Gorgonians are particularly conspicuous. Boat access is from Bunessan (NM383218).

693 Wreck of the Ostend, Loch na Lathaich. NM364227. This wreck lies at the North of Loch Caol, midway between Rubh nam Buthan and Cnoc an t-Suidhe. She lies in a depth of 8m, with about 4m of water over her. She is well broken and dispersed. Colt 45s and machine guns have been found here. The position is 56 19 20N 06 15 50W. Access is generally from Bunessan, though a shore dive would be possible for the lion-hearted.

694 Unknown wrecks, Loch na Lathaich. There are three other wrecks in this loch, but nothing is known of them.

695 Carraig Ghilliondrais, Loch na Lathaich. NM358243. This is a rock-slope with interesting gullies and lots of life to around 20m. Access is by boat from Bunessan Pier.

696 Rubh' a' Chlaidheimh, near Loch na Lathaich. NM348250. Another rock-slope to 25m, landing on sand. Access is from Bunessan. There is also a track to Camas Tuarth (NM349243).

697 Kintra Harbour, West Mull NM313256. This is a deserted salmon fishing station (near a hippie commune). A shallow dive (or good snorkelling) can be had from the quay.

698 Port Carnan a' Ghille, Iona. NM270219. Shallow, with small boulders and sandy patches. Maximum depth: 8m. Lots of fish life and lobsters. Access from Fionnphort (NM299234).

699 Eilean Musimul, Iona. NM256215. A dive to 10m and beyond with lots of small marine life.

700 Stac an Aoineidh. NM252227. Boulders and small rock-faces to 20m. The scenery is fantastic, as is the visibility usually. No large fish, but dozens of small life forms. Access as Site 698.

701 Torran Rocks (main island is Na Torrain at NM267140). This group of rocks and shoals lies over an area 3 miles by 4 miles, and extends about 5 miles South-west from the Ross of Mull. The rocks are broken up, and have deep-water channels between them. In rough weather, the whole area is a sight to behold. The tides run at up to 1.5 knots. Slack water is at +0455 Dover and −0115 Dover. The diving here is splendid, and many crawfish are to be seen. Launch at Fionnphort.

702 Wreck of the Belfast, Torran Rocks. This steamship of 1638 tons (81m-long) was lost in 1885. The position quoted is 56 14 18N 06 27 39W. This is just off West Rock, at NM233142.

703 Shackleton rock (off South Mull). NM285060 (approx). This is a shoal lying about 5 miles South of Na Torrain (Torran Rocks) at 56 10 00N 06 22 48W. It rises from 53m to 12m and is undived! It is expected to give a superb dive on rocky walls and slopes. Tides and access are as Site 701.

704 White's Rock, Rubh' Ardalanish. NM354163. A rocky bottom to 20m is swept clean by the tides and the prevailing weather so that only large kelp plants remain. Boat access is from Ardchiavaig (NM390187).

705 Sgeireig a' Bhogadain, Rubh' Ardlanish. NM360161. This site is slightly more sheltered than Site 704. It has thick weed, giving way to sandy patches at 12m. It is exposed to the South-west swells, and visibility can be disappointing on occasions.

706 Malcolm's Point, South Mull. NM485184. A steep rock and boulder slope to beyond 40m (90m just offshore!). Launch at Carsaig (NM545213).

707 Carsaig Bay, South Mull. NM525213. This bay is sandy with tube worms and flatfish. Cliffs at the West of the bay give excellent dives, as do the many small rocks to the East. Lots of small marine life.

708 Gamhnach Mhor, Carsaig Bay. NM547205. Rocks and boulders covered by kelp to 20m. A salmon net with its associated lines is operated at the East end of the reef in summertime so keep well to the West.

709 Wreck of the Meldon, Loch Buie, South Mull. NM573217. This 2514-ton collier was lost after hitting a mine in 1917. She was re-located in 1951 lying to the South-west of the loch at 56 19 03N 05 55 33W. The vessel is broken amidships, but the bow and stern are intact. The bottom is at 15m. The rudder post shows at low water.

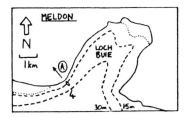  

The wreck of the 'Meldon'

710 Wreck of HMS Barcombe, South Mull. This vessel lies at 56 18 50.5N 05 52 06W, 1 mile East of Loch Buie at NM613199 in 23m of water. She was a bomb defence vessel lost in 1958, and is now broken up. There is a vessel shown ashore on the chart a few hundred metres North-west of the approximate position.

711 Wreck of HMS Maine, South Mull. This is the wreck of a 2087-ton hospital ship lost in 1918. The position is just South-east of Frank Lockwood's island (NM630196) in about 30m of water. Salvage enquiries have been made. In this vicinity there is also a wreck shown on the shore just North-west of the island.

712 Wreck of the Glen Rosa, South-east Mull. This 97-ton vessel was lost in 1958. Her position — 56 19 30.6N 05 47 28.5W — is just East of Rubh Aoineadh Mheinis, at NM662213 in about 20m. Yet another wreck is shown on the chart as being ashore, though it is about half-a-mile West of the above position.

713 Grass Point, East Mull. NM749309. Kelp-covered rock to 20m, then gravel. Lots of urchins and strong tides (see Site 716).

714 Camas a'Bhalaich. The pier here gives a poor dive on to sand at 15m. Launch boats by the pier.

715 Maol Donn, East Mull. NM749315. Similar to Site 713.

716 Black's Memorial Lighthouse, East Mull. NM754343. A good drift dive can be made here for about 1 mile to the South with a South-east-moving tidal stream. This starts to run at −0555 Dover, and may reach 2 knots (LW slack at +0105 Dover). The bottom is rocky, then muddy to 30m and beyond. Crawfish are to be found. Launch boats as for Site 714, or launch at Oban.

717 Duart Point, entrance to Sound of Mull. NM750354. A muddy slope leading down to about 25m. Rather disappointing. Launch and tides as Site 716.

Area information and services

Hydrographic charts: 2171 Sound of Mull and approaches 1:75,000; 2378 Loch Linnhe — southern part 1:25,000; 2386 Firth of Lorne — southern part 1:25,000; 2387 Firth of Lorne — northern part 1:25,000; 2392 Sound of Mull —

western entrance 1:25,000; 2617 Sound of Iona 1:25,000; 2652 Loch na Keal and Loch Tuath 1:25,000; 2771 Loch Scridain 1:25,000.

Ordnance Survey 1:50,000 maps: 47 Tobermory; 48 Iona & Ben More; 49 Oban & East Mull.

Ordnance Survey 1:25,000 maps: NM21/31 Torran Rocks; NM22/32 Iona & Bunessan; NM24/34 Treshnish Isles; NM33 Ulva; NM42/52 Loch Scridain (Mull); NM43/53 Ben More; NM44/54 Salen (Mull); NM45/55 Tobermory; NM62/72 Firth of Lorne (North); NM63/73 Duart Point (Mull); NM64/74 Loch Aline.

Local BS-AC branches: Dunstaffnage Marine Laboratory Special (1055); Fort William (1148).

Local SS-AC branches: Oban; Western Isles, Tobermory.

Air supplies: Mull Diving Centre, Salen Pier, Aros, Mull (068 03) 411; Seafare, Portmore Place, Tobermory (0688) 2277.

Outboard motor sales & service: Seafare (0688) 2277.

Boat charter: Seafare (0688) 2277; Ian Slade, Beadun, Eas Brae, Tobermory; Jim Kilcullen, 3 Dal-an-Aiseig, North Connel, Oban (0631 71) 454; Oban Divers (0631) 62755.

Harbourmaster: Tobermory (0688) 2131.

Local weather: Glasgow Weather Centre 041 248 3451; Oban Coastguard (0631) 63720.

Sea area: Malin (nearly Hebrides).

Tidal constants:

	DOVER	OBAN
Carsaig Bay	−0546	+0026
Iona	−0546	+0026
Bunessan	−0556	+0036
Ulva Sound	−0546	+0026
Craignure	−0505	+0015
Tobermory	−0500	+0020

Coastguard: Oban MRSC (0631) 63720; Tobermory (0688) 2200.

Lifeboat: Islay (Port Askaig).

Police stations: Tobermory (0688) 2016; Salen (068 03) 322; Craignure (068 02) 322.

Hospitals: Oban County Hospital (0631) 63636; West Highland Hospital, Oban (0631) 63727.

Recompression chambers: Dunstaffnage Marine Laboratory, Oban (0631) 62244; Underwater Training Centre, Fort William (0397) 3786/3136.

Vehicle recovery (AA): Glasgow 041 812 0101; Oban (0631) 62854 (office hours only).

Ferry operators: Oban-Craignure – Caledonian MacBrayne (0631) 62285 and (06882) 343; Lochaline-Fishnish – Caledonian MacBrayne (096 784) 237.

Local tourist information: Tobermory (0688) 2182.

Accommodation: Mull Diving Centre (068 03) 411. B & B and guest house accommodation is plentiful; There are chalets for rent in Tobermory.

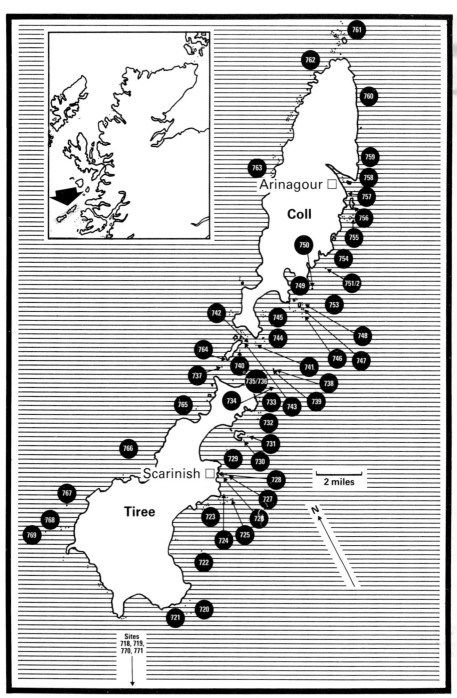

Dive Sites : Tiree and Coll

CHAPTER 5

Tiree and Coll

Coll and Tiree are the most westerly of the Inner Hebrides, (Tiree is, in fact, also further West than Harris in the Outer Hebrides). Coll is about 7 miles West of Caliach Point in Mull, while Tiree lies 15 miles West from Treshnish Point. They are both served by car-ferry from Oban, the journey taking 4½ hours to Tiree. Tiree and Glasgow are linked by the Loganair flights. Interestingly, Tiree is the sunniest place in Britain, and is surprisingly dry. But it is also one of the windiest places in the country.

Coll is 13½ miles long by 4 miles wide. Its highest point is Ben Hogh, at 104m. The northern two-thirds (owned by a Dutch business man) is composed of Lewisian gneiss, and the southern third of ancient meta-morphosed sandstones. On the coast this rock is shattered and veined, with a seaward dip. There are many raised beaches to be seen, though many of them are covered by wind-blown sand. The '100 ft' beach is well seen on the North coast; if the sea level was to return to the '100 ft' days, Coll would be divided into four islands.

Tiree measures 10 miles by 6 miles at the widest point. It is the lowest of all the Hebrides (its summit is at 141m at Ben Hynish), and its aspect is one of houses, not hills. It is made of Lewisian gneiss, but large areas are covered with blown sand, and its coast is really a succession of magnificent beaches enclosed by low, rough gneiss headlands. Much of its low-lying surface is covered with raised beach deposits.

The history of Coll and Tiree is one of Celts, followed by Vikings, followed by many years of clan feuding, then the evictions, followed by de-population during this century. In 1831, the population of Tiree was 4,450 and that of Coll 1,440. Today the figures are 870 and 140. The present-day economy depends on sheep and cattle, with some lobster creeling. The main villages on the islands are Scarinish on Tiree, and Arinagour on Coll.

Underwater around both Coll and Tiree there is a rock platform extending for some miles out to sea, with only shallow depths to be found. This shelf extends over 10 miles South-west of Tiree to Skerryvore lighthouse. Associated with it are a large number of rocks and skerries, some connected to the main islands at low tide. Coll and Tiree are separated by Gunna Sound, which is 2 miles wide, and which contains the one-mile-long Gunna Island.

The diving around these islands is one of contrasts. The wreck diving is quite good, with several significant vessels awaiting the diver, but apart from this the diving is not so exciting. Depths are rather shallow, there is a lot of sand about, and there are no submarine walls. Tidal streams are generally not very strong – the exception being Gunna Sound, and locally around Skerryvore and the Cairns of Coll on the Coll-Tiree bank.

The islands can be dived by taking inflatables on the ferry and either camping or using the self-catering accommodation that is available. Alternatively, the wrecks of the area can be used as the basis for a trip by MFV from the Sound of Mull. This has much to commend it, as the range of diving available in the general area is huge, and would amply repay several week-long visits.

Dive sites

These are described in an anti-clockwise direction from South-west Tiree, up the East coasts of Tiree and Coll, and then down the West coasts.

718 Outer Hurricane Rock. 56 26 54N 07 05 00W. This lies 3 miles West of Rinn Thorbhais (NL933400). There is a bedrock plane at 25m, with large boulders and ridges covered with soft coral. Boat access is from Balephuill Bay (NL956404). Quite strong tidal streams run between Tiree and Skerryvore; LW slack +0045 Dover, HW slack −0515 Dover.

719 Inner Hurricane Rock. 56 27 00N 07 01 54W. This site lies just West of the Rock. At 18m there are low reefs covered with barnacles. Launch as for Site 718.

720 Bo Deobedal. NL996372. This rock drops to 14m as a series of rock ridges covered with kelp. At 17m a gravel plain begins. Launch as for Site 718.

721 Hynish. NL972361. About 1½ miles South of the headland is a flat plain covered with brittle stars at 23m. Launch at Hynish Pier (NL987393).

722 Hynish Bay. NM013403. About 1.5 miles west of Mannel (NL989404) is a plain of sand and shell gravel. A poor dive. Launch as for Site 721.

723 Bogha Crotach. NM025430. A very shallow site with coarse sand filling the gaps between large boulders. A variety of sponges are to be seen. Shore access.

724 Eilean nam Gobhar. NM039432. Similar to Site 723, though rather deeper. Shore access.

725 Sgeir Fhada. NM043428. Initial small rocky gullies with kelp becoming a fairly steep rocky slope ending in sand at 19m. Lots of life under the kelp. Launch at Scarinish (NM044447).

726 Wreck of the Mary Stewart. NM048443. This wreck lies at 56 30 07N 06 48 14W in shallow water. The remains, located in 1969, will be well broken and dispersed because she was a 21m wooden sailing vessel, and the depth is only about 5m.

727 Wreck of the Lady Isle. NM050440. This 250-ton Clyde puffer sunk in 1940 in about 10m, at 56 29 58N 06 48 02W. The position is about 1 mile South-east of Scarinish.

728 Scarinish Harbour. NM045447. This site is very shallow and sandy. There is a wreck that dries out shown on the chart.

729 Gott Bay. NM057455. About 1 mile out this bay is about 9m deep, with a bottom consisting of waves of coarse shell sand.

730 Sgeir Gharbh. NM072455. A fairly steep rocky slope leading to boulders and sand at 18m. Launch at Gott Bay.

731 Cleit Ruaig. NM080457. At 200m East of the rocks there is a boulder plain at 24m. The boulders are completely encrusted with barnacles. Launch at Gott Bay.

732 Sgeir Uilleim. NM095465. Similar to Site 730, use the same launch-point.

733 Librig Mhor. NM098472. Similar to Site 730.

734 Creachasdal Mor. NM108482. A rocky slope leading to sand at about 15m. The rocks are covered with kelp and barnacles. Tidal streams of up to 2.5 knots flow through Gunna Sound; LW slack +0005 Dover, HW slack +0540 Dover. Launch at Port Ruadh (NM086492).

There are two wrecks in Gunna Sound: **735, St Claire,** and **736, Unknown.** The approximate position given by the Hydrographic Department – 56 36 30N 06 44 00W – is about ¼ mile inland! Presumably they lie just off the shore near Rosgaill (NM096487). Depths are shallow, but tidal streams are strong.

737 Gunna Sound Buoy. NM093504. The bottom here is a plain of small boulders at 15m. Tidal streams are strong (see Site 734). Interesting life on the boulders. Launch at Port Ruadh.

738 Roan Bogha Buoy. NM130483. This marks a rock awash. A kelp covered rock slope leads to a maerl (or carbonated algae) bed at 24m. Good variety of life in the kelp forest. Launch and tides as Site 734.

739 Wreck of the Hurlford, Gunna Sound. This wreck lies in 18-22m to the North-west of Roan Bogha. Although she is well broken up and thickly encrusted with marine life, there is a large section of the bow still intact, and the boiler and engine can still be seen. The best way to dive this site is to locate the rock by echo sounder and swim down the rocky slope at 320°T until the wreck is reached.

740 Eilean nam Gamhna, Gunna. NM105508. At a distance of 200m out to sea the depth here is still only 7m. Isolated rocks stick out of a sand bottom. A poor dive. Launch at Crossapol Bay, Coll (NM148530).

741 Eilean Bhoramuil, Coll. NM113546. A dive on flat sand at 10m. Not recommended!

742 Wreck of the Fisher Queen. NM112518. This ship was lost in Caolas Ban in 1973. The water is very shallow, so the wreck may be broken up. The position given for her is 56 34 00N 06 42 00W (PA), but the wreck may, in fact, lie in Traigh Halun at NM116533, on the West side of Coll.

743 Wreck of the Nessmore. The *Nessmore* was a cargo vessel of 3377 tons (107m-long) which ran aground in 1895 at 56 33 42N 06 41 24W. This position is a few hundred metres ashore, so presumably the vessel lies near Caolas Eilean Bhoramuil (about NM117510).

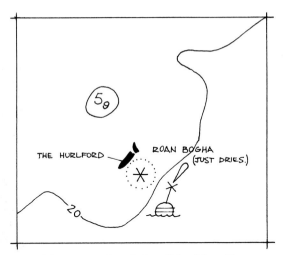

THE HURLFORD
ROAN BOGHA (JUST DRIES.)

The wreck of the 'Hurlford'

744 Sgeir nam Garbhanach. NM122502. This is an isolated drying rock lying about 0.5 mile offshore. A rocky slope covered with kelp leads to sand at 14m. Launch at Crossapol Bay.

745 Crossapol Bay. NM138518. About 1 mile offshore here the depth is 17m. The bottom is of barnacle-covered boulders and sand.

746 Boghaichean Ceann Shoal. NM156505. This is a steep, terraced rock-face descending to 45m. It is covered with hyroids and sea cucumbers. Access by boat from Crossapol Bay.

747 Eilean Iomallach. NM158508. A rocky slope leads steeply down the East of this island to 28m where there is a mud and shell bottom. Good encrusting life.

748 Wreck of the Tapti. NM158507. The *Tapti*, a 6609-ton motor vessel, was lost in 1951 close to the East shore of Soa Island. The quoted position of 56 33 40N 06 37 46W is too far to the East. The wreck is in four parts and has deteriorated considerably. It is now encrusted with soft coral and plumose anemones. The bows, which point toward the surface, are a most impressive sight. Launch at Loch Breachacha (NM159538), or at Crossapol Bay.

749 Bogha Dearg. NM172519. Off the South of these rocks is a boulder plain at 19m. Barnacles, soft corals, and hydroids, cover the boulders. Launch as Site 748.

750 Red Rock. NM169517. A few hundred metres South-west of the previous site is a rock slope to 16m, then sand.

751 Friesland Rock. NM185525. A rocky reef leading to a gravel plain at 25m, with lots of sponges on the silty rock. Launch as Site 748.

The wreck of the 'Tapti'

752 Wreck of the MV Angela. NM186524. This vessel lies at 56 35 06N 06 35 30W, on the West side of Friesland Rock. The *Angela* was lost in 1953, and what little is left is scattered among the rocks. Launch as for Site 748.

753 Trawler wreck. A trawler is recorded as being wrecked a few hundred metres to the South-east of the *Angela* site.

754 Bogha ain Mhic Airt. NM197529. To the South-east of the rock is a rocky plain turning to sand at 21m. Launch at Arinagour (NM226572).

755 Airne na Sgeire. NM220544. At the South of these islets is a kelp-covered rocky slope to 15m then a plain of boulders and pebbles. Hydroids and soft corals dominate the boulders. Launch as for Site 754.

756 Eilean Ornsay. NM225548. At the South-east corner there is a rock ridge going out to sea and dropping to a sandy plain at 20m. Kelp, then hydroids on the rock. Launch as for Site 754.

757 Meall Eatharna. NM237563. A steep rocky slope to 18m; then mud and cobbles to 30m; then rocks to below 40m. Kelp to 15m then rocks heavily-covered with hydroids. Launch as for Site 754.

758 Sloc na Faochag. NM242568. A steep rocky slope to 15m. Hydroids, soft corals, and large sponges, are prevalent. Launch as for Site 754.

759 Wreck of the Generalconsul Elissejeffe. NM248574. This 886-ton vessel ran aground in 1914 at 56 37 46N 06 29 30W. The wreck is extensively broken up, and the prop and fittings have been salvaged. The bows lie to the shore in 8m; the stern is at 15m. Launch as for Site 754.

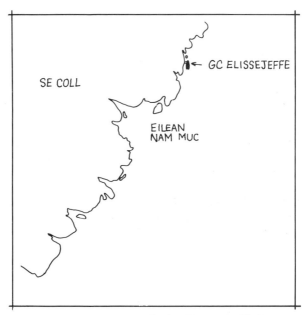

SE COLL

GC ELISSEJEFFE ←

EILEAN
NAM MUC

The wreck of 'G.C. Elissejeffe'

760 North-west Coll. I have no dives recorded for the 6 miles of coast up to Site 761.

761 Cairns of Coll. NM288666. These skerries lie almost 2 miles North-east from the northern end of Coll. The chart shows a steep slope dropping to over 100m to the North-west. There are also extensive tracts of kelp-covered rocks in depths to 20m, with rich life under the kelp. Tides up to 1.5 knots; LW slack +0145 Dover, HW slack −0415 Dover.

762 Wreck of the SS Nevada II, Rubha Mor. NM250645. The official position quoted is 56 40 46N 06 31 12W, but this vessel actually lies at 56 41 40N 06 29 45W. She was a 5693-ton (126m-long) vessel which ran aground in 1942 carrying government stores. Although the hull is intact, she is now well broken, and has been extensively salvaged. At low water the deck supports rise nearly a metre above the surface. The bows are at 3m, and the stern in 15m. Launch at Sorisdale Bay (NM272632).

Note the collier *St Brandon* was lost hereabouts in 1920.

763 West coast of Coll. I have no reports of dives on this coast. It is 13 miles long and consists of a succession of rocky shores fringing eight sandy bays. The only area that appears to have any depth is that around Rubha Hogh (NM173592).

764 West tip of Gunna. NM090510. A series of low-rock ridges and cobble areas is found here at 11m. Tidal streams are quite strong (see Site 734). There is kelp on the rocks, with anemones in between the fronds.

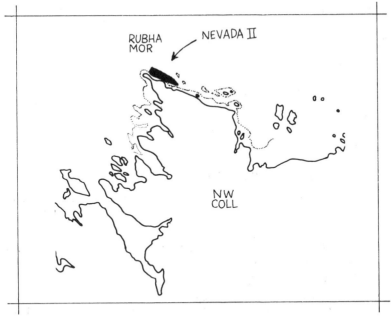

The wreck of the 'Nevada'

765 Vaul Bay area. NM063519. There is an extensive boulder, cobble, and sand, plain about 1 mile North of Vaul Bay. Urchins are very common on the barnacle-encrusted rocks. Launch at Vaul (NM051486).

766 Balephetrish Bay. NM005513. Rocky ridges with boulders in between are found at 13m. There is a lot of kelp debris on the bottom. The site is about 2 miles out. Another mile further out lies a boulder plain at 13m (NM010526). The boulders are rather bare, except for large numbers of brittle stars. Launch in the bay.

767 Bogha Sgiobaghair. NL935505. This site lies about ½ mile North of the skerry. The seabed consists of kelp-covered rocky gullies. Sponges and tunicates are found under the kelp. Launch at Hough Bay (NL938466). Tidal streams of up to 1.5 knots may be experienced; HW slack −0500 Dover, LW slack +0100 Dover.

768 Hough Skerries. NL917490. There is a rocky seabed to the North of the Skerries, with gullies covered by a kelp forest at 10-13m. Tunicates and sponges are found under the kelp. Launch as for Site 767.

769 Dubh Sgeir. NL900490. A very craggy bottom of bedrock exposed to strong tides and waves. Underneath the thick kelp is a rich encrustation of tunicates and sponges. The overhangs and gullies are particularly rich. Depths to 15m.

770 Wreck of HMS Sturdy. The *Sturdy* was a 905-ton destroyer which ran aground in 1940 and totally broke up at 56 29N 06 59W (West Tiree).

771 Wreck of a U-Boat. This wreck allegedly lies at approximately 56 28N 06 59W (West Tiree). I have no other details, though a U-Boat wreck is also rumoured to lie in Gunna Sound.

NOTE: The offshore sites of Skerryvore Lighthouse (9 miles South-west), Dubh Artach Lighthouse (20 miles South-south-east), Blackstones Bank (23 miles South-south-west), and Stanton Banks (32 miles South-west) are covered in Vol III of this series of guides. This also applies to the other outlying banks and islands.

Area information and services

Hydrographic charts: 1778 Stanton Banks to Passage of Tiree 1:100,000; 1796 Barra Head to Point of Ardnamurchan 1:100,000; 2475 Gunna Sound 1:25,000.
Ordnance Survey 1:50,000 maps: 46 Coll & Tiree.
Ordnance Survey 1:25,000 maps: NL94/NM04 Tiree; NM05/15/25 Coll (Arinagour); NM26 Coll (North).
Local BS-AC branches: None.
Local SS-AC branches: Western Isles, Tobermory.
Air supplies: None, but see Mull chapter.
Boat charter: Seafare (0688) 2277; Ian Slade, Beadun, Eas Brae, Tobermory; Jim Kilcullen, 3 Dal-an-Aiseig, North Connel, Oban (0631 71) 454.
Local weather: Glasgow Weather Centre 041 248 3451; Oban Coastguard (0631) 63720.
Sea area: Malin (nearly Hebrides).
Tidal constants:

	DOVER	ULLAPOOL
Loch Eatharna, Coll	−0530	−0110
Gott Bay, Tiree	−0540	−0120

Coastguard: Oban MRSC (0631) 63720; Duntulm (047 052) 201.
Lifeboat: Mallaig.
Hospitals: Oban County Hospital (0631) 63636; West Highland Hospital, Oban (0631) 63727.
Recompression chambers: Dunstaffnage Marine Laboratory, Oban (0631) 62244; Underwater Training Centre, Fort William (0397) 3786/3136.
Ferry operators: Oban-Mull-Coll-Tiree – Caledonian MacBrayne (0631) 62285, (087 93) 347 and (087 92) 337.
Accommodation: Some B & B facilities in the villages.
Information: The Coll Magazine (Editor: Pat Barr, Hyne, Isle of Coll, Argyll) is published annually, and makes interesting reading. It has some accommodation and tourist adverts.

CHAPTER 6

The Small Isles

These consist of the isles of Canna (with Sanday), Rum, Eigg, and Muck –
all of which lie in a group to the South-west of Skye. Their human history is
that of many other islands in the Hebrides – the arrival of Celts and Vikings,
followed by clan battles, the '45 rebellion, famines, clearances, and
present-day de-population.

A Caledonian Macbrayne steamer based on Mallaig operates round the
Small Isles three times a week. There are also ferries direct to Eigg and Rum
from Mallaig and Arisaig in the summer.

Canna is of volcanic origin; its summit is Carn a Ghaill at 210m. Sanday is
linked to Canna by tidal sands and a footbridge. In the days of the '100 ft'
raised beaches, Canna would have been two islands, split at Tarbert. The
population of Canna is just 24 people, and the island is run as a single farm,
with Sanday as a croft. There is no holiday accommodation, but it is
possible to camp on the island with prior permission.

Rum (pronounced *room*) is a beautiful island. It is almost completely
surrounded by cliffs, and has a summer population of about 40. It is the
largest island in this group at 8½ miles long; its highest point is 812m at
Askival. Rum is now owned by the Nature Conservancy Council who use it
as an open-air laboratory for the study of red deer, wild goats, Highland
cattle, and ponies. (Legend has it that the Rum ponies are descended from
animals which swam ashore after the wrecking of an Armada vessel,
presumably at Wreck Bay).

Rum's seacliffs are the breeding haunts of large numbers of puffin,
razorbills, and kittiwakes. There is also a large Manx shearwater colony on
the higher slopes of the mountains. Sea eagles have been re-introduced
from Norway, and are apparently establishing themselves.

Plant life is also prolific, having remained undisturbed on the cliffs and
summits since the end of the last glaciation. Alpines in particular are very
profuse.

The North and East of Rum are made of Torridonian rocks. The central
mountainous area is of igneous rocks (resulting from the widespread
volcanic activity that occurred in western Scotland about 50 million years
ago). West Rum has coastal rocks of granophyre, while those of South Rum
are basic. The sandstone areas have cliffs rising to 75m in places, and
feature stacks, caves, and geos. In fact, the 1:25 000 maps shows coastal
caves at 65 different sites, six natural arches, and a network of
subterranean tunnels (at NG327022).

Eigg (pronounced *egg*) was formerly called Eilean Nimban-More, which

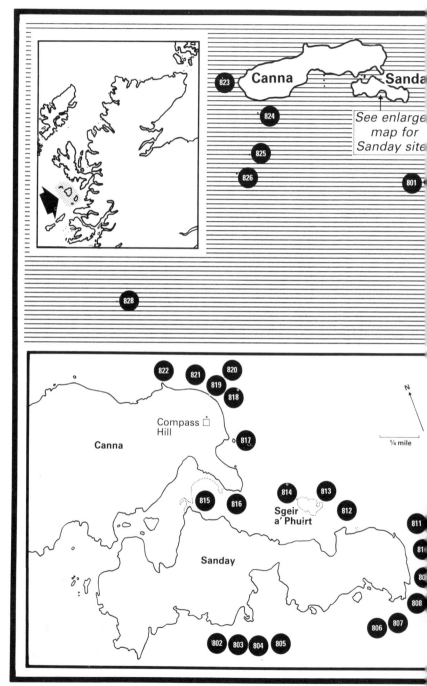

Dive Sites : The Small Isles

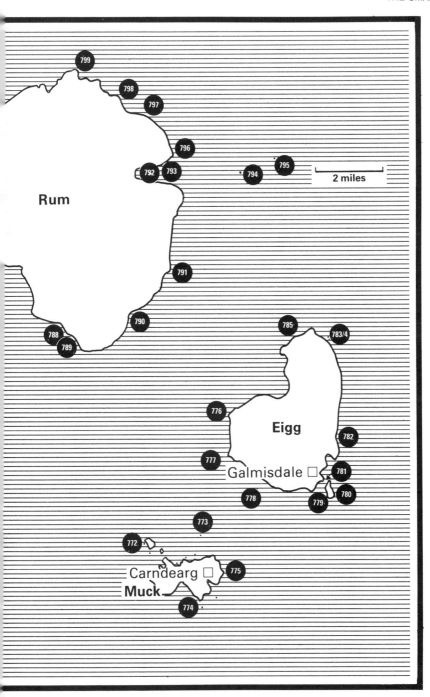

means *island of the big women*. It is the site of MacDonalds Cave, where 395 MacDonalds were suffocated to death with burning brushwood by the MacLeods. This is one of the worst examples of clan warfare, and was the culmination of a series of atrocities.

Eigg is composed almost entirely of lava flows which are well seen in the seacliffs. However, Eigg is scenically dominated by the Sgurr, a huge towering mass of columnar pitchstone (the largest in Britain), which reaches a height of 394m from the 300m contour. The view from the summit is superb.

Eigg has a population of 80 people. It is heavily dependent on tourism, with guest houses, caravans, and cottages, available for visitors.

Muck (which derives from the Gaelic for *isle of the sow*) rises to a height of 138m, and lies 2½ miles South-west of Eigg. Its population is 24, and again it is run basically as a single mixed-farm. There is a limited amount of holiday accommodation.

Muck is composed of Tertiary basalt, but one of the most striking features of the island is the large number of natural dykes which cut through the lavas and sills. On the South and East shores a total of 134 dykes are mapped (the equivalent of one every 26 metres). These dykes are 6-9m high, with vertical walls.

The diving around the Small Isles is interesting. It varies from the rather poor, shallow sites of some parts of Rum, to the sensational deep, cliff dives on the East coast of Sanday. Tidal streams around these islands can run quite strongly, and should be allowed for when planning dives. Depths vary enormously. There is an exceptionally deep (238m) channel between Sanday and Rum in which lie the recently-explored Sanday cliffs. There is also a very deep (128m) channel between Rum and Eigg (are there dramatic underwater cliffs to be found there, especially off South-east Rum?). Similar cliffs may also exist off North Eigg.

The islands of Canna and, in particular, Sanday have recently been found to give rather special dives in an area previously thought to be rather poor. I am particularly indebted to Maurice Davidson of Glasgow who supplied much of the information on the two islands for this chapter.

It would appear that Sanday (and Canna to a lesser extent) has a submerged beach around it because there is a rim of sand all around the island in the form of a shallow plain running down to 12m. Beyond that are dramatic vertical cliffs stretching down to the limits of compressed air diving. The edge of these is easily located with an echo-sounder. About 50m off the West-south-west of Sanday there is a spot depth of 168m, and the channel between Sanday and Rum is 230m deep! Tidal streams reach 1.5 knots. HW slack −0430 Dover; LW slack +0130 Dover.

While most islands in Scotland have a South-west to North-east orientation, Sanday and Canna run West to East. Consequently, parts of the islands are exposed to the tidal streams but remain sheltered from the prevailing winds and swell. It would appear that this causes the life off the East end of Sanday to be rather unusual.

Sanday is joined to Canna by a bridge and an extensive area of tidal sand. Accommodation is available with the crofters. Access is by steamer from Mallaig (25 miles) or by private charter. Visibility is up to 10-15m on flood tides, and 8-10m on ebb tides.

The outlying rocks to the South of Canna look promising for diving. To my knowledge, they are, as yet, undived.

The best way to explore these islands is to hire an MFV as a sea-base. Alternatively, and particularly if a longer stay is planned, you can camp cheaply on the islands with prior permission. A third method of visiting the area is to take an inflatable to the nearer islands. This is just about possible in good conditions.

Whatever route you choose, I am sure that you will find the diving first-class in several of the areas identified below. You might also discover some of the rather special dive sites which I believe are lurking around these islands.

Dive sites: Muck

772 Eagamol. NM388812. This site features a gently-sloping bottom of pebbles and boulders at about 25m. The boulders are covered with soft coral. Tidal streams of up to 4 knots. LW slack +0130 Dover; HW slack −0430 Dover. Boat access from Fascadale, Ardnamurchan (NM500707) 10 miles, Arisaig (NM657866) 18 miles, or Loch Scresort (NM403996) 13 miles. To travel any of these distances in an inflatable is difficult in these waters, but is about possible in good conditions with the right equipment. It is possible to hire boats from Mallaig or Tobermory.

773 Godag. NM418818. To the North-east the seabed drops steeply to about 40m in a series of rocky ridges. The lower parts of this slope are composed of boulders. The kelp forest stops at 12m, and below this the rock is encrusted with life, particularly soft corals and brittle starts. Cuckoo and ballan wrasse are common. Access and tides as Site 772. The spring rate is 3 knots.

774 South Muck. I have no sites recorded for this coast.

775 East Muck. I have no sites recorded here, but it looks promising around Eilean Dubh (NM430795), with depths to 70m shown 300m offshore on the chart.

Dive sites: Eigg

776 Rubha an Fhasaidh. NM438875. This site features a boulder slope to 20m then a plain of shell gravel. Soft corals, hydroids and sponges grow below the kelp at 15m. Boat access is from Arisaig or Mallaig (17 miles), or Rum (10 miles). Tides as Site 772.

777 Bogh' a' Churaich. NM433853. At 12m, this area is rather shallow. Sand fills many of the kelp-covered rock ridges. Visibility is usually about 12m. Tides and access as Site 776.

778 Dubh Sgeir. NM450835. A rocky slope to 16m, then boulders, pebbles, and gravel, on to 23m. An exposed, rather bare site, though there are lots of urchins. Tides and access as Site 776.

779 Eilean Chathastail. NM486838-NM485835. This is a drift dive along the West coast of the island at depths to about 5m. Sand and some kelp on rocks. Tidal rates are up to 4 knots, with slacks as Site 772.

780 Eilean Chathastail, Rubha An Iasgaich. NM491830. A steep rock slope to 14m followed by a boulder slope to 19m. Kelp to 9m, then rather bare rocks. Tides and access as Site 776.

781 Galmisdale Pier. NM465838. This site is rocky near the shore, then sandy further out. Scallops, crabs, and lobsters, are to be seen. The visibility is often good, and the diving generally is quite pleasant. Access from Arisaig (11 miles).

782 East coast of Eigg, Leac a' Ghuidal. NM494856. Steep boulder slopes characterise this coast. At the point quoted the bottom drops steeply down to about 60m, giving good diving. Tides as Site 779.

783 Unknown wreck near Bogha Ruadh, North-east Eigg. NM489911. This is a coal puffer shown as a drying wreck on the chart. The seabed shelves very gently in this area.

784 Unknown wreck. Another puffer, which came to salvage the coal from the wreck at Site 783 and was then lost. The vessel lies in 15m of water just out from the drying wreck.

785 North Eigg. I have no dives recorded at the northern end of Eigg. The North-west coast appears to have steep drops just offshore.

Dive sites: Rum

786 Wreck Bay. NM309981. I have little information on this area except that depths are less than 10m. The West headland of the bay is called Schooner Point (NM306981). At least one dive group has looked for wrecks hereabouts, but so far only shallow water and kelp have been found. There is a traveller's tale of the drinking of port on Rum from the wreck of an ocean-going sailing ship which reputedly went down to the West of the island. Such stories (like the one about the Armada-vessel ponies described at the beginning of this chapter) may well be untrue, but keep them in the back of your mind if you come across any 'bits'.

787 South-west coast of Rum. I have no dives recorded for this 6-mile stretch of coast. It appears to shelve very gradually on the chart.

788 Sgeirean Mora, South-west Rum. NM360917. A good dive on a series of rock ledges with deep cracks in them running down at 45 degrees to 20m. Lots of life on the rock in these cracks. Tidal streams run at up to 3 knots. Access from Mallaig (21 miles), where boats can be hired.

789 Papadil, South Rum. NM362916. An exposed site with smooth, stepped rocks to 25m. There is a kelp forest with sponges underneath, then purple coralline-covered rock. Access and tides as Site 788.

790 Dibidil, South Rum. NM395923. A steep rocky slope to 9m, then a boulder slope running on past 15m. A kelp forest extends to 9m and has a variety of life under it. Access and tides are as Site 788.

791 Welshman's Rock. NM420947. This is representative of a number of similar sites on South-east Rum. There is a sandy and rocky slope down to about 28m, then kelp forests with sponges and anemones. Access and tides as Site 788.

792 Loch Scresort Pier. NM415995. Out from the pier the bottom is sand and rock at 10m.

793 Loch Scresort. Towards the entrance to the loch the North side (at NM420997) is muddy sand at 6m. The South side (at NM419990) has shallow rocks to 3m, then a mud slope. Not very exciting.

794 Seagull Bank, East Rum. NM460995. This site lies 3 miles due East from Loch Scresort. The shoal takes the form of a ridge with precipitous sides, and the site is considered to be as good as Bo Fascadale (Site 852). It has a minimum depth of 18m, and drops away to the North to depths of 108m! On the North side (where the isobaths narrow) the wall starts at 20m and is vertical to 35m where there is a seabed of soft black mud. Boat access is from Mallaig on the mainland, or Tarskavaig on the Sleat peninsula on Skye.

795 Un-named shoal, 1.5 miles East-north-east of Seagull Bank. NG483005. This site has a clearance of 18m, but is as yet undived.

796 Alte Suidh' an Easbuig, East Rum. NG420015. This site consists of a rocky slope to 5m, a sand slope to 12m, then a mud slope at 29m. At 35-36m there is a rocky reef about 200m offshore. Quantities of edible crab and Norway lobster. The deep reef has a rich collection of hydroids and anemones. Tides and access as Site 788.

797 Creag na h-Iolaire, North-east Rum. NG410025. A rocky slope changing to mud at 13m. The rock is silty, with large numbers of urchins. Tides and access as Site 788.

798 Rubha Camas Pliasgaig, North-east Rum. NG399035. A rocky slope terminating in mud at 15m. Kelp and crabs are the main features. Tides and access as Site 788. Access is also possible from Elgol (NG516137) in Skye.

799 Rubha Shamhnan Insir, North Rum. NG380048. A shallow dive over rock to sand at 8m. Kelpy and not too spectacular. Tides and access as Site 798.

800 A' Mharagach, North-west Rum. NG337026. A rocky slope to 11m, then boulders to over 20m. A thick kelp forest with some sponges and dahlia anemones below. Maximum tidal stream of about 1.5 knots. Slacks at +0130 Dover and −0430 Dover. Access as Site 798.

801 A' Bhrideanach, West Rum. NG291994. Broken rocks lead down to 20m and beyond. Soft corals, hydroids, barnacles, and urchins, are all present. Tides and access as Site 800.

Dive sites: Canna and Sanday

802 South of Eilean Ghreannabric. NM273036. The underwater cliffs at this site are unspectacular. Depths to 45m. Black sea cucumbers are notable. A school of white-beaked dolphins up to 4m in length have been seen at this site.

803 South of Eilean Ghreannabric. NM275035. Very similar to Site 802.

804 South of Sgeirean nan Ron. NM277035. Very similar to Site 802.

805 South of Sgeirean nan Ron. NM280035. Very similar to Site 802.

806 Off Dun Mor. NM288034. This is one of the top dives in NW Scotland. It features a sandy plain between 9m and 12m, followed by a knob of rock which falls vertically to 50m, yielding a hugely impressive dive down a magnificent cliff. The life is not as rich as Site 813, but it is still very impressive with large sponges, orange balls of 'worms' over ½m in diameter, and large numbers of cuckoo wrasse on the boulder slope that begins at 50m. This dive is highly recommended and is considered by devotees to be better by far than the cliff on Calve Island (Site 644).

807 Off Garbh Sgeir. NM290034. A steep slope of enormous boulders from 9m to 26m, then the 'wall'.

808 Geodh Sgeir nam Crubag. NM293036. Another excellent dive, which is very craggy on the cliffs. Any depth you fancy to 60m plus! Lots of tidal streams on the corner result in a rich fish population.

809 South of Ceann an Eilein. NM294038. This site consists of a huge plain of rock sloping from 9m to over 65m. Cup corals and gorgonians (*Swiftia*) have been noted.

810 Off Ceann an Eilein. NM295040. A big wall dropping from the 9m plateau past overhangs to 26-30m. Full of life including enormous sponges (*Cliona*).

811 Off Uanh Ruadh. NM295042. A slope of very big boulders falling from 9m and covered in corals. Good fish life. Strong tidal streams.

812 Off Rubha Camas Stianabhaig. NM290046. A rock skerry dropping to 10m, then a slope to a cliff face starting at 24m with boulders at the bottom.

813 Sgeir a' Phuirt. NM286048. The best of this group of dives for marine life, which is extremely rich in species. The reef itself has seals, and cormorants can be seen underwater near the reef. The reef drops straight to 26m as a vertical and overhanging wall to a bottom of rock chasms. A photogenic dive for the rock scenery and (especially) the life.

A kelp forest extends to 8m with the rock underneath covered with purple calceolareous algae and sponges. The vertical rock below this is richly encrusted with soft coral, sponges (*Cliona, Pachymatisma, Myxilla, Suberites*), anemones (*Tealia, Sagartia*), and hydroids. Plumose anemones (*Metridium*) were common on all the deep boulders, and the burrowing anemone (*Cerianthus*) is found in the sediment. A rare sea cucumber (*Parastichopus*) has been noted, as have squid eggs. Lots of cuckoo wrasse and pollack are also to be seen. All in all, a first-class site.

814 West of Sgeir a' Phuirt. NM283049. Very similar to Site 813.

815 Canna Harbour. NM275051. A muddy bottom at 9m. Because of the shelter, rather strange marine life occurs here. For instance, cup corals are found growing on shingle. There is also a rather special reef of true branching coral *(Lophelia pertusa)*.

Diver's panoramic view of Canna

816 Rubha Carr-innis. NM279050. A 9m dive down a craggy cliff to a sandy seabed. Examples of the rare holothurian *Parastichopus tremulus* up to 0.6m long have been noted.

817 Corogon Mor (Castle). NM281055. A rocky slope to 14m covered with a kelp forest. Anemones *(Sagartia, Cerianthus, Sagartiogeton)* have been noted.

818 East of Compass Hill. NM284062. A rocky knob from 9-15m, then a boulder slope going on down. Strong tides are noted. A very pretty dive on the boulders with lobsters and wrasse.

819 Off Compass Hill. NM283063. Kelp-covered rock, then a silt slope to 25m plus. Anemones and seapens *(Pteroeides spinosum)* are noted.

820 Out from Compass Hill. NM284065. A sand slope to over 30m. Boring!

821 East of An t-Each. NM282067. To 12m on sand, then a slope to 16m followed by craggy vertical and overhanging rock. Finally, a slope to 60m plus. Rich life including gorgonians.

822 An T-Each. NM278068. A flat plain to 12m for a long way out, then small rocky steps to 24m. Kelp to 20m, then rich life including nudibranchs below.

Dive sites: Canna & outliers to South

823 Dun Channa. NG204047. A rough rocky slope with steep gullies gives way at 8m to smooth bedrock. At 18m this becomes sand and pebbles. There is a rich kelp forest with sponges below. A rather clean site, with not too much life. Tidal streams up to 4 knots. HW slack −0445 Dover; LW slack +0145 Dover. Launch from Canna Harbour, or carry your gear for 4 miles over rough ground and have a shore dive at slack water!

824 An Steidh. NG216036. These rocks ½ mile South of West Canna appear to have a drop to 18m to the East.

825 Bell Rock and Jemima Rock. NG209021. A cluster of shallow rocks in a general depth of about 25m, about 1½ miles South of Canna. Jemima Rock has been dived by echo-sounding for the shallows at 7m and then diving to the East. This gives a rocky, kelp-covered slope leading to sand at 32m. The life is pleasant but not exceptional, with large yellow sponges dominating. One wonders why it is called *Jemima* Rock − was there ever a wreck of this name here?

826 Umaolo. NG 199004. This is marked by a light-buoy about 2½ miles South of Canna. It is undived, but should be similar to Site 825.

827 Oigh-sgeir (Maiden Rock). NM161165. Lying about 6 miles South-south-west of Canna and 9 miles West of Rum, these rocks are very exposed. A 30m isobath runs close to the East side. Again, strong tidal streams are present (see Site 876).

828 Mill Rocks. These lie a further 3 miles South-west of Oigh-sgeir, at 56 56 40N 06 44 00W. They are awash at chart datum and have depths of 25m around them.

NOTE: It would be a bold, perhaps foolhardy, team that attempted these last three or four undived sites without using a charter vessel. Information would be particularly welcome on any of these sites.

Area information and services

Hydrographic charts: 1794 North Minch − southern part 1:100,000; 2207 Ardnamurchan to Sound of Sleat 1:50,000; 2208 Mallaig to Canna Harbour 1:50,000.
Ordnance Survey 1:50,000 maps: 39 Rum & Eigg.
Ordnance Survey 1:25,000 maps: NG20 Canna; NG30/40 Rhum (North); NM38/48 Eigg & Rhum (South); NM47/57 Island of Muck.
Local BS-AC branches: None.
Local SS-AC branches: None.
Air supplies: None. The nearest are at Tobermory, Oban, and Fort William.
Outboard motor sales and service: None. The nearest is at Mallaig (0687) 2304.
Boat charter: Seafare (0688) 2277; Ian Slade, Beadun, Eas Brae, Tobermory; Jim Kilcullen, 3 Dal-an-Aiseig, North Connel, Oban (0631 71) 454.
Local weather: Glasgow Weather Centre 041 248 3451; Oban Coastguard (0631) 63720.
Sea area: Hebrides (nearly Malin).
Tidal constants:

	DOVER	ULLAPOOL
Muck	−0523	−0103
Eigg	−0523	−0103
Rum	−0525	−0100
Canna	−0525	−0100

Coastguard: Oban MRSC (0631) 63720; Mallaig (0687) 2336.
Lifeboat: Mallaig.
Hospitals: Belford Hospital, Fort William (0397) 2481; Oban County Hospital (0631) 63636; West Highland Hospital, Oban (0631) 63727.
Recompression chambers: Dunstaffnage Marine Laboratory, Oban (0631) 62244; Underwater Training Centre, Fort William (0397) 3786/3136.
Ferry operators: Mallaig-Canna-Rum-Muck – Caledonian MacBrayne (0687) 24030; boat hire between Eigg and Muck – L. MacEwan, Gallanach, Isle of Muck (0687) 2362.
Local tourist information: Mallaig (0687) 2170.
Accommodation: Very limited. Some B & B available with crofters. Hotel on Muck (0687) 2365. Small hotel and limited NCC accommodation on Rum (Chief Warden, NCC, White House, Kinloch, Isle of Rum – [0687 20] 26).
Notes: The NCC produce several interesting booklets about Rum. See also "A short history of the Isle of Rum" by John Love, which is available locally.

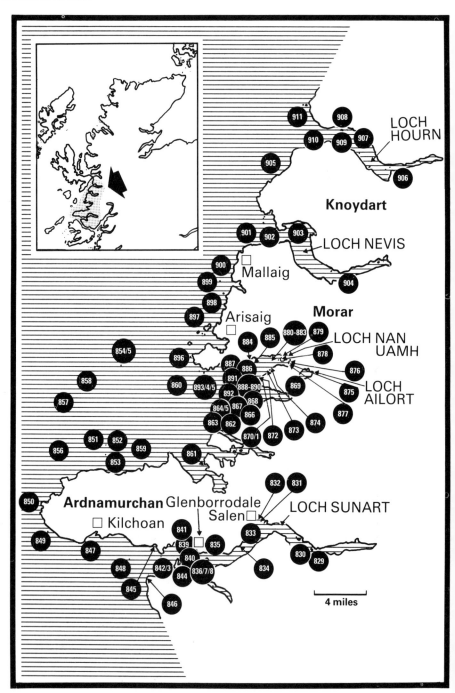

Dive Sites : Loch Sunart to Loch Hourn

CHAPTER 7

Loch Sunart to Loch Hourn

This region of Scotland contains dramatic scenery, some superb diving, and is rarely visited by divers. What more could a diver bent on exploration ask?

The peninsulas and lochs between Loch Sunart and Loch Hourn are remote and still largely inaccessible. There are no direct road routes around the peninsulas, and explorations must be made on foot or by sea. The coast has many sandy beaches, wooded burns, and harbours, and there is many a majestic view of Mull, the Small Isles, Skye, and the Hebrides.

Loch Sunart is the longest of the East-West sea lochs in Scotland. It has three basins (with depths of 93m, 152m, and 88m) as one travels West.

The middle portion of Loch Sunart is fringed with some remarkable underwater cliffs at Risga Island and Risga Pinnacle. These also include the pinnacles of Red Rocks, New Rocks, Little Stirk and Big Stirk described in Chapter 3 (Sound of Mull). Loch Teacuis runs South-east for about 5 miles from the island of Carna in Loch Sunart. As far as I know, it is undived.

The Ardnamurchan peninsula projects 17 miles out into the Atlantic. Lying 23 miles further West than Land's End, it is the most westerly point on the British mainland. Its name means *Point of the Great Ocean*.

Knoydart was the area chosen by Bonnie Prince Charlie in 1745 as being the most likely to support his cause. He landed at Loch nan Uamh, just East of Arisaig, and stayed there for a year before fleeing back to France.

Loch nan Uamh has an irregular sea-floor, with depths reaching 37m. Loch Ailort has a depth of 49m, though it is generally rather shallow.

The coast between Arisaig and Mallaig is rather shallow, and depths increase only slowly. At Morar there is a sandy inlet which only fails to connect with the fresh water of Loch Morar by about 15m.

Loch Nevis is one of the most inaccessible sea lochs in Scotland. No roads lead to it, but a ferry runs from Mallaig to Inverie on the North shore of the loch. Here, there is a 5-mile stretch of road with a cul-de-sac at each end! The inner basin of the loch is 88m deep. The outer basin is 135m deep and connects with the Sound of Sleat over a bar at about 15m.

Loch Hourn lies at the other end of the Knoydart peninsula to Loch Nevis. Its setting is even finer than that of Loch Nevis, with a great sweeping wall of mountains rising to over 900m. In fact, it is the place on Scotland's West coast most reminiscent of the Norwegian fiords. Road access to the loch is poor. A 20-mile-long single-track road winds its way down from the shores of Loch Garry to the cul-de-sac of Kinlochourn, right at the head of the loch. Alternatively, a 15-mile cul-de-sac from Loch Duich which passes through Glenelg can be used to reach Arnisdale on the North shore of Loch Hourn.

The bathymetry of Loch Hourn is complicated. There are four inner basins (with East-to-West depths of 18m, 35m, 40m, and 47m) separated by narrow channels (with depths of ½m, 8m, and 6m) before the final narrows (15m deep) connect with the main loch. This reaches a maximum depth of 185m before joining the Sound of Sleat (with depths around 85m).

Tidal streams are only significant in the various narrows in the sea lochs, and to a lesser extent off the Point of Ardnamurchan. Depths can be substantial, and visibility is generally above average, but fresh-water run-off can restrict the visibility near the heads of the sea lochs.

The area is best dived by car and inflatable, but you will have to be prepared to do a lot of driving. An MFV is also excellent, although some skippers might be reluctant to negotiate some of the narrows in sea lochs.

An exciting new dive centre – Doune Divers – occupies what may well be the most remote situation in mainland Scotland at the head of Dun Ban Bay at the western extremity of Knoydart. This rugged peninsula lies 6 miles north of Mallaig. There is no access to Doune from the UK road system; instead access is normally via *Gripper*, Doune Divers' workboat, which will collect you with all your gear from Mallaig (which is a road, rail and ferry terminal). Doune was an old shepherd's croft house that has been superbly converted by Alan and Mary Robinson helped by their sons Toby and Jamie. The house is idyllically situated on the shore of the more northerly of the twin bays of Dun Ban Bay. Here, Alan has also built a modern bunkhouse, a large boatshed and a workshop. The modern bunkhouse is warm, comfortable and well equipped on a self-catering basis. It is about 200m south of the house, on the shore of the more southerly bay. Alan has equipped this bay with a slipway and winch. Doune Divers offer several boating options. A 39ft fast launch makes distant sites accessible. Then there is the 26ft *Gripper*, usually skippered by Jamie, plus an RIB with 50hp engine which is available for divers who want to explore on their own, and a 21ft dayboat rigged as a gunter yawl. Doune offer comprehensive air facilities.

Dive sites: Loch Sunart

In recent years much of Loch Sunart has been heavily dredged for scallops. Consequently, the bottom habitats are considerably damaged and in many places it is only the rocky peaks that are of interest.

829 Laudale Pier. NM759598. A sloping mud and rock bottom with occasional boulder outcrops to 20m. Brittle star carpet, crustaceans, scallops, and lots of junk under the pier. Shore access from track leaving the A884 at NM784596.

830 Laudale Narrows. NM756602. A fierce tidal stream (of up to 3.5 knots) runs through the narrows, but this is a good dive at slack water (at +0100 and −0400 Dover). The depth is 12m, and the rocks are covered with soft coral and anemones. Around the rocks is thick silt. Access as Site 829.

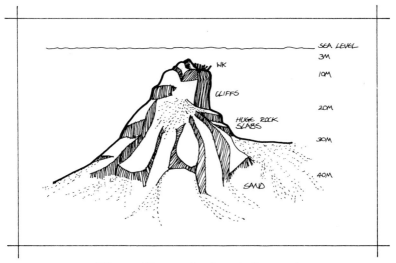

Risga Pinnacle, Loch Sunart

831 Salen Bay. NM689642. A muddy dive to 10m off the pier. The bottom is covered with 'junk' thrown in over the last 200 years. Scallops and Norway lobsters can often be seen. Shore access.

832 Just South of Rubha Bhuailte. NM684633. A dramatic cliff-face to 22m, then a boulder/cobble slope with scallops. Lots of feather stars and other starfish. Shore access.

833 Camastorsa. NM674622. A cliff face to 6m, then a boulder slope to a rough rock fang at 24m. Enormous numbers of feather stars, and lots of squat lobsters. A pleasant dive with shore access.

834 Rubha Suainphort. NM666612. Similar to Site 833.

835 Sron nam Brathan. NM628606. Steep rocks and slopes lead to boulders and sand at 40m. Cuttlefish have been seen at this site. Shore access.

836 Risga. NM610602. A sheer rock-face to 20-25m is heavily encrusted with life, especially feather stars. Twenty-two species of nudibranch were collected here on one dive in early autumn in 25m visibility! Boat access from Port na Croisg (NM583619).

837 Risga Pinnacle. NM605602. This lies 300m due West of the North-west tip of Risga. It is a sensational dive which reaches to within 3m of the surface, yet drops to 60m in the South and 40m in the West. The steeply-sloping rock walls are covered with hydroids, bryozoans, nudibranchs, gorgonians, and unusual sponges. Access as Site 836.

838 Unknown wrecks. There are the wrecks of two vessels (one a 5m fishing boat) on top of Risga Pinnacle.

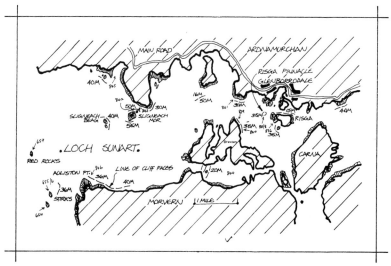

Dive sites in lower Loch Sunart

839 Oronsay. NM596599. A steeply-sloping bottom of broken rocks and occasional small cliffs to 20m. Squat lobsters, crabs, dogfish, sponges, and cup corals, have been noted.

840 Oronsay, North-east face. The underwater cliff facing Risga drops to 35m, but most of the life is on the pinnacle itself.

841 Rubha Aird Druimmich. NM596606. Another steep rocky slope very similar to Site 840. Depths to 40m. Shore access.

842 Sligneach Mor. NM563602. A near-vertical rocky cliff to 36m lies at the East side of these rocky islets. Access as Site 836. Bold souls can shore dive here. There is reputed to be a 50m cliff to the South of these rocks.

843 Rocks North-east of Sligneach Mor. NM563603. A drying rock lies about 30m North-east of the most North-easterly rock of Sligneach Mor. A mud slope off the North of these rocks gives way to a cliff to the North-east of the rocks which is charted to 54m, and is vertical from 5m to at least 31m. Lots of life make this an excellent site for the photographer, with colonial sea squirts, brown hard bryozoans, gorgonians, plumose anemones, cup corals, etc. Access as Site 836.

844 Loch na Droma Buidhe. NM588581. A very sheltered site with a muddy bottom at 10m. Scallops and Norway lobsters have been noted. Access as Site 836.

845 Camas nan Geall. NM559617. A very poor dive to a muddy bottom at 27m and no apparent life. Unrepeatable!

846 Auliston Point. NM546581. This is a splendid dive. It shelves gently to 12m, then there is a vertical and overhanging wall to 36m. A few hundred metres further east, the cliff consists of shattered faces riven by canyons. Normal encrusting life. Tidal streams of up to 1 knot. HW slack +0600 Dover; LW slack −0130 Dover. Access from Tobermory or Port na Croise, Ardnamurchan.

847 Mingary Pier. NM493627. A shore dive to a sandy seabed at about 20m. A pleasant dive in good visibility with gurnard, angler fish, dogfish, and scallops.

848 MacParlin Rock. NM526603. This lies about 1 mile North of the group of rocks (Red, New, Stirk Rocks, etc) listed in Chapter 3 (Sound of Mull), and has a minimum depth of 7m. To the North-north-east, MacParlin Rock gives an excellent dive down a 45-degree bedrock slope to 30m, where it flattens out. To the West there is a slope charted to 60m. Access as Site 846.

Dive sites: Ardnamurchan Peninsula

849 Eilean nan Seachd Seisrichean. NM424639. This gives an excellent dive over sand-covered bedrock steps to beyond 20m. Both the light and the life are good. Boat access as Site 850.

850 Point of Ardnamurchan. NM415675. Pleasant diving on rocky, sheltered slopes to about 10m. Crustaceans are to be found. The visibility can be quite good. The point itself is usually reached by boat access (either from Sanna Bay, Kilchoan Bay, or North Mull), although there are tracks to both sides of it. It has also been shore-dived from the end of the public road. But this demands a long snorkel over deep, kelp-filled gullies. Tidal streams run up to 1.5 knots. LW slack +0130; HW slack −0430 Dover.

851 Bo Fascadale, West side. NM498750 (approximately). This is an isolated underwater pinnacle which rises from about 80m to almost break the surface. It lies about 2½ miles North of the village of Fascadale (NM500708), at 56 58 00N 06 05 45W. This is best located with an echo-sounder, but at low water with a little swell running (this is a very exposed site!) the changing water colour and movement give it away. (Try running North from Port Ban for 2 miles, then look 200m West for heavy waves). A light buoy lies about a ½ mile to the North-west. Access by boat from Fascadale. Tides as Site 850.

The western, seaward, side of the rock drops gently at first, then steeply. It is fairly bare because of the pounding it gets.

Warning: If there is any size of sea running it makes it easy to find the rock, but beware the standing waves. They appear to go from a 1m swell to a 3m wall of water right under the boat. This complicates boat-handling, and makes decompression stops very bumpy, to put it mildly!

852 Bo Fascadale, East Side. Nick Tapp, one of the leading explorers of West coast dive sites, considered the East face of Bo Fascadale to be the best site he had seen until he went to St. Kilda. It offers a vertical rock wall to 55m, with a 1m wide ledge at 38m. The whole wall is hidden beneath a riotous covering of brilliant soft corals, octopus, lobster, and anemones. A 45-degree sand slope runs from 55m to beyond 60m (it is charted to 84m). A dive not easily forgotten!

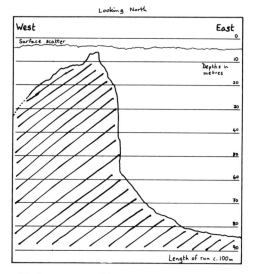

Echo sounding: Bo Fascadale

853 Elizabeth Rock, NM494735 (approximately). This lies about 1 mile South of Bo Fascadale, and rises from about 40m to the surface. The life is similar to that on Bo Fascadale, but the drop-off is nothing like as exciting. At first, there is a slope, then a smallish cliff, then another slope leading to the edge of a larger cliff. This runs to 56m before apparently sloping away again. The rock is quite hard to locate, even with an echo sounder.

854 Oberon Bank, Sound of Arisaig, West side. 56 52 21N 06 01 52W. Oberon Bank is a submarine rock ridge about ¾ of a mile long lying about midway between Eigg and Arisaig. It reaches to within 15m of the surface at one point according to the Admiralty Chart (2207) (although I have been unable to locate anything shallower than 18m at low water springs). The ridge runs north-south. The North end descends steadily to 55m, but the South end drops more steeply to 62m.

The bank can only be located by echo sounder. The best tactic is to steam West from well East of the Bank, with Eilean Chathastail Light (south Eigg) bearing 280°M. At the Bank, Fascadale House (Ardnamurchan peninsula) bears 206°M and Ardnamurchan Lighthouse bears 226°M. If weather conditions are good, then the transits on Eigg and Ardnamurchan will help. In poor conditions Decca coordinates will be necessary.

The top of the bank is a fairly distinct rocky ridge with depths generally about 20m. To the west, the ridge gradually deepens in a series of bedrock steps with shingly sand in between. These steps descend beyond 34m (charted to 55m). No wall has yet been found.

855 Oberon Bank, East side. If the western aspect was all that there was to Oberon Bank, then it would only rank as a good dive. However, the East side of the bank provides one of the most rewarding dives in Scottish waters. From the ridge, there is a slope of rocky buttresses to a fairly broad ledge and 'edge' at about 30m. Over this edge there is a vertical and sometimes overhanging rock wall which is charted as dropping to 84m!

The wall is covered with feathery hydroids, colourful anemones, and numerous feather stars together with other life. At 60m there is an overhang that slopes under the cliff at about 45 degrees – apparently into a cave. At this 60m cave there is blackness all around and below (due to the greenish coastal water and the cliff itself cutting out light). The cave has only been penetrated for about 3m, with no sign of a back wall.

Here, I must emphasise that this dive is a *very serious undertaking*. This is a place for only the most experienced of divers due to the depth (both above and below), and to the fact that a free-swimming stage decompression will probably be required.

A deep exploration of the wall (and cave) puts this dive into a risk category shared by only a very few other dives in Scotland. However, I commend it very highly to those divers capable of tackling it in reasonable safety.

856 Shoal 1 mile North of Sanna Point. (NM439703). This is one of several sites to the North of Ardnamurchan which look interesting on the chart because the isobaths appear very close together. I am not able to explain why these dramatic underwater features exist in this area, and I would welcome suggestions. The 1982 metric chart (2207) was produced from soundings taken from old surveys. It is to be expected that further uncharted shoals may exist. At this particular site, soundings of 16 and 63m are shown close to one another.

857 Bank 2 miles East of Muck. The 30m and 50m isobaths are almost coincident at the East end of the bank.

858 North-east end of Maxwell Bank (2 mile South-east of Eigg). The 20m, 30m, and 50m, isobaths are coincident here.

859 Shoal 1 mile North of Garbh Rubha. (NM538711). The 30m and 50m isobaths are coincident here.

860 Shoal 2 miles West of the Bellows. (NM624810). Soundings of 25m and 62m are shown next to each other.

Dive sites: Arisaig

All the sites (861-895) in the Sound of Arisaig area are accessible by boat from three different points – Glen Uig Bay (NM673776), head of Loch nam Uamh (NM728842), and Druimindarroch (NM684843).

861 Sgeir an Eididh, Loch Ceann Traigh. NM618713. A flat rock and sand bottom with kelp cover at the South-west of the island. Scorpion fish have been noted. A rather ordinary dive. Access by boat from Ardtoe (NM629608).

862 North channel, Loch Moidart. NM646752. Shallow, sandy narrows with tidal streams up to about 4 knots. To the North of Eilean Shona the bottom drops to 29m on to mud.

863 Am Boc. NM645777. A dive at the South of the island on to a kelp-covered, rocky bottom at 14m. Lots of small life among the kelp.

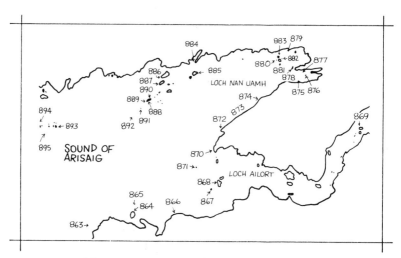

Dive sites in the Sound of Arisaig

864 Samalaman Island, Glen Uig Bay. NM662781. A shallow dive on sand and weed. The island is separated from the mainland by a very shallow sandy channel.

865 Samalaman Trench, Glen Uig Bay. NM662783. About 200m off the North of Samalaman island is a steep drop-off from 15m to 46m. Lobsters and angler fish have been noted, but otherwise the site is rather ordinary. Boat access is from the slip in Glen Uig Bay (at 673776). Otherwise, this site must be reached by means of a strenuous shore dive at low tide.

866 Rubh' a' Chairn Mhoir, Glen Uig Bay. NM676782. Kelp to 12m, then sand. Shore access from the road. A good night dive because all the life in the kelp is then out on the sand.

867 Sgeir Ghlas, Loch Ailort. NM691791. A broken rocky bottom with patches of sand to 20m. Scallops, angler fish, anemones, and urchins, have been noted. In mid-May staggering numbers of translucent jellyfish congregate here due to the wind and water movement. A pleasant dive with boat access from Glen Uig Bay.

868 Eilean nan Gobhar, Loch Ailort. NM693793. A pretty boring dive in the western bay on kelp and boulders to 14m, then sand. The ruined fort on top of the hill is more interesting!

869 Eilean Dubh, Loch Ailort. NM746813. Underwater, this chain of islands drops steeply, usually vertically, to 30-43m and a mud floor on the North-west side. The bottom is a brittle star carpet. The walls are solidly encrusted with anemones, etc, giving an breathtaking dive. The North shore of the loch has similar drop-offs. Beware of the fish farm and its large numbers of sunken cages. A strenuous snorkel out from the shore, or launch a boat at the nearby bay (NM755813).

870 Rubha Chaolais, Ardnish. NM692807. A steep drop to over 30m, then sand. The rocks are covered with cup corals, plumose anemones, and soft corals. Picturesque scenery. Boat access is from Glen Uig Bay or near the railway viaduct at Loch nan Uamh (NM727842).

871 Priest Rock, Loch Ailort. NM684798. Awash at low water, this rock is easy to spot if conditions are rough: otherwise an echo sounder is required. It lies about ½ a mile South-west from Site 868. The rock gullies are packed with life, giving an excellent dive. Launch as Site 867.

872 West of Port an t-Sluichd. NM693893. An excellent dive down a boulder slope to 38m. A seabed of shell sand then slopes away at 45 degrees, with lots of hydroids and nudibranchs on the rocks. Access as Site 870.

873 Ardnish peninsula, North-west face. NM693814 – NM706823. A 1½-mile section of coast with a craggy shore. Underwater, there is a 10m cliff, then a mud slope which runs off to the depths.

874 Ardnish cliff site. NM707826. A pleasant dive down a vertical cliff. The cliff has kelp to about 15m, then a life-filmed wall to 26m where the mud slope starts. Lots of anemones, sponges, tunicates, etc, make this site rewarding for the macro photographer. The site is easy to locate by rounding Rubha Chaolais (from Loch Ailort) as this section of the low coastal cliff juts out from the rest. There are three low rock buttresses just above the site.

875 Loch Beag, South shore. NM725833. A rocky cliff to 10m and a sandy seabed.

876 Corr Eilean, South side, Loch Beag. NM726835. A cliff face to 14m, then sand.

877 Loch Beag, North shore. NM727837. A cliff to 10m, then sand.

878 Aird nam Buth, Loch nan Uamh. NM723836. A series of walls and rock faces around the point to 20m, then sand. A pleasant, untaxing shore or boat dive with a good variety of marine life.

879 The Prince's Cairn, Loch nan Uamh. NM720844. Shore access to a rocky bottom at 7-8m, then sand with rocky outcrops. Noted for seapens and angler fish.

880 Eilean Gobhlach, Loch nan Uamh. NM715840. This island gives excellent diving. The west tip of the island drops in a series of steep faces to 30m. Access as Site 870.

881 Eilean Gobhlach, South face. NM716839. This has rock walls from 10-25m. They are well encrusted with life and there is also a legendary lobster which should be left alone as it is frighteningly large!

882 Eilean Gobhlach, East face. NM712841. There is a shallow reef running about half-way to Eilean Ceann Feidh. The sides drop to 26m.

883 Eilean Gobhlach, North face. NM716842. Very similar to Site 882.

884 Druimindarrach. NM682840. Shallow, pleasant dives can be made around the mouth of the inlet of Saideal Druim an Daraich.

885 Eilean nan Cabar, Borrodale Islands. NM684836. Access by permission from Druimindarroch (NM686844). There is a cliff on the East end of the island to about 20m, followed by steeply-shelving sand. This cliff curves round to the North, then cuts back West. Angler fish have been noted.

886 An Garbh-eilean, South tip. NM672830. A rocky slope to 14m on to a sandy seabed.

887 Sgeir Dubh, Borrodale Islands. NM673823. A thick kelp forest leading to sand at 18m. Starfish, squat lobsters, and urchins, abound in the jumbled rocks and gullies. Boat access as Site 885.

888 An Glas-eilean, South-east face. NM667824. A kelp-covered rock slope on to sand at 12m.

889 An Glas-eilean, South-west tip. NM665824. A series of rocky steps descending to 26m. Lots of anemones and feather stars.

890 An Glas-eilean, North-west face. NM666825. A kelp-covered rocky slope to 10m on to sand sloping gently to 15m, then a mud slope to beyond 34m. Apart from a few interesting anemones on the sand there is little of note.

891 Astly Rock, Borrodale Islands. NM664821. This lies 300m South-west of An Glas-eilean and is accessible from Druimindarroch. The rock is at 5m and drops to well below 20m in a series of ridges and gullies. Soft corals, anemones, lobsters, and dragonets, have been noted.

892 Gulnare Rock. This submarine rock lies 0.8 miles South-west of An Glas Eilean and has a minimum depth of 3m. It is somewhat difficult to locate by echo sounding, though it gives pleasant diving down rocky slopes to about 25m.

893 Eilean an t-Snidhe, East side, Sound of Arisaig. NM632814. Boat access as Site 891 or from Arisaig, 6 miles away. The seabed slopes away quite quickly over a kelpy rock bottom. Sea cucumbers noted.

894 Eilean an t-Snidhe, West side. NM623814. To the North of the West point the bottom becomes a maze of rocky ridges and gullies, sandy passages, and caves, at about 19m. In good visibility the scenery is superb.

895 The Bellows. These rocks lie just South of Eilean an t-Snidhe. They are awash. To their South the bottom drops steadily to 23m.

896 Meallan Odhar, Arisaig. NM604840. Access by boat from Arisaig. Large beds of kelp with their associated populations are the features of this shallow dive.

897 Eilean Ighe, Arisaig. NM635885. At Na Tairbh there are kelp-covered rock faces going down to a seabed of sand at 10m. Shore access involves a walk.

898 An Glas-eilean, Arisaig. NM645913. A 1-mile snorkel from the shore, followed by a shallow, sandy dive to 10m. Eventually, beyond the island, the sand drops to 15m and scallops are found.

899 Wreck of the Fair Morn. 56 58 30N 05 53 30W. This vessel lies about 1¾ miles due West of Morar Bay in 26m of water. She was an MFV and was lost in 1969. I have no more information, and as far as I know she has not been dived. Boat access as Site 900.

900 Bogha Dearg, South of Mallaig. NM665949. An interesting small island that has a pool at the centre. All the island, including the pool, is covered with bones. It is possible to circumnavigate the island underwater at 15m. The seabed is composed of large areas of bedrock. Anemones, tube worms, crustaceans, and angler fish, have been noted. Boat access is from Morar Bay at high tide (NM676934).

901 Mallaigvaig. NM690978. Shore access to a sandy underwater slope beyond the first few metres of boulders.

Dive sites: Loch Nevis

902 Sron Raineach. NM708981. This site features a 45-degree boulder slope which descends to over 20m. The scenery and the visibility are usually good. Note, however, that the site is extremely exposed. Inflatables have been totally swamped by heavy squalls in these waters, so beware. Launching must be carried out at Morar as there is no easy inflatable launch-point at Mallaig.

903 Headland East of Eilean Grunhais. NM732982. This is similar to the previous site, though the boulder slope drops to over 100m on the chart!

904 Loch Nevis Narrows at Sgeir an t-Sruth. NM808938. A good drift drive over a sandy bottom at about 5m. Rates up to 3 knots. LW slack +0110 Dover; HW slack −0510 Dover. Access is poor and involves a long boat journey from Morar or Mallaig.

Dive sites: Knoydart coast

905 I have no dives recorded on this coast between Loch Nevis and Loch Hourn, a distance of some 10 miles. There appear to be several interesting rocky sites.

Dive sites: Loch Hourn

906 Loch Hourn Narrows. NG889064 and NG870065. Similar to Site 967, except that depths around Eilean Mhogh-sgeir are around 15m and at Caolas Mor about 6m. LW slack +0155 Dover; HW slack −0415 Dover.

907 Sgeir nan Gealag. NG834108. Steep access from the road to a rocky shore. A steep sand and rock slope descends to over 30m. Shell-fish are noted on the sand.

Looking West across Loch Hourn

908 Caolas Eilean Rarsaidh. NG814112. A pleasant drift dive at about 1 knot at a depth of 15m. Lots of life on the shell-sand and boulder bottom. Access is from the road just above the shore.

909 Eilean Rarsaidh. NG810116. A very deep site with bedrock and boulders leading in a series of slopes and steps to beyond 50m. Quite similar to the North face of Isle Martin (Site 1131). Lots of small crustaceans to be seen. This site can be reached from the shore if you are determined. Otherwise use boat access from Arnisdale (NG846102).

910 Sgeir Ulibhe. NG775110. A drying rock near the mouth of Loch Hourn, ½ a mile South-west of Glas Eilean (NG786117). To the South of the rock there is a steep slope to over 25m, with lots of life on the rocks. Access as Site 909.

911 Sandaig Islands, South of Sleat. NG761145. The southern tip of Eilean Mor gives depths to about 15m on to sand. Shore access at low tide, otherwise launch at Glenelg (NG807189).

Area information and services

Hydrographic charts: 2207 Ardnamurchan to Sound of Sleat 1:50,000; 2208 Mallaig to Canna Harbour 1:50,000; 2392 Sound of Mull – western entrance 1:25,000; 2394 Loch Sunart 1:25,000; 2540 Loch Alsh & approaches 1:20,000; 2541 Lochs Hourn & Duich 1:25,000.
Ordnance Survey 1:50,000 maps: 33 Loch Alsh & Glen Shiel; 40 Loch Shiel; 47 Tobermory; 49 Oban & East Mull.
Ordnance Survey 1:25,000 maps: NM45/35 Tobermory; NM46/56 Ardnamurchan; NM47/57 Island of Muck; NM65/75 Morvern; NM66/76 Loch Sunart; NM67/77 Moidart; NM68/78 Arisaig & Lochailort; NM69/79 Mallaig; NM86/96 Ardgour; NM89/99 Glen Dessary; NG60/70 Mid Sound of Sleat;

NG61/71 North Sound of Sleat; NG80/90 Loch Hourn; NG81/91 Shiel Bridge.
Local BS-AC branches: Fort William (1148).
Local SS-AC branch: Western Isles, Tobermory.
Air supplies: Mull Diving Centre, Salen Pier, Aros, Mull (068 03) 411; Seafare, Portmore Place, Tobermory (0688) 2277; Fort William BS-AC.
Outboard motor sales and service: Seafare (0688) 2277; Mallaig (0687) 2304.
Boat charter: Seafare (0688) 2277; Ian Slade, Beadun, Eas Brae, Tobermory; Jim Kilcullen, 3 Dal-an-Aiseig, North Connel, Oban (0631 71) 454.
Harbourmasters: Mallaig (0687) 2154.
Local weather: Glasgow Weather Centre 041 248 3451; Oban Coastguard (0631) 63720.
Sea area: Hebrides and Malin.
Tidal constants:

	DOVER	ULLAPOOL
Loch Hourn	−0520	−0100
Loch Nevis	−0520	−0100
Mallaig	−0515	−0055
Sound of Arisaig	−0523	−0103
Loch Moidart	−0523	−0103
Loch Sunart	−0502	−0042

Coastguard: Oban MRSC (0631) 63720; Tobermory (0688) 2200; Mallaig (0687) 2336.
Lifeboat: Mallaig.
Police stations: Arisaig (068 75) 222; Mallaig (0687) 2177.
Hospitals: Belford Hospital, Fort William (0397) 2481; Oban County Hospital (0631) 63636; West Highland Hospital, Oban (0631) 63727.
Recompression chambers: Dunstaffnage Marine Laboratory, Oban (0631) 62244; Underwater Training Centre, Fort William (0397) 3786/3136.
Vehicle recovery: AA – Glasgow 041 812 0101.
Ferry operators: For local tours, etc, try either Bruce Watt Cruises, The Pier, Mallaig (0687) 2233/2320, or Arisaig Hotel & Marine Ltd, Arisaig (068 75) 224.
Local tourist information: Mallaig (0687) 2170.
Accommodation: At Knoydart, there is Doune Divers – 0687 2667; many B & B and guest houses addresses are listed for this area in the Scottish Tourist Board guide.

Divers explore the wreck of HMS Port Napier, a 150-metre long mine-layer which lies in 21m of water about 300m from the Skye shore

CHAPTER 8

Skye and its associated islands

The easy access and breathtaking scenery of the Island of Skye make it the most popular of the Hebrides with tourists.

The island's Gaelic name, Eilean a' Cheo means *Isle of Mist,* and the description is frequently apt. Skye is a big island, divided into six peninsulas by an intricate coastline of sea lochs, with each loch and penisula having quite a different character. This island is 48 miles long, and is the second largest off the Scottish coast at 672 square miles.

Skye is accessible by three ferries. The Kyle of Lochalsh to Kyleakin ferry runs continously seven days a week, the journey only taking about 10 minutes. In summer, there is another short crossing between Gleneig and Kylerhea, but this does not run on Sundays. A second summer-only, six day ferry operates between Mallaig and Armadale, the crossing taking 30 minutes. There are also ferries from Uig to the Outher Hebrides, and from Sconser to Raasay. Loganair fly six days a week in the summer from Glasgow to Broadford, with a flight time of 55 minutes.

The scenery and coastline of Skye would take a book in themselves to describe fully. If the coastline was stretched out, it would be four times the direct distance from the Mull of Kintyre to Cape Wrath! All I can do here is to pick out the main details and leave readers to delve into the books listed in the appropriate appendix.

Skye contains an enormous range of different scenic features. The best known is the Cuillin range of mountains. These provide the British mountaineer and rock-climber with the ultimate challenge. Naked fangs of rock twisted and weathered into awesome shapes make for staggering scenery in the Black Cuillins. These dramatic manifestations of volcanic activity rival even St. Kilda in their complexity. They were all formed in the same period that produced Tertiary volcanoes all along the West coast of Scotland (see the chapters on Mull). The more rounded Red Cuillins lie to the North-east of the Black Cuillins. They are made of granite as opposed to the gabbro of the Black Cuillins. The North of the island consists of a succession of lava flows which give a stepped appearance to the landscape. The dramatic features of the Quiraing and the Old Man of Stoer were caused by volcanic rock becoming stranded on top of soft clays when the glaciers melted, then slipping down through the clay. The South-east

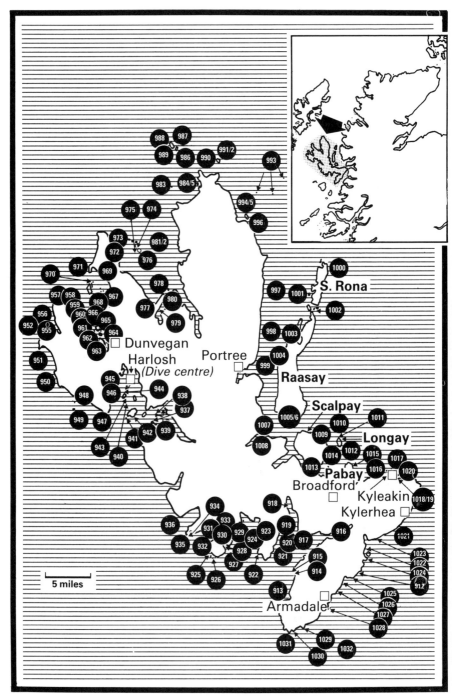

Dive Sites : Skye and its associated islands

portion of the island is structurally part of the North-West Highlands. This area is mainly Torridonian Sandstone, but there is also a little Lewisian gneiss at the very South-east of the Sleat peninsula.

Thirty thousand people left Skye in the emigrations of 1840-1888, and the current population of the islands is seven thousands. It should be noted that Skye folk, in common with many other Hebridean island communities, are rather strict in their interpretation of what activities may be carried out on Sundays. It would therefore be imprudent to flaunt your activities openly on a Sunday – better by far to have a low-profile dive somewhere out of sight.

Associated with Skye are a number of other, smaller islands. Soay lies off the South-west coast, and is 3½ miles long. This was the island from which the writer Gavin Maxwell ran his basking shark fishery in 1946. Also on the West coast lie Wiay, Harlosh Island, Isay, the Ascrib Islands, and Tulm Island. To the North are Fladda-chuain, Lord McDonald's Table, and Eilean Trodday. These are of interest to us because of the wrecks associated with them. Eilean Flodigarry, Staffin Island, Scalpay, Longay, and Pabay, lie close to the coast on the East. There is reputed to be a galleon of the Spanish Armada wrecked somewhere near Staffin Island. Coins have been found, and there are people on the island who are reputedly of Spanish descent.

Further East, between the Inner Sound and the Sound of Raasay, lie Raasay and Rona. Rona is 5 miles long, and is uninhabited except for lighthouse-keepers and Navy personnel. Raasay is 13 miles long, and has a population of 150. The view from Dun Caan, the 444m summit of Raasay, to the Cuillins (at 993m) is stunning.

From a diving point of view, Skye, with its immense coastline, is a very varied island. The southern coasts are rather featureless for divers, though Soay gives excellent diving. The West coast is not yet fully explored. Harlosh Dive Centre (see below) is situated in the middle of this West coast. There are a number of wrecks along the North-west and North coasts, and these give some interesting diving. The East coast has the deeps of the Sound of Raasay, and also Raasay and Rona with their associated dramatic underwater slopes. Right at the South-east, in Loch Alsh, there is pleasant diving both on the wreck of the *Port Napier,* and in the strong tidal streams.

Generally, the tidal streams around Skye are rather weak, though this is not the case everywhere. The visibility is usually excellent. One of the problems, however, is access to the water, especially for boats. Often one's way is cut off by high ground or sea cliffs. At other places, farmland and fences obstruct the shores. You will need, therefore, to carefully plan your access routes.

For some years now, compressed air has been available from Norman Thorpe of Portree Diving Services (0478 2274), though his main activity is professional diving. Recently, a diving centre has been opened at Harlosh, nar Dunvegan, by Mike Kirkland and his wife. This offers splendid self-catering accommodation of a delightful standard, together with com-pressed air to 275 bars and boat hire facilities. Basing yourself here allows you to explore the remote West coast of Skye. Mike is very helpful in assisting you to achieve your diving objectives, and I warmly commend his Skye Diving Centre to you.

Dive sites

The sites in this area are numbered in a clockwise direction starting at the Point of Sleat, in South Skye. For dives around the islands of North Skye (Sites 983-992) remember to allow for tidal streams of up to 2½ knots. LW slack +0415 Dover; HW slack −0145 Dover.

912 Tartar Rock. NG694090. An underwater pinnacle ½ a mile offshore which just fails to break surface. The rock walls are about 15m high and have lots of life on them. Lobsters, congers, soft coral, and anemones, noted. A good dive with a maximum depth of 24m. Access is from Knock Bay (NG671087).

913 Inver Dalavil, Sleat. NG570052. A sandy bay with rocks to the East and depths of about 15m. Angler fish and rays are found on the sand; hydroids and nudibranchs on the rocks. Boat access is from Tarshavaig Bay (NG587088).

914 Sgeir Biodaig, Tarshavaig Bay. NG570083. A very exposed site where the shallow offshore rocks drop to about 15m on to shell sand. The rocks are heavily broken up, and covered with a kelp forest. Access as Site 913.

915 Tarshavaig Point. NG575099. A boulder slope to 12m, covered in kelp, and leading to a gently-shelving sand plain.

916 Eilean Heast, Loch Eishart. NG650156. A very sheltered site with mud to 10m and beyond. Brittlestars, etc, on the bottom. Not recommended! Access from bay at NG616132.

917 Rubha Suisnish. NG584159. At Calaman cave (which is above sea level) there is a gentle bedrock slope to 6m, then boulders to 13m. The kelp forest contains all the normal life. Access as Site 916, or from the head of Loch Slapin (NG571214).

918 Rubha Cruaidhlinn, Loch Slapin. NG570186. A shallow dive over kelp-covered rock to muddy sand at 5m. Access from the shore, or by boat from the East shore of the loch. Not recommended.

919 Dun Ringill, Loch Slapin. NG563170. A rock and mud slope leads down to 16m. Kelp and urchins are common! Access as Site 918.

920 Dun Liath, Strathaird. NG549145. A flat, creviced bedrock plateau at 4m. Not too exciting! About 100m offshore there is said to be a steep slope to at least 40m. Access as Site 918.

921 Spar Cave, Strathaird. NG538128. A boulder slope to 8m, then a sandy plain dropping very slowly. Access as Site 918.

922 Suidhe Biorach, Elgol. NG515124. This is an exposed site underneath vertical cliffs. The seabed consists of rocky gullies and crevices giving way to sand with boulders. The kelp forest extends to 13m. Lots of urchins, soft corals, and other life. Access from near Elgol (NG516136).

923 Under Bidein an Fhithich, Elgol. NG515146. An exposed site with a boulder slope to 6m, then maerl to 16m, and finally a mud slope to beyond

20m. Lots of kelp at first, followed by species common to mud slopes. Access as Site 922.

924 Bogha Carrach. NG497148. This is a shoal in the centre of Loch Scavaig with a minimum depth of 3m. The bottom consists of big boulders which give way to sand and mud as depths of 20m are reached. The site has not been dredged, and gives an excellent dive with lots of life. Access as Site 922.

925 Na Gamhnaichean, Soay Island. NG431122. A superb dive. To the South-east of the low rocks above the water is a series of shallow reefs and breaking rocks. These are the highlight of diving at Soay. There are steep drop-offs in all directions to about 26m. The gullies are carpeted with anemones, and congers swim around the reefs. Crawfish and wrasse hide around the bottom rocks. All in all, a huge variety of colourful life. Weak tidal steams. LW slack is at −0445 Dover. Access from Elgol (NG516136), 6 miles. Alternatively, visitors can camp on the island.

926 A' Chearc, Soay. NG433120. Very similar to Site 925.

927 Rubha Dubh, Soay. NG458128. A pleasant shallow dive over kelp forests with very rich and prolific life. This is also a good area for basking sharks. Access as Site 925.

928 Camas nan Gall, Soay. NG455144. A sand and gravel bottom at 10m with scallops. The visibility here can be excellent.

929 Soay Sound. NG470164. A very pleasant site at 34m in the middle of the Sound. The tidal streams can carry a diver over a flat, but quite dramatic, bottom of boulders and shell sand with superb marine life. Gorgonians and the rare *Arachnactis sarsi* anemone noted. Access as Site 925.

930 North coast of Soay. NG457162. There is a fair tidal stream in Soay Sound, and it runs continuously! Boulders and kelp in the shallows, then a flat sand and gravel bottom beyond 12m. Lots of crabs, but not a very exciting dive. Access as Site 925.

931 Soay Harbour. NG450150. A flat muddy bottom to 6m. Lots of crabs and anemones. A pleasant night dive.

932 Soay, West coast. NG427146 (approx). This is actually a group of sites off the series of points that protrude form the West of Soay. They all have steep boulder slopes to sand at around 22m. Octopus, crawfish, wrasse, gobies, ling, and gurnard, have all been noted.

933 Soay Sound, West. NG440160. Access and tides as Site 930. The bottom here is of flat rock and mud at 41m. There are crabs, squat lobsters, and sea pens, to be seen.

934 Sgeir Mhor. NG394158. A very rapid descent to over 40m down a stepped rock wall with no bottom located (charted at 47m). Deep-water sponges and gorgonians *(Swiftia pallida)* noted. Access as Site 935.

935 Rubh' an Dunain, Loch Brittle. NG386163. A pleasant dive on a rocky slope to 25m and a sandy/bouldery bottom. Plenty of fish life, especially cuckoo wrasse. Access is from Glen Brittle (NG408206). (Note: access to Soay is also possible from here).

936 Geodha Daraich, Loch Brittle. NG375189. Very similar to Site 935. Near to the launch-spot the seabed is of cobbles and mud at 15m. Rather poor, but rays are often seen.

937 Sgurr nan Uan, South Loch Bracadale. NG328349. A rocky, picturesque site, shallow at first, then dropping quite steeply to 47m further out. Access is from Fiskavaig Bay (NG336345).

938 Ardtreck Point. NG335364. Rocks and boulders, then mud to 30m close to the shore. Further out depths reach 47m. The mud provides a home for lots of scallops.

939 Rubha Ban. NG344360. Similar to Site 938.

940 Submarine in Loch Bracadale. This wreck has not yet been located. The crew are buried in Portree. Most of Loch Bracadale is shallow enough for air diving.

941 Island off South-west Wiay, Loch Bracadale. NG285357. An exposed site with a vertical cliff-face to 20m and beyond. Solidly encrusted with marine life, with large amounts of soft coral. Launching: Ardtreck Pier (NG343359); Struan (NG350380); or Harlosh (NG284411).

942 Wiay Island, South face. NG284361. This site shares the same characteristics (and the same access) as Site 941. There is a dramatic rocky face covered in sponges, anemones, and other encrusting species, running to beyond 30m.

943 Shoal South-west of Harlosh Island. NG270393 (approx). An excellent dive in clear water to the top of the shoal at 18m. Lots of life on the rocky slope which gives way to boulders and, finally, a sand plain at 30m. Acces as Site 941.

944 Harlosh Skerry. NG277402. Very similar to Site 943. Lots of life, including many nudibranchs. Access as Site 941.

945 Unknown wreck, Uamh an Tairbh, Loch Varkasaig. NG256420 (approx). This vessel was lost in about 1910 at what is known locally as Bicary Point. There is a large wooden windlass on the beach, and china plates have been located in 13m of water. Launch at Harlosh.

946 Loch Varkasaid. NG270425. A rocky reef to 10m, then a sandy bottom. Lots of life under the kelp on the rocks. Shore access.

947 McLeod's Maidens, Idrigill Point. NG243361. Another very pleasant site with rocks and gullies leading down to 28m. Good for looking at crawfish! Access as Site 1024. Maximum tidal streams of about 1 knot. LW slack +0115 Dover; HW slack −0445 Dover.

948 Wreck of the SS Urlana (called 'Ulanda' by some sources), Geodha Mor, West Skye. NG197387. This was a 6852-ton vessel (possibly a Liberty ship) lost in 1968 with a cargo of wool and hides just East of the group of underwater pinnacles at 57 21 19N 06 39 20W. The vessel has been partially dispersed with explosives, and now lies in 6-9m of water. Boat access from Harlosh.

949 An Dubh Sgeir, West Skye. NG192367. Lying about 2 miles offshore, this island gives an excellent dive to about 20m. Boulders and rocky fissures are full of life, both encrusting and free-swimming. Thirteen lobsters were observed on one dive here! Access and tides as Site 947.

950 Gob na Hoe, West Skye. NG157423. Spectacular scenery underwater with rocks and boulders to beyond 20m. Noted for fish life. Boat access from Harlosh.

951 Wreck of the Dorrick (spelt 'Doric' by some sources), Moonen Bay, West Skye. NG130469. This wreck of a collier lies well broken in 10-15m of water, but gives a good dive. Large chains were located in 13m when the wreck was found by divers in 1970. The position given is East of the Neist Promontory. Contact the fishermen at Meanish Pier (NG154506) for marks and boat-hire.

952 Wreck of the Chadwick, South of An Ceannaich. NG131503 (approx). This is a 1463-ton (75m-long) collier lying in 25m. She is fairly intact, and gives a good dive. The visibility hereabouts can be over 30m, but the tidal streams reach 1.5 knots. LW slack +0400 Dover; HW slack −0200 Dover. To find the wreck from the North, round the headland of An Ceannaich (NG134504) until a tiny headland with a single large boulder is reached under the cliff of Rubha Ban. The wreck lies below this boulder just 30m off the gullies and low rocks at the North end of Oisgill Bay. She is in a fairly broken state with her keel uppermost, but many parts of the superstructure can be examined as she is somewhat twisted. Lots of fish life sheltering from the tides. Launch at Meanish Pier.

953 Near An Ceannaich at. NG130506. An unknown wreck is shown on the chart.

954 West of Meanish at. NG151508. There is an unknown wreck shown on the chart here. Chains and steel plates have been found on the bottom.

955 Meanish Pier, Loch Pooltiel. NG154506. A boulder slope to 15m lies to the North-west of the pier. Lots of fish life in evidence. There is also some twisted aluminium wreckage which may be the remains of an aircraft. Shore access.

956 Loch Pooltiel, East side. NG160513. Access from Meanish Pier. The bottom consists of sand and small pieces of shell. Scallops and crabs noted. Quite shallow.

957 Dunvegan Head. NG178568. A very exposed site with a gravel bottom covered with interesting marine life. Depths just offshore reach beyond 150m! Access as Site 959.

958 Am Famhair, Dunvegan Head. NG183560. A 45-degree boulder and sand slope leads to very deep water (and the 100m isobath). This gives a good, atmospheric, dive with profuse life. Access as Site 959.

959 Gob na Hoe, Loch Dunvegan. NG192541. An interesting site with

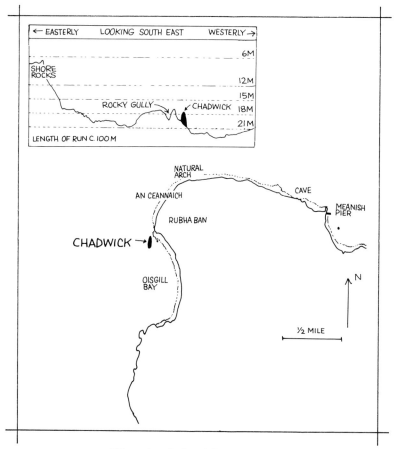

Wreck of the 'Chadwick'

shore access. There is a boulder slope to 12m, then a sand slope levelling out at 20m. Good fish life. Launch boats at Boreraig (NG192537).
Note: there is *NO* access for small boats at Husabost (NG203515).

960 Boreraig Hoe, Loch Dunvegan. NG193536. A gentle slope to 20m, then a sheer drop. According to the chart, the bottom lies at 83m!

961 Husabost Pier, Loch Dunvegan. NG203515. The "pier" does not, in fact, exist! A very sheltered shore dive on to boulders and sand to 10-15m. Fish and shellfish noted. It is a good policy to ask permission for shore access at the nearby house.

962 Eilean Grianal, Loch Dunvegan. NG225497. A sloping mud bottom and broken rock with reasonable life, especially crabs. Boat access from Dunvegan Harbour or from the South-west shore of the loch.

963 Uiginish Point, Loch Dunvegan. NG235491. Launch boats at Dunvegan Bay (NG254473). This dive is rather like those at a number of the small islands in the area. A cliff-face ends just below the surface. The bottom is then muddy and contains many sea-pens. Visibility should be about 10m.

964 Dunvegan Harbour. NG251477. Best dived at night, and preferably at weekends. Keep a close lookout for boat traffic; use an SMB, and have some means of diver recall. The bottom is a muddy slope to 10m with large amounts of junk and bottles. The site may be dived in all weathers except North-west gales.

965 Unknown wreck, Camalaig Bay, Loch Dunvegan. NG232510. The remains of a wooden vessel (21m by 6m) were located here by divers in 1970. The position is 57 27 44N 06 36 57W, which is just to the South of the drying rocks in the centre of the bay.

966 Lampay Islands. NG220551. The waters around these islands are rather shallow, but the shore-line is made up of attractive coral beaches. At low tide a spit of sand allows a strenuous shore dive to be made from the main island. Boat access is from the track past Rubha na Gairbhe (NG225544). To get there by car requires access through a locked gate, the key to which is available at Claigan House (NG233541). Alternative boat access is from Boreraig.

967 Loch Bay Pinnacle. NG250563. This is a submarine peak rising from 33m to 4m. The rock scenery is superb, as is the encrusting life of anemones and soft corals. The peak is best found by echo sounder. It lies about 500m North-east of Rubha Maol (NG247560). There is a good slip at Waternish (NG263565).

968 Sgeir nam Biast. NG237565. A shallow, sand-and-mud shore. Lots of scallops. Access as Site 967.

969 Halistra. NG240592. A shore dive down a mud-and-sand slope with some rocks. Varying depths to a maximum of about 35m.

970 Clett island. NG224583. A pleasant shallow dive can be made here on the shoreline rocks. Further out, there is a sandy plain at 20-25m with plenty of scallops. Access for boats is as Site 967.

971 Rogheadh Point, Ardmore Point. NG216602. There are two natural arches in this headland, plus another underwater in the shallows. The rocks extend to 20m, then sand takes over. Shore access is from Ardmore Bay (NG224608). Boats can be launched there too.

972 East cliffs of Vaternish, Loch Snizort. There are good-looking cliffs along about 8 miles of this coast. Underwater, there are many steep slopes which remain unexplored.

973 Eilean Iosal, Ascrib Islands. NG287654. A deep face giving a rather poor dive with strange tidal streams. Depth: 30m. Boat access is from Uig (NG392640).

974 West of South Ascrib, Ascrib Islands, Loch Snizort. NG300634. A rocky, sloping bottom to 12m, covered with kelp up to 4m long! A poorish dive. Access as Site 973.

975 Scalp Rock, Ascrib Islands. NG298633. A vertical face to 40m with dangerous vertical tidal eddies. Lots of small fish, gorgonians, and unusual anemones. Access as Site 973.

976 South of South Ascrib. NG304633. This site has a rocky cliff dropping to 10m, then a steep sand-and-boulder slope to well below 30m. Visibility of 15m can be expected. Access as Site 973.

977 Loch Diubaig, South Loch Snizort. NG330545. This site is flat, sandy, shallow, and disappointing. Boat access as Site 979.

978 Clinigin Rocks, off Greshornish Point, Loch Snizort. NG347566. An interesting dive down rocky cliffs. There are caves to a depth of 10-12m. The slope then disappears to the depths (85m on the chart). Access as Site 979.

979 Loch Greshornish, East shores. Good rocks lead down to a sandy seabed with lots of scallops. Launch at the slip for Greshornish House (NG343543). (This slip is private and permission to use it must be asked).

980 Loch Greshornish, West shore by Fanks. NG355548. Very similar to Site 979.

981 Wreck of the Mary Croan, and **982 Wreck of the Ben Aigen, Loch Snizort.** These two fishing vessels were lost in 1980 and 1978 respectively, to the East of the Ascrib Islands in 65m of water. The positions are 57 37 00N 06 27 00W and 57 36 55N 06 29 37W. Obviously, they are both too deep for amateur divers.

983 An t-lasgair. NC358747. This little group of islands lies about 3 miles West of the very North of Skye. An Dubh Sgeir is a rock to the South of the main island. It yields a dark, foreboding dive down a cliff which runs vertically from the surface to 50m and beyond. There is little life on the face apart from some plumose anemones. Boat access is from Camas Mor (NG370707), near Bornesketaig.

984 Wreck of the Rhodesia. NG410747. This was an armed naval trawler of 193 tons (33m long) which ran aground in 1915 at the South of Tulm Island. The exact position is 57 41 18N 06 20 58W. Parts of the wreck rise 1m above the surface at low water springs. The depth is 6m. The vessel is virtually intact, but is well covered in weed. A bold snorkel (watch tides in Tulm Island Sound), or a boat launch at Port Duntulm (NG412744), is required to reach the wreck.

985 Tulm Island, North Skye. NG406751. A good dive down a 45-degree boulder slope to sand at 25m. Large numbers of cuckoo wrasse noted. Access as Site 983.

986 Am Bord. NG369794. Also known as Lord MacDonald's Table, this site has a 5m cliff followed by a gradually-sloping rocky bottom to 12m and beyond. The scenery is reminiscent of St Abbs, with its rocks, weed, and gullies. Two hundred metres further out (at 18-20m) the bottom is barren and boulder-strewn. It slopes to 30m with occasional rocky clumps rising to

20m. Quite a lot of life, including squat lobsters and crawfish. Access as Site 983.

987 Gaeilavore Island, North Skye. NG366799. The small bay at the East of the island has a gully with a huge amount of kelp debris, then a slope to 22m. A rather uninspiring dive. Access as Site 983.

988 Unknown wreck, Fladda-chuain, North Skye. NG356815. The smashed remains of a small coaster lie in 1m of water at the North end of the island. The wreckage is buried under a thick layer of kelp. Launch as Site 983.

989 Wreck of the Apollo, Fladda-chuain. NG363870. This 1274-ton vessel (75m long) was stranded in 1971 at the South-west end of the island. The wreck lies in 10m of water on her starboard side. At low-water springs she rises 1m above the surface. At high water she can be found by going 75m North-west of the inlet at the above grid reference and 30m out from the shore. The wreck is breaking up, although the stern is still intact. Launch as for Site 983.

990 Wreck of the MFV Alexanders, Eilean Trodday, North Skye. NG438786. This wooden vessel was lost in 1974 and is completely broken up. The engine and prop-shaft lie at the head of a small inlet and dry 2m at low-water springs. Bits of broken equipment lie around, but are well hidden in the kelp. Launch as for Site 983.

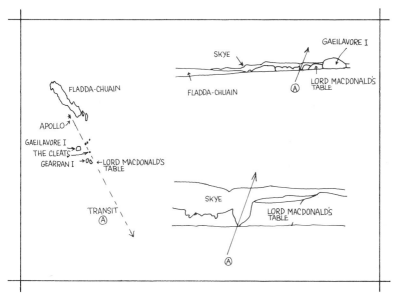

Marks for Site 989: the 'Apollo'

991 Bogha Trodday, North Skye. NG444787. Just off the South-east corner of the island rocks and huge boulders lead down to beyond 30m giving a worthwhile dive. Launch as for Site 983.

992 Wreck of the Nordhuk, Eilean Trodday. NG442793. This 1359-ton, 75m long vessel was lost in 1976. She has now broken into two. The stern has slipped back into deeper water, but the bow section lies close to high cliffs (slightly to the left of a rock pillar). A recommended dive. Launch as for Site 983.

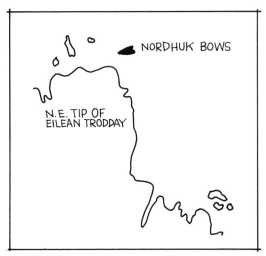

The wreck of the 'Nordhuk'

993 Shoals to the East of Trotternish. Three undived shoals are shown on the chart well offshore from Eilean Flodigarry (NG480720). One lies two miles North-east of the island, has a minimum depth of 25m, and drops to 51m to the East. Another lies three miles East-north-east of Eilean Flodigarry, runs almost East-West, has a minimum depth of 14m, and drops rapidly to 58m to the South. The third is located 5 miles North-east of Eilean Flodigarry, runs North-South, has a minimum depth of 25m, and rapidly drops to 126m to its South-east. These last two shoals look particularly interesting from the chart, as they appear to be narrow, rocky ridges with steep drops all round. Access as Site 994.

994 Staffin Island, Trotternish. NG493674. A pleasant dive on the North-east side of this island. Rocks and mud lead down to over 20m. Launch at Staffin (NG487685). The East side of the island is shallow and poor.

995 Armada wreck, Staffin Island. NG493674. This wreck is said to lie somewhere round Staffin Island. Nothing more about it is known to me.

Portree Harbour – a useful launch site for dives in the Sound of Raasay

996 Ob na Ron. NG495682. Shore access (with permission) to a shingle slope turning to sand at about 15m. A pleasant dive with all the normal life.

997 Sound of Raasay. I have no dives recorded for the next 12 miles of coastline, which is steep and impossible to reach without a boat. This is the Sound of Raasay, one of the deepest parts of the UK continental shelf.

998 Prince Charles' Cave, Skye shore, Sound of Raasay. NG518482. An extremely steep and impressive rocky and sandy slope at about 60 degrees lies out from the shore rocks. Fascinating sponges on the rocks. At 57m the slope turns into a vertical cliff which disappears into the depths (the chart shows it going to at least 90m). This is a dangerous dive to go deep on: *every precaution should be taken.* Launch at Portree.

999 Rubha na h Airde Glaise. NG512452. A 45-degree slope of soft sand that falls away to immense depths. Access as Site 999.

1000 Rubha Chuil-tairbh, Isle of Rona. NG638601. A rocky slope leading to 25m, then falling steeply to 200m! Boat access is from Portree, Staffin, or Kenmore in Loch Torridon.
Note: Rona is sometimes called South Rona to distinguish it from North Rona, the Hebridean Outlier lying 50 miles North of the Outer Hebrides.

1001 Eilean Garbh, Rona. NG604562. Off the West side of this small islet is a boring 45-degree sand slope apparently leading right down to the depths. The interesting part comes at 50m when the slope turns into a vertical rock-face. In 20m visibility no bottom could be seen. Access as Site 1000.

1002 Caol Rona, between Raasay and Rona. NG610540. Is this the ultimate drift drive? Just East of Caol Rona on the East side of Raasay (NG629536) is a depth of 316m – the deepest part of the seas around Britain. The spring rate is 1 knot. LW slack −0430 Dover (South-west-going stream begins); HW slack +0130 Dover (North-east-going stream begins). In a distance of 1½ miles the seabed climbs from 132m to 6m (at NG615535), then drops to 256m!

1003 Mannish Point, Raasay. NG569486. A steep slope to 50m. Boat access is from Portree.

1004 Mannish More, West Raasay. NG553458. The dives off the West coast of Raasay are not so deep as those off the East coast as there is a surrounding apron of sand and kelp at 10m. Beyond this, the steep slope to 50m and beyond starts. Boat access is from Portree.

1005 Ferry Pier, South Raasay. NG554341. Access by boat from Portree or Peinchorran (NH525330). Watch out for the ferry if diving around the pier. The pier supports are covered with plumose anemones. Lots of debris around the pier. Off the pier the depth drops rapidly to beyond 25m, with rich life on the mud slope.

1006 Wreck of the Spindrift. This 9m boat jammed under the pier and broke her back with the rising tide. She lies in 5m.

1007 Maol Ban, Loch Ainort. NG565292. A boulder slope to 5m, then sand and mud to beyond 15m. Norway lobsters present. Shore access.

1008 Loch Ainort, North of Luib. NG568286. A shallow, muddy slope overlain with maerl to 14m. Poor. Shore access.

1009. Rubha Doire na Boceinein, Scalpay. NG624323. A shallow boulder slope to 11m, then sand and pebbles to 15m. Urchins graze here on rocks covered with purple calceolareous algae. Plumose anemones also noted. Boat access is from Broadford (NG644243).

1010 Sgeir Dhearg. NG635332. A gentle sand slope to 10m, then rock to 26m. Rocks fairly bare except for *lithothamnion*. Access as Site 1009.

1011 Longay, North end. NG650319. A rocky and sandy slope to 35m and beyond. The kelp reaches 12m. Lots of squat lobsters. Access as Site 1009.

1012 Longay, South end. NG660305. A jumbled boulder slope to 10m, then a gentle mud slope to 20m. Lots of squat lobsters. Access as Site 1009.

1013 Rubha na h-Uamha Duibhe, South Scalpay. NG617273. A boulder-and-mud slope to beyond 15m. A poor dive. Access as Site 1009.

1014 Guillamon Island, North. NG637275. A very gradual slope of rocks and sand to 14m. Access as Site 1009.

1015 Pabay, North. NG680278. A boulder slope to 11m, then mud beyond 25m. Lots of crabs. Access as Site 1009.

1016 Ob Allt an Daraich, Skye. NG714257. A plain of muddy sand gradually dropping to beyond 20m. A disappointing shore dive.

1017 Rubha Ard Tresnis, Kyleakin. NG762259. A boulder slope to 5m, then mud and pebbles to beyond 15m. Boat access from Kyleakin (NG756265) – launch quickly to avoid the busy ferry.

1018 Head of Loch na Beiste. NG752252. Boulders to 6m, then mud to beyond 15m. Some Norway lobsters.

1019 Unknown wreck, Loch na Beiste. There is a report of a wreck in this loch.

1020 Wreck of HMS Port Napier, Sron an Tairbh, Loch Alsh. NG780254. This is a very popular dive. The vessel was a mine-layer of 9600 tons (about 150m long) when she was lost by fire in 1940. There are still some mines and ammunition left from the original cargo, though most were removed. The wreck is easy to find – it lies on its side about 300m from the Skye shore with a vertical spar projecting above the water. Some parts of the wreck dry at low water springs. Depth 21m. This wreck is thought of very highly by many divers, but I have always considered it much over-rated. The debris nearby on the shore may or may not be associated with this wreck. Launch at Kyle of Lochalsh, or Kyleakin.

1021 North of Meall Port Mealary, Sound of Sleat. NG758166. The sheer cliff above the surface stops at 1m underwater! Thereafter, the bottom consists of sloping boulders and pebbles to beyond 25m. Lots of crabs, squat lobsters, and urchins. Launch at Isle Ornsay (NG703125).

1022 Wreck of the Embrace. This lies at 57 09 30N 05 47 12W just North of Ornsay and due East of Duisdalemore at NG715136. She was a 94-ton drifter lost in 1940.

1023 Rubha Guail. NG740158. Shingle, sand, and boulders, lead to over 30m, but generally the site is disappointing. Access as Site 1021.

1024 Ard Ghunel, Sound of Sleat. NG711116. A gentle boulder slope to 11m. Large urchins, crabs, etc. Access as Site 1021.

1025 Dunan Choinnich, Sound of Sleat. NG683082. Smooth, stepped bedrock leading to a shell-and-sand plain at 14m. Squat lobsters and sea-pens noted. Boat access at Knock Bay (NG671087).

1026 Sgeir Ramasgaig, Sound of Sleat. NG667078. Access as Site 1084, or a scramble to the shore. A gently-sloping sand-and-boulder slope with maerl from 5m-15m. A poor dive.

1027 Kilbeg, Sound of Sleat. NG655058. Sand and rock outcrops to 12m, with maerl and shell fragments. Anemones *(Sagartia)*, urchins, and starfish. Shore access involves a walk.

1028 Eilean Sgorach, Armadale. NG640033. A rocky slope to 16m, then a shallow, boring sand slope with sea-pens. Access is by boat from Armadale Pier (NG641038).

1029 Ard Thurinish, Sound of Sleat. NM596998. Shallow rocks lead to sand at 12m. Access as Site 1028.

1030 Leir Mhaodail, Sound of Sleat. NM573992. Siimilar to Site 1029.

1031 Point of Sleat. NM563990. An exposed site. Shallow rocks extend for some distance from the shore, then a sandy slope leads to beyond 20m. Weak tidal streams. LW slack +0115 Dover; HW slack −0445 Dover. Access as Site 1028.

1032 Wrecks in the Sound of Sleat. There are several wrecks to the South of the Sound of Sleat marked on the charts. These are mainly too deep for sports diving, though some possibilities do exist. The area was frequented by U-boats in WW2.

Area information and services

Hydrographic charts; 1795 Little Minch 1:100,000; 2208 Mallaig to Canna Harbour 1:50,000; 2209 Inner Sound 1:50,000; 2210 Approaches to Inner Sound 1:50,000; 2479 Inner Sound − northern part 1:18,000; 2480 Inner Sound − central part 1:25,000; 2498 Inner Sound − southern part 1:25,000; 2533 Loch Dunvegan, Loch Snizort 1:25,000; 2534 Sound & Narrows of Raasay 1:25,000; 2540 Loch Alsh & approaches 1:20,000.
Ordnance Survey 1:50,000 maps: 23 North Skye; 24 Raasay & Loch Torridon; 32 South Skye; 33 Loch Alsh & Glen Shiel.
Ordnance Survey 1:25,000 maps: NG14 The Hoe; NG15 Dunvegan Head; NG23/33 Bracadale; NG24/34 Dunvegan; NG25/35 Vaternish; NG26/36 Loch Snizort; NG31/41 Soay; NG32 Loch Eynort; NG37/47 Rubha Hunish; NG42/52 Cuillin Hills; NG43/53 Narrows of Raasay; NG44/54 Portree; NG45/55 Trotternish; NG46/56 Staffin; NG50 Sleat (South); NG51 Elgol; NG60/70 Mid Sound of Sleat; NG61/71 North Sound of Sleat; NG62/72 Kyle of Lochalsh; NG63/73 Crowlin Islands; NG64/74 Applecross; NG65/75 Arinacrinachd; NG82/92 Dornie.
Local BS-AC branches: None.
Local SS-AC branches: Skye.
Air supplies: Norman Thorpe, Portree Diving Services (0478) 2274; Mike Kirkland, Skye Diving Centre, Harlosh (047 022) 366.
Outboard motor service: Skye Diving Centre (047 022) 366.
Boat charter: Skye Diving Centre. (For excursions from Kyle contact McLean & MacRae, Slipway, Kyle of Lochalsh (0599) 4209).
Local weather: Glasgow Weather Centre 041 248 3451; Oban Coastguard (0631) 63720.
Sea area: Hebrides.
Tidal constants:

	DOVER	ULLAPOOL
Broadford Bay	−0437	−0017
Portree	−0445	−0025
Uig Bay	−0450	−0030
Loch Dunvegan	−0500	−0040
Loch Harport	−0505	−0045
Soay	−0457	−0037
Kyle of Lochalsh	−0440	−0020
Glenelg Bay	−0507	−0047

Coastguard: Oban MRSC (0631) 63720; Kyle of Lochalsh (0599) 4438 Mallaig (0687) 2336.

Lifeboat: Mallaig, Stornoway, Lochinver.
Police stations: Portree (0478) 2888; Ardvasar (047 14) 222; Broadford (047 12) 222; Dunvegan (047 022) 333; Kyleakin (0599) 4650; Kyle of Lochalsh (0599) 4222; Uig (047 042) 222.
Hospitals: Portree (0478) 2704.
Recompression chambers: Dunstaffnage Marine Laboratory, Oban (0631) 62244; Underwater Training Centre, Fort William (0397) 3786/3136.
Vehicle recovery: AA – Glasgow 041 812 0101; Fort William (0397) 2099 (office hours only).
Ferry operators: Kyle of Lochalsh-Kyleakin – Caledonian MacBrayne (0599) 4218); Glenelg-Kylerhea – M.A. Mackenzie, Glenelg (059 982) 224; Mallaig-Armadale – Caledonian MacBrayne (0687) 2403 & (047 14) 248; Mallaig-Kyle – Caledonian MacBrayne (0687) 2403.
Local tourist information: Portree (0478) 2137; Broadford (047 12) 361/463; Kyle of Lochalsh (0599) 4276.
Accommodation: Skye Diving Centre, Harlosh (047 022) 366. There are also many B & B and guest house facilities (see Scottish Tourist Board guides).

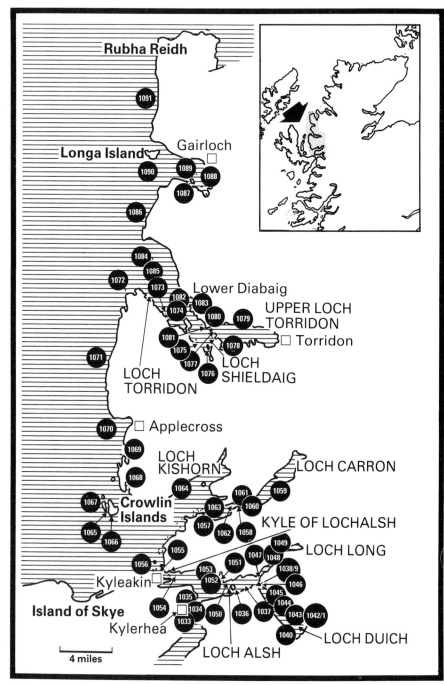

Dive Sites : Kylerhea to Rubha Reidh

CHAPTER 9

Kylerhea
to Rubha Reidh

The area covered in this chapter starts at the narrows of Kylerhea and covers Loch Alsh and Loch Duich, Loch Carron and Loch Kishorn, the Applecross peninsula, Loch Torridon, Loch Gairloch, and the coast to the headland of Rubha Reidh.

Once past the sea lochs near Skye, one begins to get that feeling of diving on a remote, northerly coast, though it is only when the next major headland is passed at Rubha Coigeach (see Chapter 10) that the true, remote magnificence of North-west Scotland is fully revealed.

At the South of this coastline, Kylerhea lies just North of the village of Gleneig. Incidentally, the view from Gleneig of the mountain ridge forming the Five Sisters of Kintail is one of the most impressive sights on the western seaboard of Scotland. Kylerhea itself is formed from Torridonian sandstone. Its 500m width is all that separates Skye from the mainland. Very strong tidal streams flow through this narrow straight, which has been called the Kylerhea *River.*

Loch Alsh (with Loch Duich and Loch Long) is rather reminiscent of Loch Cairnbawn further North. Loch Long is narrow and has a maximum depth of 47m. Loch Duich drops to 117m, but connects with Loch Alsh over a shallow sill at 10m. Loch Alsh is deep, at 112m, and it connects with the sounds leading to the open sea through Kylerhea (minimum depth 18m) and Kyleakin (minimum depth 10m). In the Ice Ages these valleys would have been filled with glaciers, though there is some doubt over the directions in which they flowed. The final separation of Skye from the mainland was the result of submergence and flooding of these glacial troughs.

The view of Loch Duich is quite superb, with the loch running into a wild tangle of spikey mountains. At the mouth of the loch, Eilean Donan Castle occupies one of the most idyllic sites in Scotland. From here, looking West over Loch Alsh to the Cuillin of Skye with the sunset colouring the scene, is a bewitching experience. The castle has a long history; it was restored in 1912, and is now open to the public.

The village of Kyle of Lochalsh is a busy ferry-point for Skye. Many steamers call here, and there is a daily boat connection to Toscaig in Applecross. The railway station marks the end of the line from Inverness.

The sandstone coast North of Loch Alsh is heavily indented and very picturesque.

From Kyle of Lochalsh to Plockton, the coast and its many islets are administered by the National Trust for Scotland.

Loch Carron has two basins separated by the gneiss ridge at Strome Ferry, which has a minimum depth of 9m. The inner loch is a basin falling to 117m. Outer Loch Carron falls steadily past 100m to reach a depth of 250m at the South of the Crowlin Islands in the Inner Sound. Loch Kishorn is an arm of Outer Loch Carron, but it does not have a separate basin. Pressure of traffic has caused a road to be built around Loch Carron after many years of long queues for the small ferry boat at Strome Ferry. The old ferry now lies wrecked in shallow water on the North side of the loch.

The Crowlin Islands are a detached part of the Applecross peninsula. They are made of sandstones and shales, cut by basalt dykes. These weather to form a series of gullies including the long gash forming Crowlin Harbour, which splits the two main islands.

Loch Carron represents a natural break on the West coast. To the North the land becomes wilder and more rugged. The rock is sandstone, Cambrian quartzite, and Lewisian gneiss, which is one of the oldest rocks in the world. These rocks form only poor soils and vast tracts of this country are wild, windswept, and virtually devoid of habitation. The sea lochs also become shorter and the seaboard more compact.

The North-west wall of Kishorn is sandstone, and this continues around the peninsula to Applecross village. The village is reached by a dramatic hill pass, Bealach na Ba, which, at 626m, is the highest road in western Scotland. Recently, a road has been built round the North end of the peninsula to reach Shieldaig. The road runs along the prominent rock platform cut by earlier seas. Depths out to sea fall only gently at first.

The North end of the Applecross peninsula runs to Loch Torridon and Loch Shieldaig. Loch Shieldaig lies between two gneiss masses and owes its form to the alternation of sandstone and gneiss. It is 135m deep and separates Loch Torridon from Upper Loch Torridon. Loch Torridon is one of the most beautiful sea lochs of western Scotland. The outer loch is 144m deep, and the inner loch reaches 88m.

The view from Beinn Alligin at 985m is outstanding and extends from Cape Wrath to Ardnamurchan (the ascent demands care if you are not an experienced hill-walker, due to narrow and precipitous ridges).

The outer coast from Loch Torridon to Rubha Reidh (or *Smooth Point*) is not very impressive. It is low, covered with boulder clay, and has bracken growing on it in many places. Part way along this coastal stretch is Loch Gairloch. This has no basin, and drops steadily from the shore, quickly passing the 50m isobath and reaching a depth of 100m at the wide mouth of the loch. The shores are of sandstone, as is Longa Island at the loch mouth. The village of Gairloch is a small holiday resort and an important fishing harbour. The loch itself has a magnificent sandy beach.

The diving described in this chapter varies considerably in quality and type. There are a number of good drift dives in Kylerhea and the narrows in the sea lochs. Loch Duich has a rich and unusual marine life. Strome Narrows in Loch Carron and Longa Island are both noted for their excellent marine life. There are also underwater rock pinnacles in Loch Torridon. The northern part of this area has still to be fully explored by divers.

Tides are not generally a problem (except in the obvious narrows).

Visibility is usually excellent, with up to 30m being expected in summer. Loch Duich can be dark at depth because of the fresh water run-off and the muddy bottom.

Most of the coast is quite accessible by car and inflatable, and there are a number of useful launch spots as well as some excellent shore dives. There is also plenty of guest house accommodation and plenty of sites for small groups to camp. Large groups may have more difficulty with camping by the shore, especially in the South of the area.

Dive sites

1033 Kylerhea Narrows. NG793224. A challenging drift dive at rates of up to 8 knots (LW slack +0140 Dover; HW slack −0420 Dover). Rates of up to 12 knots have even been claimed for Caolas an Lamhachaidh (NG793209). Depths range from 15m to 30m over a rocky bottom. Boat access is from the ferry slip (NG794213), or from the Kyle of Lochalsh (NG762271). *Note:* when the South-going stream meets a southerly wind, considerable broken water can make the narrows dangerous for small craft.

1034 East ferry slip, Kylerhea. NG794213. This shore dive is sheltered from the tide. It drops to 15m on to sand and pebbles in a small bay to the North of the slip. Bottles are to be found. Watch out for the ferry.

1035 Research Rock, Kylerhea. NG797230. A rock with a minimum depth of 6m over it. The bottom consists of flat sheets of bed rock at 20m, covered with brittle stars and soft coral. Lots of good pelagic fish life. Access and tides as Site 1033.

1036 Glas Eilean, Loch Alsh. NG847252. A low island which features a tern colony. There is a boulder slope to 30m, then a pebble-and-sand plateau. Lots of anemones *(Sagartia)* and tube worms *(Sabella)*. Weak tidal streams (up to ¾-of-a-knot). LW slack +0155 Dover; HW slack −0425 Dover). Boat access is from Dornie (NG879263).

1037 Creagan Tairbh, Loch Alsh. NG860252. From here to Eilean Aoinidh (NG873256) the bottom consists of a boulder slope dropping to beyond 15m on to muddy boulders. Sea squirts and scallops noted. Access as Site 1036.

1038 Totaig, Loch Duich. NG877254. A drift dive round the point at 20m in dark water along superb rock scenery at about 1 knot. Soft corals, brittle stars, and anemones, noted. Access and tidal streams as Site 1103. If you use the road along the South-west shore of the loch for shore access, remember it is private − don't park near the house, even though parking elsewhere may be difficult.

1039 Leacachan, Loch Duich. NG894226. A disappointing muddy slope to beyond 20m. Norway lobsters and scallops noted. Shore access.

1040 Ratagan, Loch Duich. NG920199. A steep, deep muddy slope. The darkness of the water makes the dive seem deeper than it really is. A new anemone *(Pachyceryanthus)* has been found here. Shore access.

1041 Kintail Lodge Hotel. NG937196. A pleasant dive with easy shore access and plentiful marine life.

1042 Torchuillin, Loch Duich. NG935210. A rather special site with unusual marine life, lying at the head of a sheltered sea loch. Shore access is over the small river delta. It is quite a long fin down a mud slope to beyond 40m. The water is very dark due to fresh water run-off carrying peat stains, and the top few metres may well be fresh water. Lots of anemones (including some not recorded elsewhere in Scotland), large sea-pens (1m high), and bright orange sea cucumbers *(Psolus)*.

1043 Inverinate jetty, Loch Duich. NG921216. A disappointing, poor, muddy site.

1044 Below Keppock, Loch Duich. NG897240. A silty slope with occasional boulders covered with anemones *(Protanthia)* going as deep as required. Shore access with a scramble, or boat access from Dornie (NG879263).

1045 Dun Beag, Loch Duich. NG890246. Shore access is down a steep bank from the large car-park. A very deep site (to 60m) over rocks, then mud. Large numbers of tubular sponges and tube worms, together with strange forms of bryozoans caused by the tidal streams.

1046 Eilean Donan Castle, Loch Duich. NG883257. About 400m South-east of the castle is a rough path to the water's edge from the point where the road runs through a cutting. There are a few wrecked cars in the shallows, followed by a superb steep mud slope and vertical or undercut rock face to beyond 47m. Tube worms, anemones, and brittle stars, noted.

1047 Dornie Narrows, Loch Long. NG881265. A good drift dive to a maximum depth of 7m in a current running at 2 knots with the full tidal stream (times as Site 1036). There is unusual life on the kelp due to the brackish water. Visibility of 10m noted.

1048 Loch Long, Upper Narrows. NG900294. Another drift dive at a maximum of 7 knots. At slack it is possible to dive to 24m on the cliff at the East end (NG902295). The life is not as rich as in the open sea, but there are ascidians and some unusual sponges. Access as Site 1050.

1049 Loch Long wall. NG903295. A vertical wall to 30m but with restricted life due to the dark, peaty, fresh water. Access as Site 1050.

1050 Racoon Rock, Loch Alsh. NG840256. This submerged rock lies midway between Glas Eilean (NG843254) and Ru Sgarabhaig (NG835257), and is marked with a buoy. There are small bedrock cliffs descending in 5m steps to a depth of about 20m, with very rich encrusting life. Access is by boat from Dornie. There is also a good drift dive in the channel to the North-west.

1051 Ru Sgarabhaig, West side, Loch Alsh. NG834259. A vertical cliff to 30m giving a dive with lots of atmosphere. The rock-face is encrusted with ascidians. Access and tides as Site 1036.

1052 Ard Hill, West side, Loch Alsh. NG817264. A poor dive over a barren, muddy bottom.

1053 Reraig, Loch Alsh. NG889262. As Site 1052. Shore access.

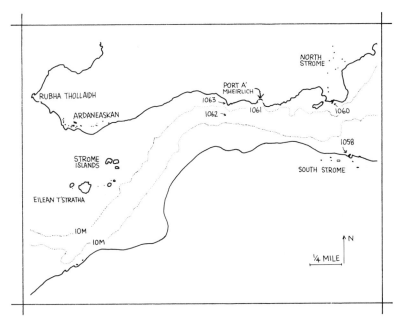

Sites in the Strome Narrows, Loch Carron

1054 Wreck of the Golden Harvest, Loch Alsh. NG767268. This 24m MFV, lost about 1970, has now been dispersed with explosives. It is full of fish and encrusting species, and seals are often seen around it. It lies in shallow water (with the tip of its mast 1m below the surface) North-east of Eileanan Dubha, just to the West of the rocks with a beacon on them.

1055 Kyleakin Narrows. NG757267. A 2½ knot tidal stream (slack at HW, Kyle of Lochalsh) gives a drift dive over a rock-and-shingle bottom at 12-25m. Watch out for the ferry boat.

1056 Eilean Ban, Kyleakin. NG738272. Down the navigation buoy chain to 13m and a bottom of pebbles and sand. Slightly closer to the island there is a flat-topped bedrock plateau. Boat access is from Kyle of Lochalsh.

1057 Plockton Harbour. NG805335. A shallow, sheltered shore dive to a clean bottom, often with spawning nudibranchs.

1058 Strome Ferry, South slip. NG865348. An interesting shallow shore dive which can yield cod-bottles, ferry company crockery, and other junk. The ferry no longer runs.

1059 Cnoc nam Mult, Loch Carron. NG897367. Shore access is across the railway line. A steep, stony slope barren of marine life to 50m. Just South of here there appears to be a 50m underwater cliff-face.

1060 North ferry slip, Loch Carron. NG863354. Walk round to the North of

The ruined castle overlooking the harbour at the Kyle of Lochalsh.

the island (to the West of the slip); then, using the flood tide (starts at +0145 Dover) drift back to the slip. Good life on the cliff in between.

1061 Conservation Bay, Loch Carron. NG856354. This is a voluntary conservation area agreed by NCC, MCS, and Inverness BS-AC. There is a huge variety of life and some very large lobsters – please leave them. The best dive is at the West of the bay down sheer, 20m cliffs.

1062 Strome Narrows, Loch Carron. NG855352. A pleasant drift dive at up to 3 knots in 15m of water. LW slack +0145 Dover; HW slack −0415 Dover. A shingle seabed with many large mussels. Access is from Strome Ferry (NG864347 or NG863354).

1063 Leacanashie, Loch Carron. NG851354. A rather nice dive from the shore round a little headland with a 20m cliff-face. Lots of life make this a super night dive. Shore access.

1064 Airigh-drishaig, Loch Kishorn. NG770367. A rock slope turning to sand and continuing to beyond 40m. Not too inspiring. Boat access is from Strome Ferry.

1065 Crowlin Islands, Inner Sound. NG690335. At the South end of the islands, and just by the channel between Eilean Mor and Eilean Mead-honach, the seabed drops to 20m. There are many seals here, and it is very pleasant to allow them to dive around you. Boat access is from Kyle of Lochalsh (6 miles), or Strome Ferry (11 miles).

1066 Eilean Mor, Crowlin Islands. NG698335. A rather poor dive over rock, then boulders, on to mud. Access as Site 1065.

1067 Wreck of the Scomber, Crowlin Isles. NG682354. This 321-ton (40m-long) steam trawler was lost in 1923. The position is 57 21 00N 05 51 00W, which is just West of the islands in Caolas Beag, where the depth is about 17m.

1068 Loch Toscaig, Applecross. NG710378. Around the pier bottles can be collected in depths of 10m. South-west of the pier is a series of stepped ledges in a rock face dropping to over 30m. Shore access.

1069 Unknown wreck, Sgeir Ghoblach, Poll Creadha. NG707414. This is the wreck of a seine netter which went aground on the rocks. She is shown on the chart as drying at position 57 24 15N 05 49 04W.

1070 Rubha na Guailne, Applecross. NG688457. Shore access to a steep boulder slope leading to a sloping, sandy bottom at 20m. Lots of shellfish among the boulders, and flatfish on the sand.

1071 Applecross peninsula. I have no dives recorded for the next 10 miles of coast. The chart shows depths increasing only slowly.

1072 Wreck of the Viscount, Murchadh Breac. NG706611. This vessel was stranded on the rocks in 1924. On the chart, she lies to the North-east of the rock at 57 35 05N 05 50 20W. The depth quickly reaches 15m and beyond, so the wreck may have slipped back into deeper water or have broken up. Nothing was found in 1975 when a search was made.

1073 Eilean Mor, Loch Torridon. NG756585. A steep boulder-and-sand slope on to sand at 28m. Shallower than 17m there are cliffs and gullies. A pleasant dive, with lots of marine life. Boat access is from Shieldaig (NG816536).

1074 Sron a Mhais, Loch Torridon. NG782572. A rough, rocky, silty face to a sandy bottom at 30m. Fish, shellfish, and encrusting ascidians, noted. Access is as Site 1073.

1075 Rhuroin Headland, Loch Shieldaig. NG800545. Shore access (but ask permission at house). Rocks lead down to 10m, where there is a sand-and-boulder slope descending to 50m. Lots of pelagic fish and shellfish.

1076 Shieldaig Island, Loch Shieldaig. NG808545. A very deep site with a series of rock steps to 50m and beyond. A deep and eerie dive with only sparse life on the rocks. Access as Site 1073.

1077 Eilean a' Chaoil, Loch Torridon. NG813563. There are good, if shallow, underwater pinnacles to the South-east of this island. These give a good second dive. Access is from Shieldaig or the head of Loch Torridon at Fascag (NG895565).

1078 Ob Mheallaidh, Loch Torridon. NG830540. A shallow dive to 5m on to sand with urchins. Shore access.

1079 Inver Alligin, Loch Torridon. NG840570. A shallow dive to 10m on to weed and sand. There is a sewage outfall nearby! Beyond this there is a steep mud slope to 50m. Shore access.

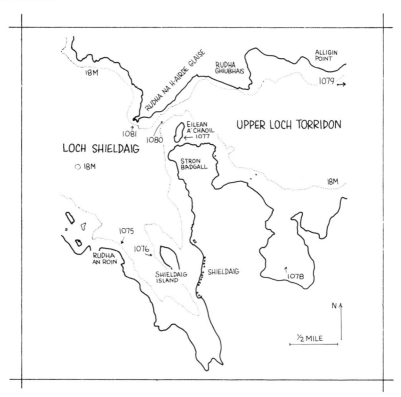

Sites in The Narrows, Loch Torridon

1080 Torridon Narrows. NG813563. A pleasant drift dive at rates of up to 3 knots. LW slack +0200 Dover; HW slack −0425 Dover. The bottom features large boulders covered with hydroids. Access as Site 1077.

1081 Rubha na h-Airde Glaise, Loch Torridon. NG807567. Sandstone cliffs drop underwater to 26m on to shell and gravel at this site. The cliffs are covered with soft corals; the seabed has crawfish. Access as Site 1077.

1082 Rubha na h-Airde, Loch Torridon. NG786593. The rocks drop off on to sand at 16m. This then drops away to over 50m. There are scallops on the sand, and sea squirts on the cliffs. I have a sighting of dolphins hunting salmon hereabouts. Boat access as Site 1077, or launch at Diabaig (although this involves a very steep hill which demands a powerful towing vehicle).

1083 Diabaig Pier, Outer Loch Torridon. NG707598. A shore dive off the end of the pier (do *not* park on the pier itself). Initially 8m deep and pretty, then a steep slope to 40m further out. Large skate noted.

Outer Loch Torridon offers varied diving with plenty of fish including large skate.

1084 Sgeir na Trian, Outer Loch Torridon. NG731650. A small island 1½ miles offshore with a shoal ½-a-mile to the South-east with a minimum depth of 3m. The sandstone island drops to 25m on to shell sand. Lots of fish, both bottom dwelling and pelagic. Access is from Shieldaig.

1085 Sgeir na Trian shoal. NG735643. The shoal can be located by echo sounder ½-a-mile South-east of Site 1084. The bottom quickly drops to 50m to the South-east. Access is from Shieldaig (9 miles).

1086 Loch Torridon to Loch Gairloch. Other than sites 1084/5, I have no dives recorded for the 12 miles of coast from Diabaig to Loch Gairloch. The bottom appears fairly shallow from the chart.

1087 Unknown wrecks, Badachro beach, Loch Gairloch. NG781738. Two wooden hulks were reported in 1976 at 57 41 55N 05 43 40W.

1088 An Aird, Loch Gairloch. NG802750. This is a rock-spur running down to about 25m and a sandy bottom covered with brittle stars. Access is by boat from Charleston Pier (NG806749).

1089 Glas Eilean, Loch Gairloch. NG793753. A slope of boulders and bedrock to 25m, then shell sand to 40m. This is a good site, with all the normal encrusting life and grazing urchins. Access as Site 1088.

1090 Longa Island, Loch Gairloch. NG734771. A superb site with a boulder slope to beyond 25m. Massive shoals of fish, congers, cuckoo wrasse, lobsters, and normal encrusting life, noted. Access as Site 1088.

1091 Rubha Ban to Rubha Reidh. I have no dives recorded for this 7 miles of coastline. Depths appear to be fairly shallow, though Rubha Reidh (NG739918), with its 2-knot tidal streams, might well be worth a look.

Area information and services

Hydrographic charts: 1794 Little Minch — southern part 1:100,000; 2210 Approaches to Inner Sound 1:50,000; 2479 Inner Sound — northern part 1:18,000; 2480 Inner Sound — central part 1:25,000; 2498 Inner Sound — southern part 1:25,000; 2509 Rubha Reidh to Cailleach Head 1:25,000; 2528 Lochs Kishorn, Carron & Gairloch 1:15,000; 2540 Loch Alsh & approaches 1:20,000; 2541 Lochs Hourn & Duich 1:25,000.

Ordnance Survey 1:50,000 maps: 19 Gairloch & Ullapool; 24 Raasay & Loch Torridon; 33 Loch Alsh & Glen Shiel.

Ordnance Survey 1:25,000 maps: NG62/72 Kyle of Lochalsh; NG63/73 Crowlin Islands; NG64/74 Applecross; NG65/75 Arinacrinachd; NG76 Red Point; NG77 Loch Gairloch; NG78 Melvaig; NG79 Rubha Reidh; NG81/91 Shiel Bridge; NG82/92 Dornie; NG83/93 Stromeferry; NG84/94 Upper Loch Carron; NG85/95 Upper Loch Torridon; NG87/97 Loch Maree (North).

Local BS-AC branches: Ullapool (970).

Local SS-AC branches: None.

Air supplies: Wester-Ross Marine, South Erradale, Gairloch; Camusnagaul Diving Centre, Sail Mhor Croft, Camasnagaul (085 483) 224.

Outboard motor service: The garages in Kyle of Lochalsh and Gairlock are worth a try.

Boat charters: Contact Camasnagaul Dive Centre in the North; for the South try McLean & Macrae, Kyle of Lochalsh (0599) 4209.

Local weather: Glasgow Weather Centre 041 248 3451; Oban Coastguard (0631) 63720.

Sea area: Hebrides.

Tidal constants:

	DOVER	ULLAPOOL
Gairloch	−0435	−0015
Shieldaig	−0440	−0020
Applecross	−0435	−0015
Plockton	−0435	−0015
Kyle of Lochalsh	−0440	−0020

Coastguard: Oban MRSC (0631) 63720.

Lifeboat: Mallaig, Lochinver, Stornoway.

Police stations: Gairloch (0445) 2017; Lochcarron (052 02) 222.

Hospitals: Belford Hospital, Fort William (0397) 2481.

Recompression chambers: Dunstaffnage Marine Laboratory, Oban (0631) 62244; Underwater Training Centre, Fort William (0397) 3786/3136.

Vehicle recovery: AA — Glasgow 041 812 0101; Fort William: (0397) 2099 (office hours only).

Local tourist information: Kyle of Lochalsh (0599) 4276; Torridon (044 587) 221; Gairloch (0445) 2130.

Accommodation: There are plenty of B & B and guest house facilities in this area (see Scottish Tourist Board guides).

CHAPTER 10

Rubha Reidh to Rubha Coigeach

This part of the coast contains some of the best diving areas in North-west Scotland. These include Loch Ewe, Gruinard Bay, Little Loch Broom, Loch Broom, and the mainland coast East of the Summer Isles. The Summer Isles themselves are discussed in Chapter 11.

Within the large, unnamed bay containing the Summer Isles, whose South shore includes the lochs listed above, I have details of over 100 sites. This is a reflection of two things – firstly, the quality and popularity of Summer Isles diving over the last few years; and secondly, the relatively recent establishment of the Camusnagaul Dive Centre at Sail Mhor Croft on Little Loch Broom. This is run by Dave and Linda Neville, and offers excellent facilities including high-class bunk-house accommodation, compressed air to 280 bars, and boat hire. It is refreshing to see someone attempting to open up a good, remote diving area by establishing simple facilities (rather than setting up a centre near good lines of communications, but poorer diving, just to make money). Dave has explored the coast around his base, and I am indebted to him for supplying details of quite a number of the sites in this chapter.

Much of the coast covered by this chapter is accessible from the main road (A832) that skirts the southern shores. The more northerly parts of the bay (and the Summer Isles) are accessible from the minor road to Achiltibuie. Access by hire boat is very convenient, and is available from Dave Neville.

From Rubha Reidh, the sandstone coast has fossil cliffs and geos leading to Loch Ewe. Loch Ewe is fairly broad, and quite shallow (58m) by West coast standards. It also contains an island – the Isle of Ewe.

Loch Maree is a fresh-water loch 45m above the present-day sea level (it would have been connected to the sea in raised beach times). A most ruggedly beautiful loch, 102m deep, it has a number of islands, the largest of which – Eilean Subhainn – has four lochs of its own! One of these, measuring 230m by 65m, has a maximum depth of 20m, and possesses three *islands*. So these are islands in a loch on an island in a loch!

The other point of note about Loch Ewe is that it provides the setting for the world-famous Inverewe Gardens, near Poolewe. These were created in 1862 by Osgood MacKenzie on a peninsula of barren ground which he

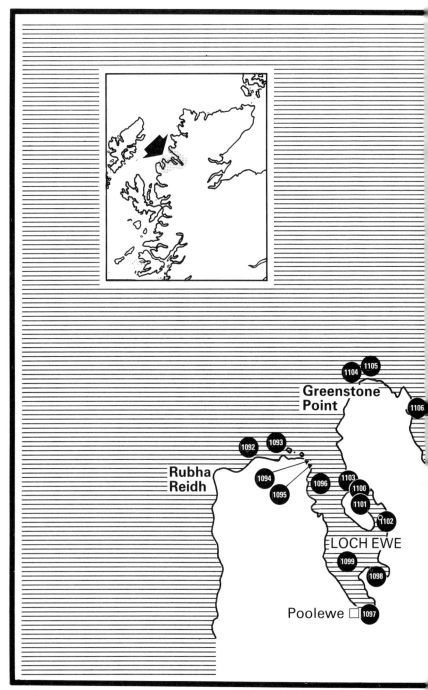

Dive Sites : Rubha Reidh to Rubha Coigeach

turned into one of the best sub-tropical woodland gardens in Europe. Plants from as far afield as China, the Himalayas, Chile, and the Pacific Islands, now thrive at a latitude that passes through Hudson Bay and Siberia.

East of Loch Ewe lies the peninsula of Rubha Mor, which terminates in Greenstone Point. This is composed of sandstone and has a raised platform which is cut by the present-day sea to form many geos in the North. These may well repay further diving examination. On the West side of Rubha Mor at Mellon Charles is a large traditional crofting community.

Rubha Mor forms the West coast of Gruinard Bay (or *Shallow Fiord*). This is a wide bay with depths falling steadily from the shore to over 100m at the mouth. There are magnificent raised beaches near Little Gruinard.

Gruinard Bay also contains the mile-long Gruinard Island. This was experimentally infected with anthrax during WW2 and landing is prohibited. Apparently, the island could be decontaminated, but this is considered too expensive. As it is, it may not be safe until the middle of next century.

Little Loch Broom lies to the East of Stattic Point, and consists of one large basin with a maximum depth of 110m, and a sill whose depth is 41m. The shores are wholly composed of sandstones which, though locally steep, are rather monotonous.

Loch Broom is mainly surrounded by sandstone, but South of Ullapool the loch crosses into Cambrian beds and the Moine Thrust. There are many examples of raised beaches, and the fishing village of Ullapool actually stands on one. The inner part of Loch Broom has a maximum depth of 68m, rising to 22m in the shallows near Corry Point and staying fairly shallow for about 2 miles until Ullapool is passed. Here, the bottom falls to 84m as the open sea is approached. Both Loch Broom and Little Loch Broom are glacial features which follow the lines of former river valleys.

Ullapool has a population of 600 and is the tourist centre of the Northern Highlands. It has hotels, guest houses, and a caravan and camping site. It is also an important fishing port, ranking third on the North-west coast. Boats may be hired from the harbour, where plenty of small craft run sea-fishing and shark-fishing excursions.

Just North of Loch Broom lies Isle Martin, which has a spit running to the mainland. The North of Isle Martin features a cliff dropping into a loch basin at 99m, then rising just as rapidly to the sandstone wall of Camas Mor. This basin is cut off from the open sea by shallower water (58m deep). Presumably, this was cut by a glacier descending Strath Kanaird in a former Ice Age.

The coast past the Summer Isles is shallow and formed from sandstone. Isle Ristol is connected to the mainland by a low-water reef.

The headland of Rubha Mor (the second headland of this name in this chapter, and one of 11 in Scotland – the name means *Great Headland*) has many minor features caused by faults. The whole headland has cliffs behind a rock platform cut by former seas. In such times, Achnahaird Bay and Badentarbat Bay would have been connected by the sea, and Rubha Mor would have been an island. The point of the headland is called Rubha Coigach (meaning *Fifth Headland* – presumably counting from Cape Wrath).

Diving in this area is splendid, with excellent headlands, dark and eerie submarine cliffs, isolated rock shoals, wrecks, and rich marine life. Visibility can be expected to be very good. Tidal streams are not very significant, except off exposed headlands. The area is well worth a visit, both for the diving itself and for the stirring scenery above water.

Dive sites

1092 Rubha Reidh to Eilean Furadh Mor. I have no sites recorded for this 4-mile stretch of coastline. It is fairly shallow on the chart, though there may be a worthwhile dive at Sron a' Gheodha Dhuibh (NG771929).

1093 Wreck of the William H Welch, Eilean Furadh Mor. NG796934. This was an American liberty ship of 7176 tons (134m long) which was lost in 1944. She ran aground in Black Bay, just outside Loch Ewe, and 62 out of her 74 passengers and crew were lost. The vessel broke in two, and the bow section floated away before sinking. The stern lies in 1m of water on a rock 40m off the West of Eilean Furadh Mor. Because of the exposed nature of this site, the wreck is very broken and nothing stands more than about 3m clear of the rocky seabed. The wreck is scattered over about 100m. Boat access is from Camas Dubh, Cove (NG810906).

1094 Unknown wreck, mouth of Loch Ewe. NG815925. This may be the bows of the *William H. Welch.* The position is just off the rocky islet of Sgeir Maol Mhoraidh Shuas. Access as Site 1093.

1095 Rhubha nan Sasan, Loch Ewe. NG817920. Cliffs underwater give way at 8m to a sandy slope running to 15m and beyond. The cliffs have a good variety of life. The headland here was used as a gun emplacement in WW2. The guns were salvaged, but a considerable amount of debris still lies in shallow water. Shore access.

1096 Cove, Loch Ewe. NG811911. Sheer rocks covered in kelp to 5m, then boulders. Quite a pleasant little dive, with small encrusted rock-faces among the kelp. A few armaments for the guns at Site 1095 lie here too. Shore access.

1097 Poolewe, Loch Ewe. NG848800. A poor, sandy dive to 5m. Shore access.

1098 Ploc an Rubha, Loch Tournaig. NG962840. A rock face to 20m, then a sand slope. Lots of crustaceans. Access is by boat from the jetty near Tournaig Farm (NG873838).

1099 Resolution Rock, Loch Ewe. NG842852. A rocky pinnacle rising from 18m to 7m with lots of life, making for a good dive. The bottom consists of coral sand with muddy patches. Access as Site 1098.

1100 Loch Ewe. this loch was used as an anchorage for naval and convoy vessles in WW2. Although there are no naval wrecks, there is considerable debris including ships' bells, portholes, and bottles. The Sound to the East of Isle Ewe is probably as good a place as anywhere to start searching. Depths here reach 20-30m. Access is from Aultbea (NG873888).

1101 Unknown wreck, Acairseid Bheag, Loch Ewe. NG849892. The hulk of a barge was reported to be lying at the low water line in this position in 1975. Access as Site 1100.

1102 Off Drumchork, Loch Ewe. NG874881. Shore access to a sandy, shallow, rather poor dive.

1103 Gob na Lice, Isle of Ewe. NG844901. A kelp-covered bottom down to about 20m. Lots of life under the kelp. Boat access is from the slipway at Mellon Charles (NG844901).

1104 Greenstone Point, Rubha Mor. NG860985. Deep gullies descend from the shore to pebbles and sand at about 20m. Lots of fish and some crawfish. This site is very exposed and there is a tidal stream of up to about 1½ knots. (LW slack +0500 Dover; HW slack at HW Dover). Boat access is from Mellon Udrigle (NG891957), or as Site 1103.

1105 Wreck of the MFV Gratitude. NG861988. This vessel was lost in 1958 and lies at 57 55 35N 05 36 48W. (This is 356 degrees and 400m from the triangulation mark on the point.) The wreck is well tangled with nets and floats and lies in about 30m. Access as Site 1104.

1106 Meallan Udrigill, Gruinard Bay. NG899932. An area of shallow surge gullies with depths to about 5m. There is much life in these gullies, but calm conditions are required. Shore access.

1107 Fraoch Eilean Mor. NG947912. A shallow shore dive around the island to 10-15m. Anemones on the rocks. Fish life plentiful.

1108 Gruinard Island. NG944940. This is the anthrax-infested island. Landing is totally forbidden (and totally stupid), and warning notices are displayed around the island. As far as I know, no-one has dived here. It

The contamination of the mile-long Gruinard Island with anthrax in the 1940s rules it out as a dive site. Other sites in the surrounding Gruinard Bay offer plenty of underwater interest.

appears shallow all round (less than 8m), except to the West where it drops to 15m. Presumably there is some danger underwater due to the anthrax organisms being washed into the sea by heavy rain, though I have no detailed information on this.

1109 Stattic Point. NG973963. The seabed at this site slopes gradually down to 30m and beyond. It seems a long way to the pebbles and mud, with scallops around. Boat access is from the jetty in Gruinard Bay (NG960926), or at Badluchrach (NG996948).

1110 Ardross Rock, Little Loch Broom. NG980965. This rock rises from 54m almost to the surface at a point about 700m East-north-east of Stattic Point. The scenery is rather variable, ranging from flat areas to sudden 20m vertical faces with lots of encrusting life. Some divers speak highly of it, others think it over-rated. Boat access is from the jetty near the mouth of Little Loch Broom (NG996948), or at Badluchrach at high tide. The rock is usually buoyed by Camusnagaul Diving Centre.

1111 Stac Cas a' Bhruie, Little Loch Broom. NG982957. Kelp-covered rock gullies lead down to sand beyond 15m. A very pleasant dive in the gullies, with nudibranchs, cup coral, anemones, and dogfish, noted. Access as Site 1110.

1112 Leac an Ime, Little Loch Broom. NG988957. Similar to Site 1111. About 800m out from the shore the flat-topped rocks give way to sand. The gullies at the shore are very pleasant when dived at high tide. This site is sheltered from the prevailing South-west winds. Shore access. Launch as Site 1110.

1113 Badluchrach jetty, Little Loch Broom. NG996948. A shallow, sandy bottom at around 5m. Brittle stars are found a little deeper. Nudibranchs also noted. Shore access.

1114 Leac a' Bhaid-bheithe, Little Loch Broom. NH037907. A steep slope over sand, mud, and boulders, to beyond 25m. Lobsters and scallops noted. Shore access.

1115 Conger Stack, Little Loch Broom. NH063903. This large rock rises from 50m-plus to within 7m of the surface. There is an underwater pinnacle on the South side of the rock with a sheer drop to over 30m. On the North there is a drop to mud at 22m. Excellent scenery on the drop-offs. Lots of life, often including Cyanea jellyfish. (*Caution:* the sting of these jellyfish is normally just a mild irritant, but can be dangerous to sensitised people.) The stack can be located by echo sounder, though Dave Neville usually has it buoyed. Boat access is from Camusnagaul (NH067892), or Dundonell (NH081885).

1116 Cadha nam Muc, Little Loch Broom. NH037925. Deep cliffs and boulder slops to 100m! Also some vertical boulder patches which have been eroded to give exciting 15m-long 'through routes'. These boulders lie at 20m on the point just South of the little bay, and are easily missed. Angler fish noted. Access as Site 1110.

1117 Creag a' Chadha, Little Loch Broom. NH036932. A series of cliff-faces down to 30m. Lots of life. Boat access as Site 1110.

1118 A' Chailleach, Cailleach Head. NG985986. Gullies and small, shallow caves, thickly covered with kelp. Depths to 18m. Angler fish, dogfish, and lobsters, noted. Otherwise, not too exciting. Maximum tidal streams of 1 knot. LW slack +0210 Dover; HW slack −0415 Dover. Access as Site 1110.

1119 Sgeir na Crubain, Cailleach Head. NH000987. A 60 degree slope of rock and boulders dropping to about 30m. Tides and access as Site 1118.

1120 Iolla Dearg, Cailleach Head. NH012996. Small gullies leading down to 10-12m with lots of fish life. Access and tides as Site 1118.

1121 Unknown wreck, Cailleach Head. NH012996. This is the wreck of a collier. At low water the drying rocks form a 50m-wide 'U' shape facing North. Swim out of the 'U' to find the wreck. Access and tides as Site 1118.

1122 South of Camas a' Mhaoraich, Loch Broom. NH090959. A vertical cliff dropping to 18m and containing a steep mud slope to 60m. The face is rather bare of life. Boat access is from Ullapool, or from the beach at the camp-site (NM124938).

1123 Rubha Blar Bog, Loch Broom. NH164890. This site goes very deep very quickly, but is muddy. A poor dive, relieved only by the excellent bar lunches at the Tir-Aluinn Hotel.

1124 Corry Point, Loch Broom. NH143923. A drift at up to 1 knot over sandy mud. Depths to 30m. Shore access. LW slack +0210 Dover; HW slack −0415 Dover.

1125 Wreck of a fishing vessel, Ullapool Harbour. NH130938. This vessel lies in about 15m of water on a muddy bottom in the area of the moorings to the East of the pier. The exact position can be checked with the owner of the *Sunset Queen*. It is his wreck, and his permission is needed to dive it. Shore access.

1126 Off Ullapool campsite, Loch Broom. NH124938. This site features a sloping muddy bottom littered with junk. Eventually 30m can be reached. Lobsters are often seen in the old tin cans, etc. Shore access.

1127 Rubha Cadail, Loch Broom. NH095973. Rock outcrops in 10m of water at either side of the bay. The middle of the bay is sandy and eventually reaches 30m. Shore access from the car-park path.

1128 Ardmair Bay, South cliffs. NH104979. Shallow rocks dropping on to sand at 12m. Rich life in deep gullies and caves make this a good second dive. This site can be reached either from the shore, or by boat from Loch Kanaird at NH112985.

1129 Ardmair Bay. NH105983. The centre of the bay is flat and sandy. Depths are 15-20m Flatfish noted. Shore access.

1130 Isle Martin, South-east face. NH099995. A steep wall leading to 30m on mud. This cannot compare with Site 1131.

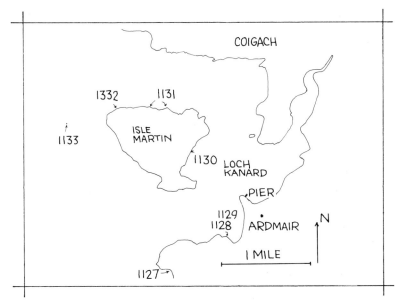

Isle Martin sites

1131 Isle Martin, North face. NC092001. The wall down the North face of Isle Martin is one of the most imposing submarine cliffs in Scotland. It drops almost vertically to a depth of 143m. Facing North, it is nearly always in shadow and gives an exceedingly gloomy, oppressive dive similar to the infamous Loch Lomond wall. At 50m, there are small ledges every few metres. The life on the wall is sparse. Boat access is from Loch Kanaird (NH112985). This is not a dive for the faint-hearted, or for those not comfortable with a 'black pit' beneath their fins.

1132 Isle Martin, West end of North face. NC085001. A vertical cliff from 3m to 36m, then a mud slope onwards. Lots of sponges and anemones in the shallows. There is reputed to be a cave in this face. Access as Site 1131.

1133 Martin Bank, West of Isle Martin. NH076999. A steep ridge rising to within 15m of the surface with depths of 54m on either side. This is undived as far as I know, but I would expect it to be a good dive if the seabed is rocky. Access as Site 1131.

1134 Leuim an Fheidh, mainland North of Isle Martin. NC084016. Dramatic cliffs fall steeply to the sea and carry on underwater as vertical sandstone walls dropping to over 40m. Then a steep slope to 90m. These give a very pleasant dive with lots of life including cup corals and hydroids. I have a report of 40m visibility at a depth of 45m in February! Access as Site 1131.

1135 Coulnacraig, mainland North-west of Isle Martin. NC067030. A steep boulder slope, then a sand slope to 45m. A pleasant dive with good visibility. Flatfish, rays, and angler fish, noted. Access as Site 1131.

1136 Badenscallie Point, Horse Sound. NC035061. A good second dive off the shore over rocks with kelp to sand at 6m (and on to 29m if required). Nudibranchs and lots of other small life under the kelp. Shore access.

1137 Skerry South of Rubha Dunan. NC024067. A shallow dive over a boulder slope to sand at 12m.

1138 Badentarbat Bay. NC013097. A shallow shore dive or a deeper boat dive on to flat sand. Depths run down to 30m, but are generally about 10-15m. The South of the bay is the deepest part. Flatfish and rays noted.

1139 Badentarbat Pier. NC008095. The rocks descend to 15m on to sand. A pleasant dive, usually with good visibility. Rays noted. Shore access.

1140 Dorney Sound. NB983099. A pleasant drift dive with tidal streams that are reported to reach 2 knots on springs. From the shore, boulders lead to 12m. There is then a sand slope dropping down to 30m-plus.

1141 Dorney Sound to Rubha Coigeach. I have no dives recorded for this 8-mile stretch of the mainland coast. The chart shows a number of interesting-looking rocks and headlands.

Area information and services

Hydrographic charts: 2500 Loch Broom & approaches 1:25,000; 2501 Summer Isles 1:25,000; 2504 Rubha Coigeach to Staerhead 1:25,000; 2509 Rubha Reidh to Cailleach Head 1:25,000; 3146 Loch Ewe 1:12,500.
Ordnance Survey 1:50,000 maps: 15 Loch Assynt; 19 Gairloch & Ullapool.
Ordnance Survey 1:25,000 maps: NB91 Rubha Coigeach; NC00/10 Strath Kanaird; NG79 Rubha Reidh; NG88/98 Loch Ewe; NG89/99 Gruinard Bay; NH08/18 An Teallach; NH09/19 Ullapool.
Local BS-AC branches: Ullapool (970).
Local SS-AC branches: None.
Air supplies: Dave Neville, Camusnagaul Diving Centre, Sail Mhor Croft, Camasnagaul (085 483) 224; Barry Todd, Ullapool (0854) 2036.
Outboard motor services: Try Ullapool garages.
Boat charters: Contact Camasnagaul Dive Centre; try fishing hire vessels on Ullapool Pier; Barry Todd, Ullapool (0854) 2036.
Local weather: Glasgow Weather Centre 041 248 3451; Oban Coastguard (0631) 63720.
Sea area: Hebrides.
Tidal constants:

	DOVER	ULLAPOOL
Summer Isles	−0425	−0005
Ullapool	−0420	0
Mellon Charles	−0430	−0010

Harbourmaster: Ullapool (0854) 2091/2165.

Coastguard: Stornoway MRSC (0851) 2013; Oban MRSC (0631) 63720; Ullapool (0854) 2014.
Lifeboat: Mallaig, Lochinver, Stornoway.
Police stations: Ullapool (0854) 2017; Aultbea (044 582) 222.
Hospitals: Raigmore Hospital, Inverness (0463) 34151.
Recompression chambers: Dunstaffnage Marine Laboratory, Oban (0631) 62244; Underwater Training Centre, Fort William (0397) 3786/3136.
Vehicle recovery: AA – Glasgow 041 812 0101; Inverness (0463) 33213 (office hours only).
Local tourist information: Inverewe (044 586) 229; Ullapool (0854) 2135.
Accommodation: Camus nagaul Dive Centre (085 483) 224; there are also many B & B and guest house facilities (see Scottish Tourist Board guides).

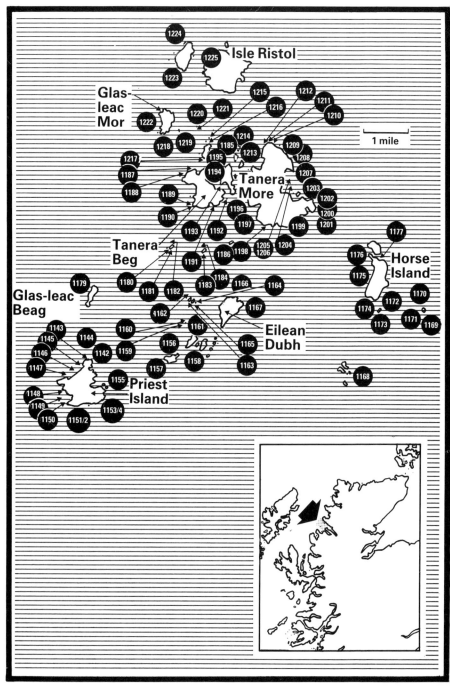

Dive Sites : The Summer Isles

CHAPTER 11

The Summer Isles

Islands have always figured bodly in man's imagination. Remote, northern stacks and isles, set in turbulent seas off a windy coast, excite more than their normal share of wanderlust, and the desire to dive such places is well-nigh irresistible when the water is clear and teeming with life. Add to this the topside exploration of islands steeped in history, but where wild creatures now reign supreme, and you have a heady environment. The Summer Isles of North-West Scotland are such places.

These enchanted isles lie just off the mainland, about 47 miles South-south-west of Cape Wrath. Some 30 islands (depending on how the term "island" is defined) and many more stacks make up the group. These are strung out in two lines – one running from Isle Ristol in the North to Priest Island in the South-west, the other following the coast in a South-east direction from Isle Ristol to Horse Isle. Their total area is 5½ square miles, and they are largely uninhabited.

Geologically, the Summer Isles represent a continuation of the sandstone of the nearby mainland, though the gneiss foundation shows through in places. The main feature of the Summer Isles is that they are rugged and rocky. Their coasts are irregular, with many caves and headlands.

The outer Summer Isles (with the exception of Priest Island) are formed of coarse felspathic sandstones, with a succession of ridges running North-north-east to South-south-west. The scarps of the cliffs face West, as on Priest Island.

Plant life on the islands is prolific. Heather dominates, but there is also a lot of turf. In early summer, the flowers create a very pleasant backdrop to island exploration.

The wildlife on these islands is one of their attractions. Birdlife on the larger islands is rich, with 43 species recorded on Tanera Mhor. Priest Island and Horse Isle are also noted for their birds. Priest Island has a breeding flock of grey lag geese. Glas-leac Beag draws several hundred barnacle geese in winter. Horse Isle has a herd of white goats. (Perhaps it should be called *Treasure Island* because a gold coin was found here last century, supposedly from the hidden gold of an Armada ship.)

There are seals in the waters around the Summer Isles, and some breed on Tanera Beag. Porpoises and dolphins are also seen here, and further West out in the Minch whales have been sighted.

Although the waters of the Summer Isles are sheltered by the Outer Hebrides across the Minch, considerable seas still occur when the predominant South-west and West wind blows. One of the advantages of the islands, however, is that there is always shelter to be had to the East, away from the prevailing winds. The tidal streams are generally weak between the islands, with a maximum rate of ½-a-knot. The spring range is 3-4m. The underwater visibility is usually very good too, with horizontal visibility often reaching 20m or more, especially around the remoter rocky stacks and headlands. The bottom in this area is made up largely of sands and muds. But there are also significant underwater cliffs, the bases of which are often steep boulder slopes which lead down to the depths. To my knowledge, no bedrock is exposed on the seabed.

The normal way to dive these islands is by means of a substantial inflatable. Camping used to be the order of the day, but divers can now take advantage of the facilities at the Diving Centre at Camusnagaul on Little Loch Broom.

It is a 10-mile boat trip to the first of the Summer Isles from Camusnagaul, with another 6 miles to the furthest. When conditions are too rough for this trip, a beach launch can be made at Achiltibuie, though this requires a road journey of 106 miles from Camusnagaul. Regrettably, beach camping at Badentarbat Bay near Achiltibuie is no longer allowed and the official camp-site at Achnahaird Bay (NC014137) must be used. There are caravans and guest houses available at Achiltibuie.

All in all, the Summer Isles should provide you with plenty of idyllic memories of long, sunny summer days filled with wide skies, seabirds, clear visibility, plenty of fish life, and exciting underwater cliffs.

Dive sites

Tidal streams with spring rates of up to ½-a-knot run in the channels between the Summer Isles, but their direction and the times at which they begin are irregular. The best launch for inflatables is over the shingle beach at Achiltibuie (NC017093). Alternatively, the islands can be approached from Little Loch Broom and the Diving Centre at Camusnagaul.

In so far as is possible with a complex archipelago, the sites are described South to North, and West to East.

1142 Priest Island, Stoll Eilean a' Chleirich. NB927030. At the North-east tip of Priest Island there is a flooded tunnel, the east entrance of which has several 12m-deep gullies. This is a good dive with kelp on the flatter surfaces, and sponges covering the vertical walls.

1143 Priest Island, North Tip. NB925030. This is another tunnel at the more westerly peninsula at the North of the island. Depths vary from 3m to 14m. The marine life is similar to Site 1142.

1144 Unknown wreck, North of Priest Island. There is a report of a 6m craft foundering here in the 1950s. Six people were lost.

1145 Priest Island, North-west face. NB922026. Depths to 30m down a rock-face. Shoals of pollack, numerous wrasse, and the ever-present seals, noted.

1146 Wreck of MFV Silver Reward, Priest Island. NB922026. This 50-ton trawler was lost in 1964 at 57 57 45N 05 31 18W in 20m of water.

1147 Priest Island, West face. NB917025. A steep, rocky cliff to about 10m leading on to bedrock with deep gullies and a flat plain of boulders at 16m. Kelp and soft corals noted.

1148 Priest Island, South-west face. NB920018. This drops to 42m on to sand. Rather gloomy at depth, but the rock-faces are interesting.

1149 Wreck of MFV Guiding Star, Priest Island. NB919017. This 39-ton wooden MFV was lost in 1964 at 57 57 25N 05 30 58W in a charted depth of 8m.

1150 Priest Island, South-west tip. NB918016. The bottom is made up of large boulders, sloping rock faces, and rocky bluffs, becoming less steep around 26m. Soft corals and seals noted.

1151 Priest Island, South point. NB923015. A steep, rocky slope. About 75m East of the point a sheer rock-face starting at 10m runs at an angle of 45 degrees to the shore. Numerous fish, anemones, nudibranchs, and soft coral.

1152 Priest Island, bay West of South point. NB922015. Broken rocky gullies to 20m, then smooth sloping rock with small vertical faces. Feather stars, cup corals, squat lobsters, and crabs, noted.

1153 Priest Island, East point. NB932022. A steep, rocky bottom extending beyond 20m.

1154 Bay North of Site 1153. NB931022. In the bay immediately North of Site 1153 there are splendid shallow rock faces covered with life.

1155 Ard Glas, Priest Island. NB933023. Steep bedrock-and-boulder slope giving way to boulders and sand at 18m. Just offshore there is a steep pinnacle of rock extending from deeper than 16m to within 5m of the surface. This is not marked on the chart. It is covered with a kelp forest, with lots of life under the plants.

1156 Sgeir Mhor. NB952029. These rocks only just show at high water. Excellent diving on all sides. Pelagic fish everywhere, together with ling and lobster. To the South-west there are sloping boulders becoming steeper to the North, and eventually vertical. These extend below 32m.

1157 Bottle Island, South-west point. NB953018. Unusually for the Summer Isles, there can be quite a strong tidal stream around the point. There is a steep slope, vertical in places, to over 35m. The superb display of anemones and soft coral, along with seals and cormorants underwater, make this a first-class site, though it is very exposed to the South-west.

1158 Carn Deas, South point. NB964023. Rocky at first, then gently-sloping sand to 30m. Scallops, Norway lobster, skate, and seals, noted. Not the best site in the Summer Isles!

1159 Twelve Foot Rock, West face. NB957034. This lies about ½-a-mile North-west of the North point of Carn Iar, and about ½-a-mile North-east of Sgeir Mhor. The top of the rock lies 5m below the surface and an echo sounder is needed to locate it. To the West, the bottom drops steeply in a series of ledges to over 35m. All the usual life.

129

1160 Twelve Foot Rock, North face. NB957034. A vertical wall goes down from 15m to 40m and provides a splendid dive.

1161 Twelve Foot Rock, South face. NB957034. This rock has steep, gouged surfaces to 22-30m, with boulder slopes carrying on down. Below the kelp the rock surfaces are curiously bare of life.

1162 Sgeir nam Mult, North-east side. NB962040. A sloping bottom of rock and kelp on sand. Eventually 25m is reached, but it's a rather boring dive.

1163 Sgeir nam Mult, South-west side. NB961038. A fairly steep drop to a little over 50m. Good rock formations in the shallows.

1164 Sgeir nam Mult, off the East side. NB964048. A gentle slope of smooth bedrock turning to boulders at 14m and shell gravel at 17m. Kelp to 17m.

1165 Unknown wreck, Sgeir nam Mult, South side. NB960037. This is the wreck of a motor prawn boat of 10 tons, lost in 1970. The position given is 57 58 42N 05 27 00W (PA). This is about 100m South of the main islet where the depth is about 30m. The boat was 10m long.

1166 Eilean Dubh, North side. NB974041. Rocky, gullied cliffs to 9-11m; boulder beds to 20m; then sand. There is a kelp forest with cup corals noted at the base. Rocks covered with purple algae.

1167 Eilean Dubh, East side. NB978038. A rocky cliff to 8m, then boulders leading to sand at 14m.

1168 Carn nan Sgeir. NC013015. The skerries at the South end of the inlet are bedrock and boulders to 15m, then sand and mud to beyond 30m. Seals noted.

1169 Iolla Bheag. NC039036. This rock rises 3m above the surface and lies about 400m off the mainland shore at Rudha Dubh Ard. The South end drops to 27m on to mud.

1170 Mary Rock. NC037039. This just breaks the surface 300m North-west of Iolla Bheag. Off the North-east, there is a slope to 25m.

1171 Unknown wrecks, Iolla Bheag. The wrecks of two unknown trawlers lie very close to Iolla Bheag. One is just to the West and one just to the South.

1172 Iolla Mhor. NC024035. These rocks rise 4m above the surface. On the North side there is a slope leading down to 23m. The other parts of the skerries are shallow.

1173 Wreck of the MFV Silver Spray, Iolla Mhor, NC027033. This 20m-long, 40-ton wooden vessel sank after hitting Iolla Mhor in 1965. The position is 57 58 32N 05 20 14W in about 36m of water, 300m South-east of Iolla Mhor.

1174 Horse Island, South end. NC023038. A pleasant dive to 23m down a rocky face.

1175 Horse Island, West side. NG020047. An exposed, but good, site. There is a vertical rock-wall to 15m, then a boulder-slope to 30m followed by sand leading into the depths. Lots of encrusting life on the rock.

1176 Horse Island, North-west tip. NC021053. A boulder slope to 15m with shell sand and mud beyond.

1177 Skerry North of Horse Island. NC024052. Shallow rocks to 12m. The usual life, but at this site it is profuse.

1178 Horse Island, Armada wreck. Legend tells us that an Armada wreck was lost in these waters. A Spanish gold coin has certainly been found on Horse Island, reputedly from the treasure buried from an Armada vessel.

1179 Glas-leac Beag. NB928054. The North tip appears from the chart to be a rock-face to 27m. The West side appears to be a very steep slope on to sand at 45m, though there is reported to be much kelp in the shallows. A whale was washed up here in 1984, so there may be large bones lying about underwater! A very exposed island. Its name means *Little Grey Slab.*

1180 Stac Mhic Aonghais, South tip. NB955057. A steep boulder-slope to 19m covered in kelp. A pebble-and-sand slope runs gently on.

1181 Stac Mhic Aonghais, South-east face. NB953056. A splendid dive down a rocky slope to 50m. Lots of fish life.

1182 Stac Mhic Aonghais, North-west tip. NB954057. A steep bedrock drop with gullies to 28m and beyond, on to a seabed of large boulders covered with life.

1183 Sgeir Neo-ghluasadach, South end. NB964053. A stepped, rocky slope to 22m, with kelp cover to 13m. Small, rocky faces covered in plumose anemones.

1184 Sgeir Neo-ghluasadach, North-west tip. NB965056. A superb dive. Visibility up to 25m, together with unpredictable underwater contours. There is an 18m vertical wall, though the seabed flattens quickly beyond this depth. The main feature of this dive is the vast shoals of fish that abound here in the late summer.

1185 Sgeir nan Feusgan. NB976089. A rock-and-boulder slope to 30m, where there is a good reef.

1186 Sgeir Revan, South end. NB973057. Strangely for the Summer Isles, this rock does not give a very good dive. Perhaps it is too shallow and exposed.

1187 Tanera Beg, North end. NB963083. A broken rocky slope gives way to a sandy plain at 13m, with rocky outcrops. Lots of kelp on the rocks.

1188 Tanera Beg, North-west face. NB958079. A steep boulder slope to beyond 22m dominated by a kelp forest to 15m.

1189 Sron Ghlas, Tanera Beg. NB962068. A rocky slope with lots of gullies and boulders to a depth of 28m.

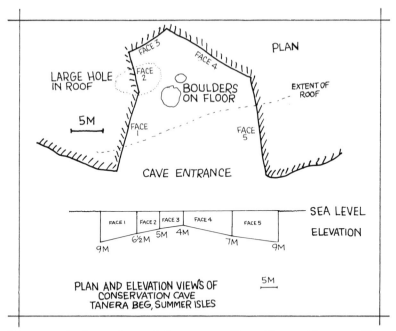

PLAN AND ELEVATION VIEWS OF
CONSERVATION CAVE
TANERA BEG, SUMMER ISLES

Plan and elevation of Conservation Cave, Tanera Beg

1190 Conservation Cave, Tanera Beg. NB963069. There is an underwater cave here that is 6m deep. This contains a very fragile system of unusual marine life. This is considered to be one of the best dives of its type in western Scotland and is an NCC conservation area. Please respect this site. Be careful to do no damage.

1191 Carn Sgoitte, Tanera Beg. NB970068. A slope of rock and boulder to 18m and a sandy plain.

1192 Rocks off the East of Tanera Beg. NB973073. An interesting second dive down a 10m cliff covered in plumose anemones.

1193 Tanera Beg anchorage. NB970076. A very sheltered site with a soft mud-and-sand plain at 8m. There are also boulders and small cliff-faces with soft coral and light kelp cover.

1194 Eilean Fada Mor, North-west side. NB971082. A vertical cliff to 5m, then a slope of rocks and mud to beyond 12m. Ascidians and anemones noted.

1195 Eilean Fada Mor, North tip. NB973084. A series of rock skerries with depths from 6m to 15m. Pleasant dives amid the kelp and associated life.

1196 Sron na Moil Moire, Tanera More. NB979069. Boulders in the shallows, then a steep sand-and-mud slope to beyond 30m with all the usual life.

1197 Mol Mor, Tanera More. NB980067. The mouth of the bay has a thick maerl bed on top of dead maerl sand at depths of 20m.

1198 Mol an Sgadain, Tanera More. NB986063. Rocky gullies running out to 18m. Beyond these the seabed drops away to over 38m.

1199 Earbull Dhuin, Tanera More. NB993063. Rocky slopes to about 10m with a kelp forest. Sand leading on down. Lots of urchins and squat lobsters.

1200 Rubha Dubh, Tanera More. NC004068. Boulder slopes to 14m, then a slope of sand to beyond 20m. Kelp and urchins noted.

1201 Out from Rubha Dubh, Tanera More. NC003065. A gentle slope of muddy sand with occasional boulders. Little life noted except infrequent squat lobsters.

1202 North Rubha Dubh, Tanera More. NC001073. A shelving muddy sand plain at the South of the Anchorage. Various shell-life noted.

1203 Eilean Mor, Tanera More. NB997075. A muddy bottom to over 17m, with huge scallops after initial rocks. No signs were found of the bottles supposed to be here from an old pub. Take care you do not offend the local fishermen by diving too closely to the salmon cages hereabouts.

1204 Tanera More Pier. NB992075. A sheltered site with a sandy slope turning into mud at depth. A few isolated boulders. Sparse life.

1205 Tanera More Anchorage. NB991076 – NB993081. Shallow and muddy near the shore, deeper and muddy further out! Good mud life at 30m.

1206 Unknown MFV wreck, Tanera More Anchorage. This is a recent wreck and lies at 22m. I have no further details.

1207 Rubh' Ard-na-goine, Tanera More. NB995080. A shallow dive down rock faces covered in plumose anemones, urchins, and starfish. Scallops on the sand. A good night dive.

1208 Sron na Moil Baine, Tanera More. NB995085. A plain of cobbles covered with kelp to 13m; then a steep boulder slope to 20m; and finally a muddy sand slope to 26m. Normal marine life for this area.

1209 Skerry North east of Tanera More. NB992088. A good site because of the life. It is a rocky slope to over 30m, with a band of boulders at 12-15m.

1210 Sgeir a' Chapuill, Tanera More. NB988090. This rock lies just to the North of Tanera More, and dries 2m. It provides an excellent, if shallow, second dive. The main rock is invisible beneath plumose anemones of all colours, shapes and sizes. Otherwise the bottom is of kelp with sandy patches.

1211 West of Sgeir a' Chapuill, Tanera More. NB989090. A slope of shell-sand and scattered boulders at about 20m. Good range of species present.

1212 Creag Ard, Tanera More. NB986090. A rocky cliff, then a boulder slope, then a sand slope to beyond 24m. Brittle star beds at depth.

1213 Eilean a' Ehuic, North end. NB978084. There are skerries around here with depths of 6-15m round them. Pleasant dives under the kelp.

1214 Sgeir nam Feusgan, North end. NB977089. Similar to previous site.

1215 Rock North of Eilean a' Char. NB967091. There is a shallow channel between two islets with a kelp-covered rocky seabed at 6m.

1216 Eilean a' Char, North end. NB967089. Similar to Site 1213.

1217 Eilean a' Char, South-west end. NB963085. A steep rocky slope to sand at 28m, with rock faces at about 18m. Seals, nudibranchs, sea pens, and anemones, noted.

1218 South of Glas-leac Mor. NB957089. Bedrock at 30m overlaid with some sand and large boulders. Urchins and feather stars noted.

1219 West Black Rock. NB957093. Kelp-shrouded rocky gullies with sand patches at 18m for some distance to the east. These are followed by a series of ledges and drop-offs to about 30m. The best approach is to find the edge of the drop-off by echo-sounder before diving.

1220 Sgeir Dubh, North side. NB963095. An interesting boulder-slope to beyond 30m. Cuckoo wrasse noted in some numbers.

1221 Sgeir Dubh, West side. NB962095. A boulder slope to 32m, with ledges and little faces in it, then sand going on down. Varied life includes four species of wrasse.

1222 Glas-leac Mor. This is apparently undived. The North end appears to drop very steeply to 32m. The rest of the island has depths to about 20m.

1223 Eilean Mullagrach, South end. NB958113. There is a 'boatable' tunnel through the cliffs. The diving is quite shallow, but interesting.

1224 Eilean Mullagrach, North-west end. NB958122. There is a steep, rocky slope here to 23m on to a seabed with boulders.

1225 Isle Ristol, West side. NB965116. The chart shows the depth here as about 13m. However, I have report of a boulder-slope with kelp to 30m.

1226 Unknown Armada Wreck, Isle Ristol. There is a local legend of an Armada vessel wrecked in the northern bay off Bo Bhuiridh on Isle Ristol. This links interestingly with the Horse Island information (see Site 1178).

Area information and services

Hydrographic charts: 2500 Loch Broom & approaches 1:25,000; 2501 Summer Isles 1:25,000; 2509 Rubha Reidh to Cailleach Head 1:25,000.
Ordnance Survey 1:50,000 maps: 15 Loch Assynt; 19 Gairloch & Ullapool.
Ordnance Survey 1:25,000 maps: NB90 Summer Isles; NB91 Rubha Coigeach; NC00/10 Strath Kanaird.
Local BS-AC branches: Ullapool (970).

Local SS-AC branches: None.
Air supplies: Dave Neville, Camusnagaul Diving Centre Sail Mhor Croft, Camasnagaul (085 483) 224; Barry Todd, Ullapool (0854) 2036; Jim Crooks, 6 Inver Park, Lochinver (057 14) 362.
Outboard motor service: Try Ullapool garages.
Boat charterers: Camasnagaul Dive Centre; fishing hire vessels on Ullapool Pier; Barry Todd, Ullapool (0854) 2036; Jim Crooks, 6 Inver Park, Lochinver (057 14) 362.
Local weather: Glasgow Weather Centre 041 248 3451; Oban Coastguard (0631) 63720.
Sea area: Hebrides.
Tidal constants:

	DOVER	ULLAPOOL
Summer Isles	−0425	−0005

Coastguard: Stornoway MRSC (0851) 2013; Ullapool (0854) 2014.
Lifeboat: Lochinver, Stornoway.
Police stations: Ullapool (0854) 2017.
Hospitals: Raigmore Hospital, Inverness (0463) 34151.
Recompression chambers: Dunstaffnage Marine Laboratory, Oban (0631) 62244; Underwater Training Centre, Fort William (0397) 3786//3136.
Vehicle recovery: AA – Glasgow 041 812 0101; Inverness (0463) 33213 (office hours only).
Local tourist information: Ullapool (0854) 2135.
Accommodation: Camusnagaul Dive Centre (085 483) 224; accommodation is also sometimes available on Tanera More.

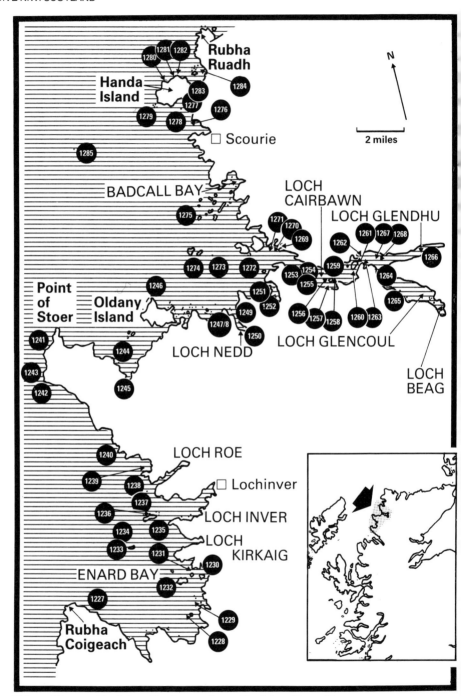

Dive Sites : Rubha Coigeach to Rubha Ruadh

CHAPTER 12

Rubha Coigeach to Rubha Ruadh

This chapter covers the penultimate group of dives on the Western seaboard of Scotland. These run from Enard Bay, to Lochinver, Point of Stoer, Eddrachillis Bay, Loch Cairnbawn and Kylesku Ferry, and the Badcall Islands and Handa Island.

The landscape of the rocky desert of Assynt and the Reay Forest has a fantastic quality about it – several miles of rough ground lead from the shore to great sandstone peaks standing in total isolation. At first sight, it seems improbable that such dramatic scenery can exist in the British Isles.

The craggy shoreline throws down a gigantic challenge to the exploring diver. Some exploration has been done by one or two pioneering individuals, but much remains.

The whole area is made up of Lewisian gneiss, except for the sandstone of Handa Island, the Stoer peninsula, and the South-west of Enard Bay. The break between the sandstone and the gneiss occurs at Lag na Saille in Enard Bay. From there to Lochinver the coast is broken into bays and islands, with fossil cliffs backing most of the coast.

Lochinver is a beautiful village of white-painted cottages lying at the head of Loch Inver. At the mouth of the loch, 3 miles away, lies Soyea Isle. Lochinver is an important fishing village, and the landing of the catches there is a sight indeed.

Behind Lochinver rises the amazing mountain cone of Suilven. The name comes from the old Norse for Pillar Mountain, and so it must have appeared to the Viking raiders and colonists. It has been likened to a whale or a galleon riding in a sea of gneiss.

Loch Kirkaig, Loch Inver, and Loch Roe, are all short lochs, which cannot be regarded as fiords, even though they have been modified by ice. It appears that they have a tectonic origin and that in Tertiary times they were part of a large river valley draining to the East.

From Lochinver to the Point of Stoer is a series of beautiful sandy bays – at Achmelvich, Clachtoll, Bay of Stoer, and Balchladich – divided into subsidiary bays by ribs of sandstone. There used to be free access to these areas, but now the locals have realised that money can be made by fencing them off and charging for entry. The main rock hereabouts is sandstone, running out to the Point of Stoer.

At the bleak Stoer Point there is a lighthouse and high sandstone cliffs which dip to the East and rise 120m to the North-east and 60m to the West. Beyond lies the 60m high stack of the Old Man of Stoer. This was first climbed in 1966 by Dr Tom Patey, the Ullapool doctor so tragically killed while descending another sea stack off Whiten Head on the North coast.

Beyond the Point of Stoer is Eddrachillis Bay, with its feast of islands. The two largest of these are Oldany Island and Handa Island, but there are also about 40 rocks and islands in the South of the bay, and about another 40 skerries and islets composing the Badcall Islands

There is a winding road running round the North of Assynt and passing the Stoer headland. It skirts the South shores of Eddrachillis Bay, and passes the sandy Clashnessie Bay, Oldany Island (separated from the mainland by a fault flooded with sea-water), and Lochs Nedd and Ardbhair (in which there are well-developed salt marshes). This road gives delightful views over Eddrachillis Bay and its island-fringed shores to the mountains further inland.

Loch Cairnbawn (also called Loch a' Chairn Bhain) is a major inlet which splits into Loch Glencoul and Loch Glendhu. The general trend of this loch system is to the South-east and is continued as a structural line down the freshwater Loch Shin. The probable origin is tectonic, as no significant streams drain into the lochs. The mouth of Loch Cairnbawn is 34m deep, but this falls to 108m before rising to 13m at Cailas Cumhann, the narrows near Kylesku Ferry. There is a 63m basin just East of the ferry, where the loch splits. Loch Glendhu is quite shallow (15m maximum) and has no further basins, whereas Loch Glencoul has a basin at 51m connecting over a sill at 20m with the main loch. Finally, after shallows at 2m, Loch Beag has a small basin at 25m.

The coast from Kylesku to Handa shows a great number of minor crags and valleys, which follow fault lines and dykes.

The new road bridge over Cailas Cumhann at Kylestrome (which in 1984 replaced the famous Kylesku Ferry) connects to the road running along the East of Eddrachillis Bay, giving excellent views of the glaciated Badcall Islands. It then leads to Scourie, Tarbet, and Handa Island.

Handa Island is completely made of sandstone. It dips to the East at about 25 degrees, so its East coast is low lying, but its West coast has dramatic, vertical sandstone cliffs reaching 120m. These include a classic sea stack rising to the level of the cliffs tops. The distance from the main cliff to the Great Stack is 25m. This gap was first crossed in 1876, hand over hand on a rope suspended over the 105m drop.

The Stack has a long, low natural arch (or tunnel) in its base, through which an inflatable can be taken at low tide on calm days.

Handa was occupied in the last century by twelve families who lived on potatoes, fish and seabirds. Their lives are reminiscent of those of the St Kildans. They had their own parliament (which was recognised on the mainland) and queen, who was the oldest widow on the island. The great potato famine of 1848 made the people emigrate, and the island is now uninhabited and is administered by the Royal Society for the Protection of Birds. It is, in fact, an incredible seabird reserve. Landing is still permitted, but it is good policy to ask the warden, who is one of the lobster fishermen in Tarbet. He is able to ferry you there for a small charge.

Leaving Handa, the gneiss coast continues to Rubha Ruadh (or *Red Point*).

The best way to tackle the diving is by car and inflatable, as there are a number of good launch spots, though some (eg: the south coast of Eddrachillis Bay) present certain difficulties.

Diving from this piece of coastline is an experience unlikely to be forgotten. The visibility is usually excellent, and the tidal streams are insignificant, except by Kylesku Ferry. Boating along this coast in the long, idyllic days of high summer is a marvellous experience, which has a dream-like quality about it.

Dive sites

An excellent local contact is Jim Crooks at 6 Inver Park, Lochinver — Lochinver (05714) 362. He has a base with hot showers on Lochinver Pier from which he supplies compressed air, and hires out tanks. He has a 6m dory with twin 55 HP outboards (carrying six divers) for charter. Its range includes the whole of Enard Bay.

1227 Cliffs South east of Rubha Coigeach, Enard Bay. NB980182 — NC014147. A 3-mile stretch of coast with great diving potential. The chart shows depths reaching 18m quite close to the shore and fairly quickly reaching 36m a little further out. Excellent diving is reported among drop-offs, caves and gullies. The spring tidal stream off the point runs at 2.5 knots. LW slack +0515 Dover, HW slack at HW Dover. At NC012148, the bay called Camas nan Soithechean on the maps is named Vessel Bay on the chart. Boat access with an awkward launch at Achnahaird Bay (NC020126).

1228 Green Island, Enard Bay. NC056152. Very pleasant scenic diving amongst cracks and caves with lots of life in depths of 12-20m. There appears to be a steep slope to beyond 40m on the North-west side. Boat access is from Loch an Eisg-Brachaidh (NC075176) or Lochinver.

1229 Meall an Iaruinn. NC065156. There is a tunnel right through the rock below the vitrified fort. The fish life among the reefs is excellent. Access as Site 1228.

1230 Loch an Eisg-Brachaidh, Enard Bay. NC074174. Rocky skerries accessible from the shore with a sandy seabed at a maximum of 15m. Normal life.

1231 Eilean Moineseach. NC065178. Between the North-east of this island and the mainland headland to the North there is an uncharted reef at a depth of 25-28m. This has good marine life, including scallops. Boat access as Site 1228.

1232 Eilean Mor. NC052174. The West point gives a very pleasant dive to about 25m with plenty of life. Access as Site 1228.

1233 A' Chleit Island. NC027205. The West point gives a splendid dive down a cliff reported to beyond 50m, though it is only charted to 32m. The North and South sides have drops to 20m or thereabouts. Access is from Loch Kirkaig (NC078195) or Lochinver.

1234 A' Chleit Shoal. NC028213. About half a mile North of A' Chleit there is a rocky shoal reaching up to 8m from a general depth of 20-30m. Diving reports indicate that there is a dramatic wall to the West of the shoal which drops to over 50m. Access as Site 1233.

1235 Trawler wreck off Kirkaig Point. This lies about 1 mile West of Kirkaig Point, near the mouth of Loch Inver. The exact position can be obtained from Jim Crooks. The wreck is of a 20m wooden vessel which is slowly breaking up.

1236 Soyea Island, mouth of Loch Inver. The North and West sides give good scenic diving in the 12-18m depth range. The islet of Scaraveg has a very narrow channel running between it and the main island, which could yield interesting gullies. Boat access is from Lochinver or Loch Kirkaig (NC078195). About a-quarter-of-a-mile North-west is a shoal rising from 36m to 16m.

1237 Ondine Rocks, south of Loch Roe. NC051237. A group of skerries reaching to within 8m of the surface from a depth of about 40m. I have no details, but these must surely give excellent diving down steep rock slopes. Access is from Achmelvich Bay (NC055249).

1238 An Fharaid Bheag, South Achmelvich Bay. NC049249. A super shore dive off the rocks at the end of the peninsula. Depths 15-18m. Lots of life.

1239 Achmelvich Bay. NC053254. A beautiful sandy beach with rocky spurs running into the sea. About a mile out, the seabed is of flat sand at 45m. Huge *Cyanea* jellyfish have been observed here, with their tentacles spreading out over as much as 30m. By lying flat on the seabed the usually-good visibility allows you to see 'bumps' in the sand. When investigated these often turn out to be rays, flat fish, or angler fish. A deep sandy dive, best done on sunny summer days. Launch in the bay itself.

1240 A' Chlach Thuill, South of Bay of Clachtoll. NC037267. Sandstone cliffs and reefs lead on to a white shell-sand seabed at 25m. Lots of rays and angler fish. Access by boat from Bay of Clachtoll or Achmelvich Bay. Alternatively, a shore dive is possible.

CAUTION: There are few places in Scotland where inshore fishermen are aggressive towards divers, but this appears to be one of them. I have had my inflatable menaced by Lochinver fishermen coming to empty a salmon net. I have another report of an inflatable being shot at, though this report suggests that the culprits may have been tinkers. Be warned, and steer clear of salmon nets. Report any trouble to the Police at Lochinver [Lochinver 222].

1241 Stoer peninsula. I have no dives recorded for the 10 miles of coast from Clachtoll to Clashnessie Bay, with the exception of the next two sites. The Point of Stoer (NC022457) looks promising.

1242 Cluas Deas. NC002413. Difficult shore access from the road just South of the lighthouse. A fairly pleasant dive to 12m sloping over kelp covered rocks to 20m some distance out from the shore. Good for fish life. Tides as Site 1227.

1243 Lighthouse Bay. NC004422. Similar to the previous site except that

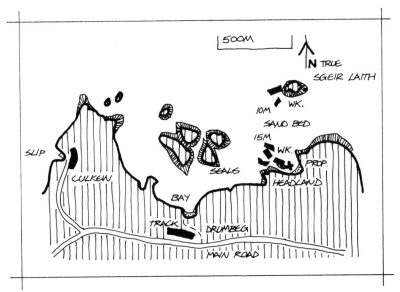

The wreck of the 'S.S. Bermuda'

the boulders are much larger. Good visibility and lots of life. Shore access.

1244 Port Achnancarnan, North of Clashnessie Bay. NC051323. A narrow, shallow gully entering the open sea at a depth of 13m. Shore access.

1245 Clashnessie Bay. NC067317. A gradually sloping sand and boulder bottom with an interesting variety of seaweeds. At the West of the bay are rock gullies, 3-4m deep, descending to 22m on to a good bottom with lots of life. Shore access.

1246 Oldany Island. Apparently undived, the North-west and North-east sides appear to drop to depths of about 20-30m. Boat access from jetty at the end of the track to the South of the island at. NC099335, or as Site 1247.

1247 Wreck of the liner Bermuda, Eddrachillis Bay. NC128335. A 19,086 ton (160m-long) vessel which drifted ashore when its towing hawser parted in 1933. She now lies at 58 15 00N 05 11 31W at the East side of the headland of Rubh' Dhubhard. Wreckage is visible ashore and extends to a depth of 12m. The wreck has been salvaged, and is now broken into three large pieces, with the stern being the only recognisable part. Boat launch at Culkein Drumbeg (NC101338).

1248 Wreck of a puffer, near Site 1247. This was lost during the salvage operations on the *Bermuda*. I have no position for her.

1249 Unknown wreck, Loch Nedd. NC139329. The wreck of a drifter, blown up but full of scrap, in about 10m. The position is about one third of the distance up Loch Nedd from the open sea. Launch at the head of the loch (NC143317).

1250 Unknown wreck, Loch Nedd. NC139321. Shown on the chart as on the West shore near the head of Loch Nedd. I have no further information.

1251 Loch na Drioghniche. NC163345. Kelp-covered rocks at the shore lead down to sand at 15m. Access as Site 1252.

1252 Loch Ardbhair. NC167335. A muddy bottom at 11m. Lots of seals. Note that the land around the loch is owned by Mr J. Payne, who is erecting a salmon farm. He has a compressor. Access to the loch is over his ground so his permission should be sought.

1253 Loch Cairnbawn, Kerrachar Bay to Poll a' Ghamhna. NC180350 – NC208328. This area was used in WW2 for midget submarine training. There are buoy chains and huge 5-ton mooring blocks lying around that were for a destroyer, which was used as a base for the submarines. There is a steep drop-off to a sandy bottom at 35m with scallops and crabs to be seen in good visibility. Boat access from Kylesku Ferry (NC230339).

1254 Wrecks of two midget submarines, Loch Cairnbawn. NC193342 and NC194342. Lost in WW2, these two vessels are charted as lying close together in the centre of the loch in 65m of water, which should make them interesting for submersible pilots! During WW2 the jetty at NC195335 was used for mooring a destroyer which was used as a base for these submarines. There was an anti-submarine net arranged around the destroyer at a radius of ⅓-of-a-mile. The two midget submarines (one with crew) were lost within this net according to the destroyer's captain. Several 24m long M-craft were also tested here, but none was lost.

Divers enter the waters of Loch Cairnbawn from an access point near the Kylesku ferry. Marine life in the loch includes soft corals, sea squirts, and sponges.

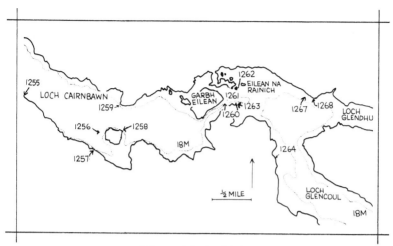

Sites 1255-1268

1255 Under Torr an Airbhe, Loch Cairnbawn. NC195334. Access from the jetty (or as for Site 1370) to an excellent dive site down a rocky slope turning to sand and reaching 40m. Lots of soft corals, sea squirts, and sponges, noted.

1256 Eilean a' Ghamhna. NC203334. A warhead (presumably from a torpedo) has been found just West of this island. It lies at 18m on a gently-sloping bottom.

1257 Loch Cairnbawn, opposite Eilean a' Ghamhna. NC202331. Shore access from the road. A cliff face to 20m with plenty of feather stars and anemones.

1258 Eilean a' Ghamhna, North East tip. NC207334. Bedrock slabs dropping to over 30m, with bizarre life forms. These include feather stars, sea squirts, worms, starfish, nudibranchs, and, surprisingly, brachiopods, together with cup corals. Launch as Site 1253.

1259 Rubh' an Fhir Leith, Loch Cairnbawn. NC207339. Very similar to Site 1254. Same access. A good night dive, but watch the depth, as it reaches 52m.

1260 Caolas Cumhann (Kylesku Narrows), Loch Cairnbawn. NC226337. A drift below the old ferry point at 25m. There are vertical down-eddies at full tide, so beware. The tidal streams can reach 2.5 knots. LW slack +0220 Dover, HW slack −0340 Dover. The top of the col is gravel and shell-sand. The slopes are more stony, with an interesting life of sponges and anemones. At slack water the channel can be traversed from the South by descending the very steep rock-face to 25m, then crossing the channel (note that the charted depths are inaccurate). The stipes of the kelp plants are 3m high and 10cm thick!

1261 Garbh Eilean, Loch Cairnbawn. NC229340. Take a line from the telegraph pole by the north ferry slip to the East end of Garbh Eilean. Swim about 100m along this from the ferry, then go South-east until reaching an edge at 10m. This descends to 18m, or 34m to the West. Lots of soft corals and tube worms. Watch the tides (see Site 1260), especially at the base of the cliff.

1262 North Ferry Slip, Kylesku. NC230341. This gives access to the drift of Site 1260, or to the small skerries to the East of the slip. These are about 10m deep, kelp-covered, and the haunt of seals.

1263 South Ferry Slip, Kylesku. NC231338. A splendid shore dive down cliffs to 25m on to a coarse sandy bottom, covered in brittle stars. The wall extends for several hundred metres to the West and has fascinating encrusing life. Watch the tide (see Site 1260).

1264 Loch Glencoul, West shore. NC238324. After the last fascinating site, this is rather a disappointment. A muddy bottom at 15-20m with kelp then brittle stars. Rather poor. Shore access.

1265 Eilean a' Chon' a Chreige, Loch Glencoul. NC249314. To the North-east of these rocks lies a mud slope to beyond 20m. Shore access or boat from the ferry slip.

1266 Unknown wreck, Loch Glendhu. NC271336. The wreck of a drifter lying in 15m of water. The position is under the crags of Creag Ruadh. Boat access from the ferry slip.

1267 Bottle site. NC242342. The Duke of Westminster used to keep a yacht anchored just West of Site 1268. Bottle finds have been made.

1268 Point West of Maldie, Loch Glendhu. NC246339. Apparently undived. The chart shows a very steep slope to 20m, then a further slope to 40m.

1269 Loch Shark, entrance to Loch Cairnbawn. NC180363. Despite its fascinating name, a poor dive. Sand and mud bottom with a maximum depth of 15m. There is a low ridge across the mouth of the bay. Boat access from Kylesku Ferry (NC230339).

1270 Unknown wreck, Loch Shark. NC177364. The wreck of a small vessel lies on the low ridge mentioned in the previous site, in about 5m depth. Access as Site 1269.

1271 Loch na Creige Ruaidhe. NC176367. At the South-west tip of the loch there is a wall to 15m with sand and some rocks at the base. Good for scallops. Boat access as Site 1269.

1272 Ravens Rock, South of Calbha Beag, Eddrachillis Bay. NC154362. This lies about 350m South-west of the South tip of Calbha Beag island, and dries 1.8m. Off the South-west of the rock, depths fall to about 40m. It is mainly sandy with some rocks, and lots of jellyfish in summertime. Boat access from Culkein Drumbeg (NC109338) or Badcall Bay (NC163415).

1273 Sgeir a Chlaidheimh. NC134370. Undived, but there appears to be an excellent steep drop to over 50m at the Southern end of the shoal. There are also shoals at Lachlan Shoal, and another halfway between Lachlan Shoal and the main island. These both look promising. Access as Site 1272.

1274 Meall Mor and Meall Beag, Eddrachillis Bay. These are both undived, but the chart indicates a number of possibilities, with depths to 35m. Boat access as Site 1272.

1275 Badcall Islands, Eddrachillis Bay. A fascinating group of more than 30 islands and many rocks and shoals. As far as I know these have not been dived. The chart indicates many possibilities – eg. Clansman Shoal, Ox Rock, Dubh Sgeir, Meall Earca Shoal, Eilean Garbh etc. Launch at Badcall Bay (NC163415). Note that there is a fish farm in Badcall Bay – it might be a good idea not to go too close, unless invited.

1276 Creag a' Mhail, Scourie Bay. NC143457. Vertical rocks to 25m then in steps to a depth of 35m. The site is just off the shore – note that Chart 2503 is not accurate here regarding depths. Slightly further North there is a boulder slope running beyond 40m. Good visibility and lots of ling and cuckoo wrasse. Launch at Scourie Village (NC155448) over shingle.

1277 Port an Eilein, Handa Island. NC146473. A good dive in 10m along the ledges and crannies of the cliff face. Lots of life and (usually) super visibility. Launch as Site 1276.

1278 Glas Leac, South Handa Island. NC137467. To the South-west of the islet there is a steep boulder slope dropping to more than 40m. Ling and

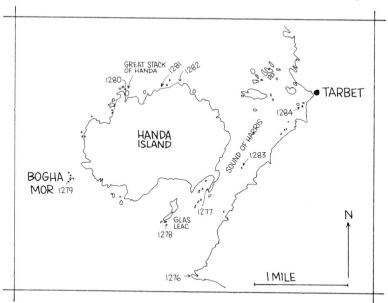

Dive sites around Handa Island

DNWS – 10

cuckoo wrasse are to be seen amidst the dramatic scenery. Launch as for Site 1276.

1279 Bogha Mor, Handa Island. NC122473. Another steep boulder slope to beyond 40m amid dramatic scenery. This site is exposed to rough seas. Access as Site 1276.

1280 The Great Stack of Handa. NC132488. Superb diving down tremendous rock gullies of 8-10m high. There is a considerable debris of eggs and dead birds from the seabird cliff above, (the presence of birds is obvious from the noise and smell!) There is a navigable channel through the base of the stack. Underwater there are fascinating glimpses of guillemots and other seabirds 'flying' around one's bubble stream. Not a dive to be missed. Boat access as Site 1276.

1281 North face of Handa Island. NC135488 – NC139490. The 120m cliffs provide an impressive backdrop to this dive which is around the rocks and skerries to about 10m. Boat access as Site 1276.

1282 North point of Handa Island. NC142491. Just off the cliffs there is a large rock which slopes off to 34m and beyond. The usual dramatic rock scenery and prolific fish life. Access as Site 1276.

1283 Bogha Morair, Sound of Hand. NC151475. A rock with a minimum coverage of 1.8m and a maximum of about 8m, in the middle of the Sound of Handa. Tidal streams run up to 3 knots. LW slack +0400 Dover, HW slack −0200 Dover. There are heavy overfalls in the vicinity of the shoal, so slack water is essential. The Sound can be drift dived, with depths ranging from 16m at the North end to 35m at the South end in a distance of about 1 mile. Launch as Site 1276.

1284 Tarbet Bay. NC162489. Just South of three small skerries lies a 200 years old anchor in 8m on a bottom of kelp covered cobbles. Shore access.

1285 Unknown wreck, West of Handa Island. This lies 5 miles West of Creag a' Mhail in deep water, the minimum clearance being of 28m. The position is approximate, so the wreck is only of academic interest. Depths range from 60-100m.

Note: About one sixth of the 58 sites discusssed in this chapter have not been dived to the best of my knowledge. I think it is reasonable to include them here to draw attention to potentially good sites. As can be seen from a study of the maps and charts, the potential for diving in this area is so great that far more sites could easily have been included.

Area information and services

Hydrographic charts: 2502 Eddrachillis Bay 1:25,000; 2503 Lochs Laxford, Inchard & approaches 1:25,000; 2504 Rubha Coigeach to Staerhead 1:25,000.
Ordnance Survey 1:50,000 maps: 9 Cape Wrath; 15 Loch Assynt.
Ordnance Survey: 1:25,000 maps: NB91 Rubha Coigeach; NC01/11 Loch Sionascaig; NC02/12 Lochinver; NC03/13 Drumbeg; NC14 Scourie; NC15 Ardmore Point; NC22/32 Inchnadamph; NC23/33 Loch More.

Local BS-AC branches: Ullapool (970).
Local SS-AC branches: None.
Air supplies: Jim Crooks, 6 Inver Park, Lochinver (057 14) 362; Dave Neville, Camusnagaul Diving Centre Sail Mhor Croft, Camasnagaul (085 483) 224; Barry Todd, Ullapool (0854) 2036.
Boat charters: Jim Crooks, 6 Inver Park, Lochinver (057 14) 362.
Local weather: Glasgow Weather Centre 041 248 3451:
Sea area: Hebrides.
Tidal constants:

	DOVER	*ULLAPOOL*
Badcall Bay	−0415	+0005
Loch Nedd	−0420	0
Loch Inver	−0425	−0005

Coastguard: Stornoway MRSC (0851) 2013; Oban MRSC (0631) 63720; Ullapool (0854) 2014.
Lifeboat: Lochinver, Stornoway.
Police stations: Lochinver (057 14) 222.
Hospitals: Raigmore Hospital, Inverness (0463) 34151.
Recompression chambers: Dunstaffnage Marine Laboratory, Oban (0631) 62244; Underwater Training Centre, Fort William (0397) 3786/3136. At this distance, one might also consider Glasgow Western Infirmary 041 339 8822, and Aberdeen Royal Infirmary (0224) 681818.
Vehicle recovery: AA − Glasgow 041 812 0101; Inverness (0463) 33213 (office hours only).
Local tourist information: Lochinver (057 14) 330.
Accommodation: There are many B & B and guest-house facilities (see Scottish Tourist Board guides).

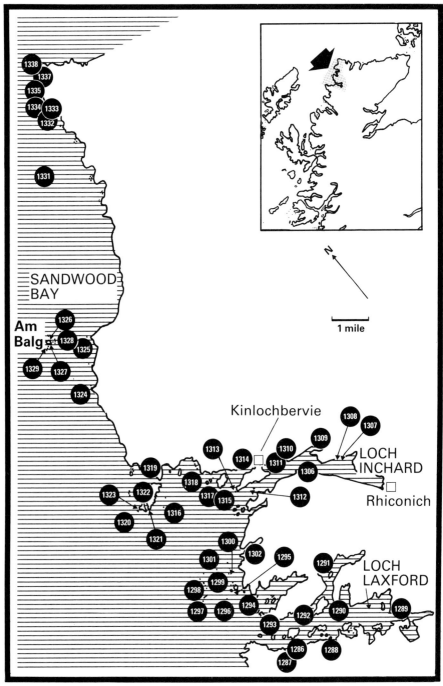

Dive Sites : Rubha Ruadh to Cape Wrath

CHAPTER 13

Rubha Ruadh to Cape Wrath

This is it! The final stretch of that most incredible of coastlines – the Western Seaboard of Scotland. Diving here is superb, climaxing in the fantastic headland of Cape Wrath and its challenging outlier, Duslic Rock.

Loch Laxford and Loch Inchard are both totally enclosed by Lewisian gneiss. The origin of Loch Laxford is probably tectonic. It does not have a basin separated from the sea by a shallow bar. Its maximum depth is 71m, though the inner half of the loch is quite shallow (maximum 18m). Loch a' Chadh Fi is also shallow, reaching a maximum depth of 20m at its junction with Loch Laxford. Loch Dughaill shares the same entrance to the sea with Loch Laxford. Its maximum depth is 47m.

The scenery in Loch Laxford is stunning, with many bays and inlets. It is famous for its salmon fishing, and is also the fishing ground for the occasional otter.

Ceathramh Garbh is the rough country between Loch Inchard and Loch Laxford. It reaches 137m, and is dissected into innumerable valleys and crags. Glaciation followed by submergence is mainly responsible for giving this coast its picturesque quality.

Loch Inchard is 4½ miles long and has a 60m basin connecting it with the sea over a bar at 22m. It has been subject to glaciation, but is also thought to owe its origins to faulting, the fault extending out to sea through Loch Clash.

Loch Clash lies just North of Loch Inchard. It deepens steadily towards the sea, reaching a depth of 42m at its mouth. At its head is the quiet little fishing village of Kinlochbervie. Its harbour, however, is the busiest in the North-west Highlands. It stands astride a neck of ground and has jetties in both Loch Clash and Loch Inchard. At the time of writing it is being considerably extended. It is possible to hire boats here on occasions for journeys to the North and the far northern outliers.

The coast running North-west from Loch Clash is formed into a series of sandy bays separated by gneiss headlands. Shiegra is the last centre of habitation before the 10 miles of coast leading to Cape Wrath. At Shiegra the gneiss changes to sandstone, which continues to Sandwood Bay, where it forms the detached pinnacle of Am Buachaille. There are two rocks awash that are the bases of collapsed former pinnacles, showing that erosion is severe. All of this sandstone is embedded with semi-precious stones.

The beach at Sandwood Bay is considered to be the finest in Scotland. However, it is rarely visited, as this involves a walk of over 2 miles along a wild and boggy path after a 2-mile drive along a rough cart track. Its remoteness adds to its charm, and its 2-mile sweep approaches perfection. Sandwood Loch is backed by gneiss rocks and connects through the dunes to the sea by the very short Sandwood River. If the sand were to be removed, the shallow loch would become a fairly typical sea loch. The variety of land forms, plants, and wildlife, makes Sandwood Bay one of the most attractive spots on the Scottish coastline.

Just over a mile out to sea is the island and group of rocks that make up Am Balg. The main island is 153m high and is formed of Lewisian gneiss. It is an important seabird breeding station, with a large colony of great black-backed gulls nesting on the summit. Many seals also live around the island. It is steep all round, so landing is difficult, though the scramble to the top is relatively straightforward.

From the North of Sandwood Bay the rock is sandstone almost to Cape Wrath, though the Cape itself is composed of gneiss. This coast is a succession of bold, craggy cliffs and small bays.

Cape Wrath is a steep cliff, 113m high, topped by a lighthouse that can be seen for 27 miles. There is no public road within 10 miles of it, though a private road goes to it, and is connected to the public road by a passenger ferry at the Kyle of Durness on the North coast of the mainland. A minibus runs along this road in summer, but the only effective way for a diver to reach Cape Wrath is in his own boat, launched near Kinlochbervie or at Balnakiel Bay on the North coast.

One mile North-east of Cape Wrath is the final outlier of the Scottish West Coast – the rock of Duslic. This rises from a 30m-deep bank and gives a superb dive.

Cape Wrath is one of Britain's magical places – the top corner of Scotland where its majestic and celebrated West coast and its wild and rugged North Coast meet. The English name, Cape Wrath, is significant, though the word comes from the Viking word *hvarf* meaning *turning point*. On a clear day the view from Cape Wrath is superb. The Outer Hebrides show as a faint, low line 50 miles to the South-west. North Rona, 47 miles North-west, can be seen occasionally by virtue of atmospheric refraction. Sule Stack, 31 miles North, can be seen as a white speck. And the 335m-high Hoy cliffs in Orkney are visible 63 miles to the East.

The plant life in this part of Scotland is typical of the northern moors and coasts, with few, if any, trees. The animal life includes deer, otter, and wild cat. The bird life is rather special – the moors having a number of unusual species such as greenshank, hen harrier, and short-eared owl. The usual spectacular colonies of seabirds breed on the sea cliffs.

Camping sites and accommodation can be found West of Kinlochbervie and around Scourie. With the exception of the roads to these villages, there are few roads giving useful access to the sea. Basic supplies are available at these villages.

The diving is dominated by the prevailing weather, as the area is not protected very much by the Outer Hebrides, except against the strongest of the predominant South-westerlies. The visibility can be excellent as there are few sediments to be stirred up by storms – 30m might be expected on occasions. The spring tidal streams can run at up to 2 knots at Cape Wrath, and these streams, coupled with the usual swell and frequent winds, can make for difficult diving conditions.

The dives that can be made around Cape Wrath and the coast to the South are fabulous. The tunnels and walls of the Cape itself almost defy description. Am Balg, with its seabirds and seals, gives a marvellous diving outing, and the coastal cliffs hereabouts must give good dives too – though they have yet to be fully explored.

Dive sites

1286 Fanagmore Bay, North east headland, Loch Laxford. NC181500. Shore rocks, then a reef in the sand at 20m with the usual encrusting life. Shore or boat access from Fanagmore (NC178498).

1287 Fanagmore Pier, Loch Laxford. NC178498. Shallow water with sand and rock. Shore access.

1288 Bagh na Fionndalach Moire, Loch Laxford. NC194489. Access from Foindle slip to shallow water to 14m with sand and rock. Lots of kelp with life under it.

1289 Laxford Bay, Loch Laxford. NC225477. Very shallow diving (or snorkelling) from the disused slip as the road swings inland. Otters have been observed in this vicinity, feeding on eels in shallow weedy water.

1290 Loch a' Chadh Fi, Loch Laxford. NC213512. Shallow and muddy, to the North of Eilean a' Chadh Fi at a depth of about 13m. Access by boat from Skerricha (NC230508), where it is very shallow.

1291 Rubh na h-Airde Bige, Loch Laxford. NC206501. A steep drop to a muddy bottom at 20m at the entrance to Loch a' Chadh Fi. Boat access as Site 1289.

1292 Eilean an Eireannaich, West tip, Loch Laxford. NC197503. A steep muddy slope to 34m on to a muddy bottom. Boat access as Site 1289.

1293 Ardmore Point, Loch Laxford. NC182516. Shallow diving in the skerries at the North west of the loch. Depths to about 20m. Boat access from Fanagmore Pier (NC178498).

1294 Rubh' a' Cheathraimh Ghairbh, Loch Dughaill. NC183524. A slope of sand and pebbles to 40m. Boat access as Site 1293.

1295 Eilean na Saille. NC179532. There is a series of shallow underwater gullies and skerries here. Access as Site 1293.

1296 Eilean na Saille Skerry. NC173533. Similar to Site 1295.

1297 Whale Islet, Dubh Sgeirean. NC166539. To the South-west the depth quickly plunges to beyond 34m down rocky walls and overhangs to give excellent diving. The visibility and the marine life are excellent. Access as Site 1293.

The landscape at Loch Laxford is stunning, with many bays and inlets. Underwater, the scenery includes kelp forests and shallow reefs.

1298 Dubh Sgeiran, North-west. NC169546. These islands lie about 1 mile West of the mainland between Loch Laxford and Loch Inchard. The diving involves many rocky gullies and skerries covered in marine life. Boat access as Site 1293.

1299 Dubh Sgeirean, East. NC172544. Similar to Site 1297.

1300 Unnamed skerry. NC180540. To the West this exposed site gives excellent diving over a very rough bottom. Access as Site 1293.

1301 Unnamed skerry. NC179547. Similar to Site 1300.

1302 Loch an Roin. NC192543. This loch is only just tidal, and the large waterfall brings in large quantities of fresh water. There is a blaze of unusual red anemones, sponges and hydroids due to the freshwater. Boat access from Fanagmore Pier (NC178498) or Kinlochbervie (NC220563).

WRECKS OF LOCH INCHARD. There are at least three wrecks shown on chart 1785, lying at various distances almost due West of Loch Inchard. They are all rather deep, but may still be of interest to the armchair diver:

1303 5.7 miles due West of Eilean a' Chonnaidh. This site has clearance of 64m in about 70m of water.

1304 7.5 miles due West of Eilean a' Chonnaidh. This site has a clearance of 15m in a depth of about 52m.

1305 14.3 miles due West of Eilean a' Chonnaidh. This site has a clearance of 28m in 87m depth.

1306 Loch Inchard, South-west shore. NC231552. There is a vertical underwater wall at this site that runs from the surface to 45m, where it meets a 45 degree slope. All the usual life may be seen in the normally good visibility. Access is from Kinlochbervie (NC220563).

1307 Achriesgill West, Loch Inchard. NC247543. Access from the shore via a steep field. Rocky faces and ledges lead down to 17m where sand takes over. There are scallops, plus 'castoff' from the crofts nereby.

1308 Rhuvoult, Loch Inchard. NC243546. Access is from the shore via a track down a field from the road end. There are stepped rock faces leading down to 30m off the nearby point. Kelp cover near the surface gives way to a covering of ascidians and anemones deeper down.

1309 Loch Shiegra, Loch Inchard. NC242554. A poor dive in shallow water over muddy sand. Shore access is from the road just West of Inshegra (NC248552).

1310 Bay West of Creag Ceum an Leim, Loch Inchard. NC230558. This dive features vertical cliffs to 18-20m, then a sand slope to beyond 30m. A variety of life is to be seen. Shore access from end of track, then over a field.

1311 Loch Bervie, Loch Inchard. NC222558. Shore access from pier (or by boat). Shelving rock bottom with kelp in the shallower water. Small white sea cucumbers were noted living in the rock crevices, but otherwise a very poor dive.

1312 Bodha Ceann na Saile shoal, Loch Inchard. NC212558. This is a shoal lying half a mile West of Loch Bervie. It reaches to within 3m of the surface from a depth of 25m. Undived, but the rocky cliff to the North looks promising. Boat access from Loch Clash (NC219566).

1313 Rubha na Leacaig. NC205563. The site lies in the channel on the East side of the small island. The depth in this channel is 10-20m and the rock face is considerably undercut to form a cave of sorts. The lip is at 10-12m while inside the depth rises to 8m; the seabed is at 18-20m. This is an excellent dive with lots of life in the crevices and on the rock faces. Access as Site 1312.

1314 Loch Clash. NC218565. Shore access to a sloping muddy bottom with much fishing debris from the very busy pier to the South of the bay. Large starfish noted. Disappointing.

Rugged cliffs and rocks around Handa Island.

1315 Eilean a' Chonnaidh. NC201568. Off the South west tip is a steep slope of rock and boulders to 30m. This gives a pleasant dive with all the normal marine life. Boat access as Site 1312.

1316 Unnamed shoal, West of Eilean a' Chonnaidh. NC178576. The southern tip of this shoal reaches 30m and beyond on a seabed of rolling bedrock waves. Plenty of fishlife. The visibility is usually excellent. Access as Site 1312.

1317 Wreck of the "Winchester", North of Eilean a' Chonnaidh. NC201575. A 94 ton (26m-long) steam drifter lost in 1933 after running aground. She then slipped back into deeper water (about 20m) at position 58 28 00N 05 05 00W. I have no diving information, but from the position it would be reasonable to expect the vessel to be well broken up.

1318 Lochan nam Meallan, Oldshoremore. NC200590. A sandy bay with shore access. The East rocks at the point become a 10m cliff face with a good variety of marine life.

1319 Port Chaligaig pier. NC185593. A superb shallow site straight off the pier, usually in very clear water. The North side of the bay has cliffs and rocky slabs with two caves. The South side has pinnacles, canyons and tunnels. There is also a cave right through the South headland at NC186587. Recommended.

1320 Wreck of the Valonia, off Eilean an Roin Beag. NC165586. An MFV lost in 1975. The position of 58 28 10N 05 05 10W lies about ½-a-mile West of the above island in about 35m of water. I have no diving information, though at this depth the vessel should be reasonably intact. Boat access is from Oldshoremore (NC200595).

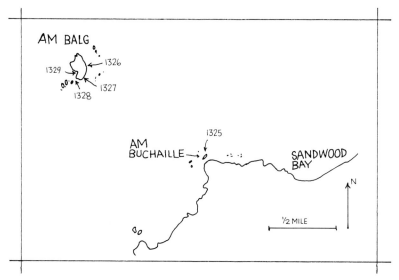

Dive sites: Am Balg

1321 Eilean an Roin channel, South. NC173581. The remains of an old wreck lie here, in the form of steel girders, an old anchor and some 12-inch copper nails. Access as Site 1320.

1322 Eilean an Roin channel, North. NC174585. A pleasant dive to 20m on a rocky, kelpy bottom with lots of life. Access as Site 1320.

1323 Eilean an Roin Beag. NC170584. A beautiful dive to 32m, with a cliff-face to 25m followed by a boulder slope. Rare crabs *(Lethoides)* have been recorded here. Access as Site 1320.

1324 Rubh an Fhir Leith. NC187635. A rather poor dive on a boulder slope then sand at 30m. Rather strong currents. Access as Site 1320.

1325 Am Buchaille, South Sandwood Bay. NC201652. This pinnacle is on the shore rocks, though two collapsed former pinnacles are out to sea. The depths reach 17m very quickly, giving a pleasant dive in fantastic surroundings. Boat access as Site 1320. A Spitfire plane lies buried in the sand of the bay above sea-level. This appeared in 1983 and then was covered by the sand again.

1326 Am Balg islet. NC187662. This lies about 1 mile North-west of Am Buchaille, and about 6 miles South-west of Cape Wrath. Boat access as site 1320 (8 miles). A superb diving site; the depth is 25m all round and the life is very rich. Seals play around the rocks and gullies. The islet is a seabird nesting station. Highly recommended, though good weather is vital. There are significant tidal streams of up to 1.75 knots; LW slack −0530 Dover, HW slack +0045 Dover.

The western approach to Cape Wrath – the "most exciting headland in the British Isles."

1327 Am Balg, South east corner. NC188660. The remains (hull and engine) of a trawler sunk in 1975 lie here.

1328 Am Balg channel. NC186660. The channel between Am Balg and its South-west skerry is a broad gully with lots of subsidiary gullies full of inquisitive seals.

1329 Am Balg, West. NC185661. There is a huge underwater cave on the West of the islet that has been hollowed by the rough seas. It can be found by locating a deep depression North of the channel. It is 20m deep with house-sized boulders, and passageways full of seals. Outside, the bottom drops beyond 30m. An absolutely superb dive in calm conditions.

1330 Wreck of the Majorka. 58 34 00N 05 13 40W (PA). The position is about 3 miles North west of Am Balg (at about NC1569) in 30m of water. The vessel was a Norwegian sailing ship of 1684 tons, lost in 1917. A mast used to show 2m at low water. The chart shows the depth as 50m with a clearance of 15m. Undived as far as I know, this would be a real worthwhile dive, and should be fairly easy to find with a hard boat (possibly hired from Kinlochbervie).

1331 Ten-fathom bank. NC234717. This lies 2.5 miles South-west of Cape Wrath. It rises from 32m to 18m to the East of the shoal, and can be located by echo-sounder. The seabed is rocky. Access as Site 1320.

1332 Wreck of the Sunnyvale. 58 36 30N 05 01 00W (PA). The position is about half-a-mile South of Am Bodach at NC248730, in about 30m of water. The vessel was an MFV lost in 1971. I have no other information.

1333 Am Bodach. NC249736. A splendid dive in a swell-ridden cave behind the stack of Am Bodach. To seawards the depths fall to 20m. Boat launch as Site 1320, but note that the distance is 13 miles, and there is no possibility of shelter in bad weather.

1334 A' Chailleach. NC249736. Another sea stack that provides lots of interesting clefts to explore. Depths reach 28m on the seaward side. Access and tides as Site 1326.

1335 Uamh Cham. NC253744. A small inlet about a third of a mile South of Cape Wrath. At its head is a cave to explore. The South point of the inlet gives a dive down rocky walls to 25m on to a sandy seabed. The rock walls are all covered with solidly encrusting marine life. Access and tides as Site 1326.

1336 Wrecks West of Cape Wrath. An examination of Chart 2720, particularly the old pre-metric edition, will show a number of wrecks lying well offshore in deep water, though some are in diving range. This area was an old WW2 U-Boat hunting ground, and should certainly repay investigation in a hire boat. I have no further details, and none of the wrecks has been dived to my knowledge.

1337 Cape Wrath Channel. NC247747. An incredibly narrow, winding channel dividing Stac an Dunain from Cape Wrath itself. The tide runs hard through here, and slack water would be necessary to explore it fully (slacks at −0530 and +0045 Dover). Vast quantities of life make for a superb dive. Access as Site 1338.

1338 Cape Wrath Tunnel. NC257749. Cape Wrath is not the most northerly point on the Scottish mainland, nor is it the most westerly. It is simply the most exciting headland in the British Isles. It is the best dive of its kind in our waters. And no praise can be higher than that! There are two natural arches – one large and manageable, the other small and only passable to a diver. The smaller, more seaward, archway gives an unforgettable dive. It is 15m deep, with walls covered with colourful sponges, ascidians, anemones, and the like. Tides are strong, and access is difficult (14 miles from Kinlochbervie, 10 miles from Balnakeil Bay). But it is a dive that must not be missed!

Area information and services

Hydrographic charts: 1954 Cape Wrath to Pentland Firth 1:200,000; 2503 Lochs Laxford, Inchard & approaches 1:25,000.
Ordnance Survey 1:50,000 maps: 9 Cape Wrath.
Ordnance Survey 1:25,000 maps: NC14 Scourie; NC15 Ardmore Point; NC16/26 Strath Shinary; NC24/34 Arkle; NC25/35 Rhiconich; NC27/37 Cape Wrath.
Local BS-AC branches: None.
Local SS-AC branches: None.
Air supplies: None in the area. The nearest is Jim Crooks, 6 Inver Park, Lochinver (057 14) 362; also Dave Neville, Camusnagaul Diving Centre Sail Mhor Croft, Camasnagaul (085 483) 224; Barry Todd, Ullapool (0854) 2036.

Boat charter: None known, though fishing vessel skippers from Kinlochbervie may do an occasional informal charter for divers if the fishing is quiet.
Local weather: Glasgow Weather Centre 041 248 3451.
Sea area: Hebrides.
Tidal constants:

	DOVER	ULLAPOOL
Cape Wrath	−0355	+0025
Loch Bervie	−0405	+0015
Loch Laxford	−0410	+0010

Coastguard: Stornoway MRSC (0851) 2013; Oban MRSC (0631) 63720; Ullapool (0854) 2014.
Lifeboat: Lochinver, Stornoway.
Police stations: Rhiconich, Kinlochbervie (097 182) 222.
Hospitals: Raigmore Hospital, Inverness (0463) 34151.
Recompression chambers: Dunstaffnage Marine Laboratory, Oban (0631) 62244; Underwater Training Centre, Fort William (0397) 3786//3136. At this distance one should also consider Glasgow Western Infirmary 041 339 8822, and Aberdeen Royal Infirmary (0224) 681818.
Vehicle recovery: AA − Glasgow 041 812 0101; Inverness (0463) 33213 (office hours only).
Local tourist information: Lochinver (057 14) 330; Durness (097 181) 259.
Accommodation: There are B & B and guest-house facilities available in the villages and townships (see Scottish Tourist Board guides).

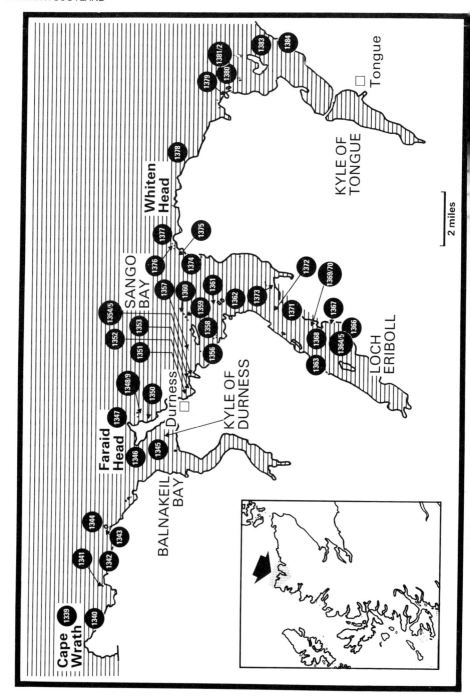

CHAPTER 14

Cape Wrath to Kyle of Tongue

This is a magnificent area with the coast bounding the Parph, the "wildest 100 square miles in Britain", which is that area of land lying South and East of Cape Wrath. It is inhabited by golden eagle, greenshank, and wild cat, and excepting the lighthouse-keepers no people live there. In fact, in the whole of Sutherland, human habitation is so sparse that the relatively few sheep outnumber people by 20 to 1!

Running East from Cape Wrath, the coast is largely steep rocky cliffs with the occasional bay for about 10 miles. In fact, the cliffs at Clo Mor are the highest in mainland Britain at 272m. The Kyle of Durness is flat, shallow, and sandy. Balnakeil Bay to its East is a superb 1½-mile-long sweep of shell-sand.

The geology of this part of North-west Scotland is rather complicated. It is here that the Moine Thrust occurred, and the rocks are a mixture of Lewisian gneiss, Torridonian sandstone, Cambrian quartzite and limestone, Moine schists, and *mylonised* (crushed and pressure-melted) rock. There is also much evidence of thrust planes and faults. The so-called Moine Thrust resulted from the waves of folding of the Caledonian mountain-building episode (about 400 million years ago) pushing against the ancient Archean 'foreland' of hard Lewisian gneiss and tough Torridonian sandstone lying to the West.

The village of Durness (population about 400) is the main settlement of this area. It offers four hotels, many bed-and-breakfast houses, several shops, two petrol stations, public toilets, and a public tap (by the most easterly shop/filling station). The name *Durness* comes from the Norse *Dyra-ness*, which meant *wolf cape*, as the district was plagued by wolves in Viking times. Directly seaward of Durness is the superb sandy beach of Sango Bay. This is swept by the Arctic rollers, and always appears quite pristine. There is a steep track down the centre which allows boat launching using a Land Rover in calm weather.

On the headland to the East of Sango Bay is the curious limestone formation of Smoo Cave (from the old Norse word *Smuga*, or cleft). The stream of Allt Smoo flows at 34m above sea-level at the top of the cliffs; and 60m back from the geo it drops 24m down a vertical shaft to reappear from the large cavern just above the beach. There is a fine view from the cliff-top over Eilean Hoan and the mouth of Loch Eriboll, to the pale, Lewisian cliffs of Whiten Head.

Loch Eriboll is long, deep (106m in places) and well protected by its flanking steep mountains. It was used as a fleet anchorage in both world wars. During WW2 it was used for assembling North Atlantic convoys, and it is here that German U-boats surrendered to the Royal Navy in 1945. One imagines that a detailed diving examination might be repaid, even though the bottom is of rather boring mud. There are many small sand-and-shingle beaches along its shores.

Whiten Head and its 150m-high cliffs are rather special. Access by land is difficult and demands a 6-mile walk over rough, trackless moorland broken by winding stream gorges.

The moorland road over the A' Mhoine peninsula (ie: Whiten Head) first passes the north end of the 56m-deep freshwater Loch Hope, and then gives spectacular views of Ben Hope (the most northerly *Munro* – ie: mountain over 3,000 feet). It then goes by the small villages of Talmine and Melness before the shallow and sandy Kyle of Tongue is reached. This is now crossed by a long causeway to reach the pleasant village of Tongue, which lies at the eastern extremity of the area covered in this chapter.

Accommodation is available in many bed-and-breakfast establishments in the region as well as in the few hotels. Camping is possible at Durness, Balnakeil, Talmine, and other smaller sites. None of this wild area makes good camp-sites, as it is largely boggy moorland. There is only one road in the area. This largely follows the coast.

The caves on Whiten Head are the only place on the British mainland where the Atlantic grey seal – the world's rarest seal – is known to breed. Dolphins, and even whales, are seen from time to time in the coastal waters.

The diving along the western end of the North coast of Scotland is really rather splendid. Cape Wrath is in range (from Balnakiel or Sango Bays), and (with the outlying Duslic Rock) is quite magnificent.

The sites between Cape Wrath and Faraid Head have yet to be explored fully, but the details which are known are extremely encouraging. In particular, An Garbh Eilean and Faraid Head give super diving. To the East of Sango Bay, An Dubh Sgeir is memorable, and the Whiten Head sites leave little to be desired.

Tidal streams run rather strongly off the major headlands, but otherwise can generally be ignored. The water here is that of the Arctic Ocean – blue, cold, and subject to big swells. Visibility is usually very good, but is reduced by the spring plankton bloom, which usually occurs slightly later than in the South-west of Scotland. Access to the water is somewhat difficult, though there are strenuous beach launches at Balnakeil and Sango Bays, and several places in Loch Eriboll. Boating is straightforward, but there is very little commercial traffic and virtually no pleasure craft, so visitors must aim to be self-sufficient in this respect.

Dive sites

These are described from West to East as we pass along the coast. The best chart for the West of this area is F.6680 (1:50,000), but this is restricted to Navy personnel only. Loch Eriboll is well covered (at 1:17,500) by 2076. The only other chart is 1954, with a not-very-helpful scale of 1:200,000.

1339 Duslic Rock. NC267759. A very challenging dive as the rock lies about 1 mile North-east of Cape Wrath, and water conditions can be exceedingly rough. It was first dived, with some difficulty, by members of Inverness BS-AC, who explored its North and East faces. Both of these have steeply sloping rock faces, with small, vertical steps. On the areas where boulders could lodge, many potholes up to 3m wide have been cut. Some of these interconnect. Just away from the rock, no bottom was located up to a depth of 40m. Visibility is usually excellent, and the marine life is prolific. The tidal streams are strong, and the vertical eddies around the rock require particular care. LW slack −0530, HW slack +0045 Dover. Boat access is from Balnakeil Bay (NC391687) or Sango Bay (NC407677).

1340 Lighthouse jetty, Store Cove. NC273737. This gives some shelter in heavier weather. The West side of the cove gives shallow diving over rocky slopes to about 10m. Access as Site 1339.

1341 Stack Clo Kearvaig. NC295737. A sandstone pinnacle replete with its quota of breeding auks. Its underwater cliff-face is worthy of exploration, though the depth is unlikely to exceed 20m. Access as Site 1339.

1342 Clo Mor cliffs. NC306734 (approx). These 200m-high sea cliffs are the highest in mainland Britain. The diving at their base is not very deep, due to cliff erosion. However, this is an excellent place to see auks underwater in the shallows. Access as Site 1339.

1343 An Garbh-eilean, South-west tip. NC332734. This gives dives to 25m to a seabed of sand and boulders with lots of crustaceans. Note that both this island and the Clo Mor cliffs are used for target-practice by the

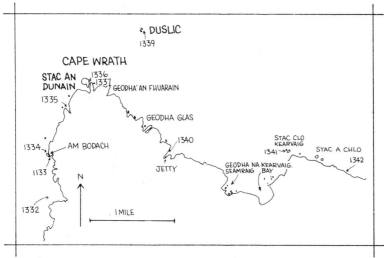

Dive sites: Cape Wrath

Navy for 3 weeks every summer (check dates in advance!) Access as Site 1339.

1344 An Garbh-eilean, North end. NC334736. The North end of the island falls to a 20m plateau. There are deep, 3m-wide underwater geos cleaving this plateau in a North/South direction to depths well below 40m. The deep blue water and the gullies full of fish life and nudibranchs make this an exceptional dive. Access as Site 1339.

1345 Wreck of a U-Boat, Balnakeil Bay. NC375706 (approx). It is rumoured that a U-Boat was lost hereabouts, though I have no further information.

1346 Faraid Head, West point. NC377714. A dive to 30m on to huge boulders with a shingle seabed in between. Seals abound, especially in the kelp of the shallows. Access as Site 1339. It is possible to drive a Land Rover along to the North end of the beach to the East of Balnakeil Bay to NC393696. Further penetration depends on how much sand has been drifted across the road – it is usually not possible to get further than about NC392702.

1347 Gob nan Leac, Faraid Head. NC393719. Superb diving down vertical, life-encrusted cliffs to 25m. This corner seems to pick up any swell that is running, and magnify it! Access as Site 1339.

1348 Clach Mhor na Faraid, Faraid Head. NC398712. There is a 25m-deep rock cauldron in the seabed here. Its vertical walls are teeming with life including nudibranchs and octopus. Many channels lead out of the cauldron, and all have walls covered with life. Access as Site 1339.

1349 Clach Mhor na Faraid, Faraid Head. NC398711. Excellent dives to 25m among house-sized boulders covered in life. Lots of fish and crustaceans. Access as Site 1339.

1350 Geodh' a' Lochaidh, Faraid Head. NC394703. Interesting rock turrets and archways 20-30m offshore at depths of 15-20m. Plenty of life. Access as Site 1339.

1351 Sango Bay. NC413682. Flat, featureless sand at about 10-20m. This bay picks up big swell in some sea states, and this can cause a significant seaward tidal backwash along the seabed near to shore. Boat access is from Sango Bay (NC407677).

1352 Sango Bay, South-east cliffs. NC415679. Very pleasant cliff diving to depths of 20m on to flat sand. The cliffs are vertical and have many nooks and crannies. Underwater, they are encrusted wtih life. Access as Site 1351.

1353 Leirinbeg headland. NC417679. A cliff-face with underwater caves and a sandy bottom at 22m. Plenty of crustaceans on the face. Access as Site 1351.

1354 Geodha Smoo. NC420676. The diving here is shallow and unspectacular. Though well sheltered, the inlet seems to collect all the loose kelp ripped out by storms. Shore access.

Sango Bay combines large, featureless tracts of sand with some spectacular underwater cliffs and caves.

1355 Smoo Cave. NC419672. This cave can be explored by divers using powerful torches. It is filled with fresh water from the stream to a depth of about 1m. Take care: the farther reaches are for experienced potholers only.

1356 A' Ghoil-sgeir, North side. NC432672. The name means *boiling water skerry!* Gullies lead off the North side of the island to a cliff-face dropping to at least 22m. Noted for crustaceans. Access from Sango Bay (NC407677), or Rispond Bay (NC452654).

1357 An Cruachan. NC435678. The North face of this skerry drops quite quickly to 24m and has good marine life on the rocky slopes. Access as Site 1356.

1358 Eilean Hoan, South side. NC444672. There are cliff-faces around the island to 12m and a flat sand bottom. Plenty of interesting life on the faces. Access as Site 1356.

1359 An Dubh-sgeir, South-east side. NC456680. A superb and challenging dive into a pitch-black cave with seals abounding. Your torch will shine back bright red from seals' eyes! The cave penetrates perhaps 100m, with mussel-covered walls and no sediment. Then it comes to a dead end. This is a fantastic dive and is highly recommended to suitably-experienced divers. Access as Site 1356.

1360 An Dubh-sgeir, North-east side. NC457681. There is a shallow slope to 26m, then a steeper one to over 40m. It consists of waves of limestone bedrock covered with brittle stars, and gives an excellent dive in usual visibility of 20m. Access as Site 1356.

1361 Eilean Cluimhrig, North side. NC462661. The 15m cliffs fall to a boulder beach bounded by shallow water. Access as Site 1356.

1362 Eilean Cluimhrig, South end. NC463656. An excellent dive in beautiful bedrock scenery with overhangs and caves at depths of about 25m. Follow the isobaths around to the West of the island. An excellent night (or dusk) dive. Access as Site 1356.

1363 Portnancon, Loch Eriboll. NC428603. A shallow, rather muddy, dive off the pier. This site provides quite a good night dive, and there are reports of migrating Norway lobsters being seen here.

1364 Wreck of a minesweeper, Loch Eriboll. NC444583. This wreck lies at a point much closer to the shore than the one given on the chart (the above grid reference is fairly accurate). The wreck, which was an armed trawler, is sometimes buoyed. It lies in 30m of water and is well silted – the first pair down usually ruin the visibility for the rest of the party.

1365 Unknown wreck, Loch Eriboll. A Navy vessel from which the 4-inch guns were removed in 1977. The deck is rotten. The bottom is at 18m and sandy.

1366 Near Kempie, Loch Eriboll. NC447580. A muddy bottom descending below 17m, with scallops. Shore access.

1367 Camas an Duin, Loch Eriboll. NC449588. A shallow site with a muddy sand bottom and shore access. There is a report of interesting bottles being found here.

1368 Ard Neakie, Loch Eriboll. NC445596. An interesting cliff-face extends right round the peninsula at depths of 10-20m.

1369 Bay North of Ard Neakie isthmus, Loch Eriboll. NC448598. A pleasant dive over gravel and rock together with shelving small cliffs inhabited by lobsters. Depth: about 18m. Shore access.

1370 Geodh' an Sgadain, Loch Eriboll. NC450602. A steeply-shelving silty bottom extending to beyond 40m. Shore or boat access.

1371 Under White Head light, Loch Eriboll. NC458618. A boulder slope to 15m, then a steep sand-and-mud slope to beyond 40m. Cuckoo wrasse noted. Access as Site 1356.

1372 Wreck of an MFV, Loch Eriboll. This is shown as (PA) at 58 31 18N 04 39 12W near the edge of the 50m isobath, about 600m North-west of White Head light. As far as I know, it is undived.

1373 Rubh' a' Mhuilt. NC473626. An area with lots of interesting-looking clefts and sea caves. Unexplored as far as I know.

1374 Geodh' a' Bhrideoin, Whiten Head. NC489667. An area of ragged caves and natural arches which can be explored by a small boat. The main system has three entrances and is 20m deep. The walls are full of life, and

Whiten Head is a rugged area of sea stacks, natural arches, and caves, some of which can be explored by boat.

the sunlight streaming through the holes illuminates large shoals of fish. Access as Site 1356.

1375 Mol Mhor, Whiten Head. NC495682. This is a big shingle beach, with seals abounding. Out to sea, the bottom levels out at 25m, with rock walls full of life in excellent visibility. I have an exciting report of two divers being 'looked over' by a 9m-long rorqual whale. Apparently the whale twice swam past them, and as it passed it rolled on to its back and inspected them. The seabed was teeming with sand eels, so the whale was presumably feeding on them. Access as Site 1356.

1376 An Stac, Whiten Head. NC495687 (approx). The rocks called Bodack Dearg and The Sisters give exciting exploratory diving with depths reaching 20m. Access as Site 1356.

1377 Whiten Head. NC503687. Superb diving on dramatic, vertical, life-encrusted cliffs that reach a rugged seabed at 25m. The dives here are very similar to those at Cape Wrath. LW slack +0545, HW slack −0030 Dover. The spring rates can reach 3 knots, though close to shore they are slower. Access as Site 1356.

1378 Rubha Thormaid, Whiten Head. NC548681. Between Whiten Head proper and Friesgill Head to the South lie 2 miles of coast that are strewn with sea caves. These are exciting to explore, both by diving and by boat. Depths reach 22m down cliff-faces. Access as Site 1356.

1379 Port Vasco. NC585651. Shallow, though quite pleasant, diving at 9m. Good for snorkelling. Shore access.

1380 Wreck of Ashbury, Dubh-sgeir Mhor. NC598646. A 3,000-ton vessel wrecked in 1944. Half of the wreck lies each side of the rocky reef. The bottom is sandy, with usual visibility of about 10m. The depth to the boilers is about 20m. Access as Site 1383.

1381 Wreck of Nitedal, Sgeir an Oir. A 5,000-ton wreck of a merchantman with a cargo of timber, which was found in two pieces in 1977. Three-quarters of the forward section lie to the west of the island. The stern quarter

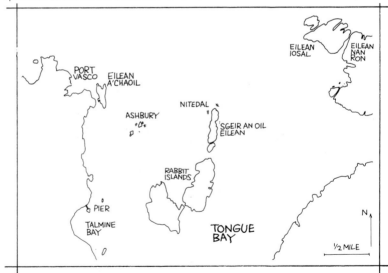

Wrecks of the 'Ashbury' and 'Nitadel'

168

lies to the North-east of the island. At about 20m there is a sandy bottom. A bell bearing the name *Nitedal* has been recovered. Access as Site 1383.

1382 Unknown wreck, Sgeir an Oir. A timber boat is recorded. This is almost certainly the *Nitedal*, but there may be another wreck off this island.

1383 Rabbit Islands, Tongue Bay. NC611635. These islands generally give boring, weedy diving at depths of less than 9m. There is a good camp-site and an easy beach-launch at Talmine (NC585630).

1384 Skullomie Harbour, Tongue Bay. NC617614. An average dive on to silty rocks at 12-15m. Shore access. Boats can be launched at the harbour for exploring the islands North of Tongue Bay. There is a camp-site on the isthmus to the west of the harbour.

Area information and services

Hydrographic charts: 1954 Cape Wrath to Pentland Firth 1:200,000; 2076 Loch Eriboll 1:17,000; F.6680 Cape Wrath to Faraid Head 1:50,000.
Ordnance Survey 1:50,000 maps: 9 Cape Wrath; 10 Strathnaver.
Ordnance Survey 1:25,000 maps: NC25/35 Rhiconich, NC26/36 Kyle of Durness; NC27/37 Cape Wrath; NC45/55; NC46/56 Whiten Head; NC66/76 Bettyhill.
Local BS-AC branches: None. The nearest ones are Ullapool (970) and Thurso (119).
Local SS-AC branches: None.
Air supplies: None in the area. The nearest are Jim Crooks, (6 Inver Park – Lochinver [057 14] 362), and Thurso BS-AC.
Boat charters: None known.
Local weather: Glasgow Weather Centre 041 248 3451; Wick Coastguard (0955) 2332.
Sea area: Fair Isle (close to Hebrides).
Tidal constants:

	DOVER	ULLAPOOL
Cape Wrath	−0355	+0025
Kyle of Durness	−0350	+0030
Rispond	−0345	+0035
Kyle of Tongue	−0330	+0050

Coastguard: Stornoway MRSC (0851) 2013; Wick MRSC (0955) 2332.
Lifeboat: Lochinver, Stornoway, Scrabster.
Police stations: Tongue (080 05) 270.
Hospitals: Dunbar Hospital, Thurso (0847) 63263; Raigmore Hospital, Inverness (0463) 34151.
Recompression chambers: Dunstaffnage Marine Laboratory, Oban (0631) 62244; Underwater Training Centre, Fort William (0397) 3786/3136; Glasgow Western Infirmary 041 339 8822; Aberdeen Royal Infirmary (0224) 681818.
Vehical recovery: AA – Glasgow 041 812 0101; Inverness (0463) 33213 (office hours only).
Local tourist information: Durness (097 181) 259; Bettyhill (064 12) 342.
Accommodation: There are B & B and guest-house facilities in various villages and towns (see Scottish Tourist Board guides).

BEST VALUE

BEST EQUIPMENT

BIGGEST CHOICE

AT

AQUATRON FACTORY SHOP

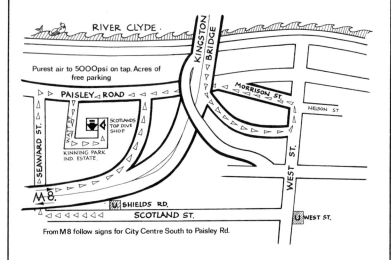

From M8 follow signs for City Centre South to Paisley Rd.

Whatever you want? We've got it—At the right price! From design to manufacture—Suits, Valves, Compressors, charging systems—Maintenance and Repair.
We have the most comprehensive range of "in house" facilities to satisfy the requirements of the most discerning diver—sport or commercial. See for Yourself at—

AQUATRON MARINE LTD, 3 HOUSTON PLACE, GLASGOW
G5 8SG
Tel. 041-429 5902/3

CHAPTER 15

Kyle of Tongue to Skirza Head (Duncansby Head)

The coastline of this region of Scotland is not very well known by divers. Most of the diving is shore-based, and the off-lying shoals and wrecks have not really been explored. Some of the diving is first-rate, however, and that of the Duncansby Head area is particularly interesting.

At the West of this area Eilean nan Ron gives excellent diving among sandstone cliffs and natural arches. These gullies and narrow channels have resulted from the erosion of lines of weakness of the faults caused by the Moine Thrust.

North of the village of Strathy, a side road runs for 3 miles along a cliff-lined peninsula to the lighthouse at Strathy Point. During gales, clouds of spray dash against the lightroom window, 40m above sea level; but in fine weather the superb view from this window takes in Cape Wrath, Dunnet Head, and the Orkney islands.

The 12-mile section of coast between the Kyle of Tongue and Melvich Bay is very jagged. This is due to the Moinian rocks which run out to sea being differentially eroded to form narrow channels. At Melvich Bay, the Old Red Sandstone of Caithness appears, and the Lewisian rocks and Moine Thrust are almost left behind. The sandstone of the East end of the North coast of Scotland has many minor faults and dykes of igneous rock. These have the habit of eroding into either magnificent stacks and clefts, or superb geos – long, deep, finger-like indentations filled with water. These usually provide excellent diving.

The sandstone cliffs extend from Strathy Bay for about a mile before giving way to a picturesque coast of Moinian rocks around Portskerra. To the East, the sands of Melvich Bay are separated by several miles of cliffs before Sandside Bay is reached. The eastern end is dominated by the steel sphere of Dounreay's experimental fast-reactor nuclear power station.

The cliffs of Brims Ness are low, but rise in height as Holborn Head is reached. This has magnificent sandstone cliff scenery including the off-

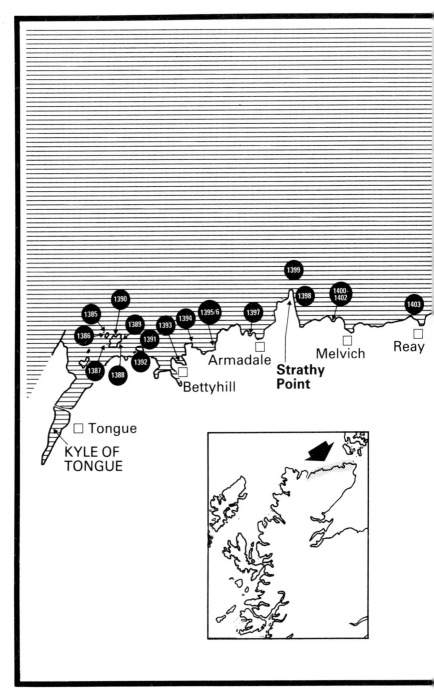

Dive Sites : Kyle of Tongue to Duncansby Head

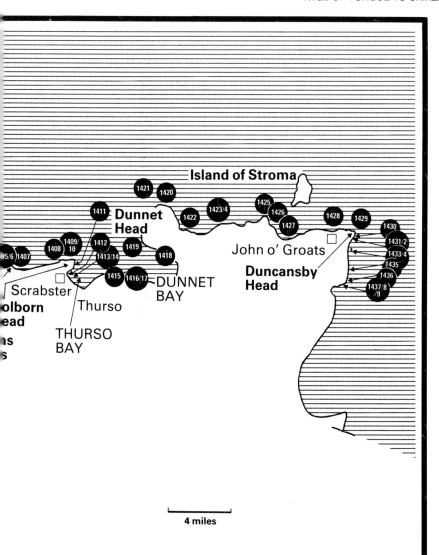

Island of Stroma

**Dunnet
Head**

John o' Groats

**Duncansby
Head**

Scrabster

olborn
ead

ns
s

Thurso

THURSO
BAY

DUNNET
BAY

4 miles

lying Clett, a great mass of sandstone that the sea has cut away from the main cliff to form a huge sea stack standing on 'legs' surrounded by sea caves. The sea works upwards in these caves so that eventually a vertical passage is made to the surface and a blowhole is formed. Holborn Head, like those of Dunnet and Duncansby, is an ancient hill of sandstone that the sea has cut back.

The port of Scrabster originated as a flagstone-exporting centre, but now handles ferries to Orkney, the Faeroe Islands, and Iceland, and also shelters fishing vessels. Across Thurso Bay lies Thurso. With a population of about 9,000, this is the most northerly town on mainland Britain. It provides a wide range of facilities including a thriving branch of the BS-AC.

Dunnet Bay lies East of Thurso and has a wide beach backed by large sand dunes. At low tide, this truly is one of the most strenuous boat-launching sites in Britain!

Dunnet Head is magnificent, with 90m cliffs topped by a lighthouse with a superb view, as befits the most northerly point of mainland Britain. The view extends from Cape Wrath, 60 miles to the West, to the Old Man of Hoy and most of the rest of the southern Orkney islands, to the North-east.

To the East of Dunnet Head, the coast is low and composed of Thurso flags. Between St John's Point and the Orkney island of Hoy runs the *Merry Men of Mey,* the wildest of all the Pentland Firth's boiling races. The Admiralty state that, "the extreme violence of the race, especially with West or North-west gales, can hardly be exaggerated". Be warned! At the Ness of Duncansby there are extensive shell beds.

The village of John O'Groats, which falsely claims to be the most northerly part of the British mainland, lies just West of Duncansby Head. There is the usual tourist kiosk here. The village is otherwise totally unexceptional.

Duncansby Head, however, is well worth a visit. A memorable walk can be had along the 60m-high cliffs to view the magnificent chasms, arches, and castle-like stacks, carved out of the sandstone by the power of the sea. There is a large geo – Long Geo – immediately North of the lighthouse; and just to the South is the precipitous Geo of Sclaites. The end of this has the famous natural arch of Humlies Hole. The 20m-high stack of The Knee lies a little further South, with the Rispie tide race seething between it and the mainland cliffs. Half-a-mile South of the lighthouse are the twin Stacks of Duncansby (66m and 89m), with the natural arch of the Thirle Door just to their North. A mile further South is Wife Geo with its fine twin entrances, one of which is in the form of a tunnel. There are then three more major geos before Skirza Head is finally reached.

Accommodation is widely available throughout the area covered by this chapter. The area to the East at Thurso is particularly well equipped. There are also a number of caravan and camping sites by sandy beaches.

Diving is generally relatively straightforward (with the notable exception of the wild and turbulent Pentland Firth). To take a boat into the Pentland Firth you *MUST* have a very experienced boathandler who is well able to assess conditions accurately.

Dive sites

The sites in this chapter are described from West to East along the coast. I have included sites up to 4 miles South of Duncansby Head because this completes a natural headland.

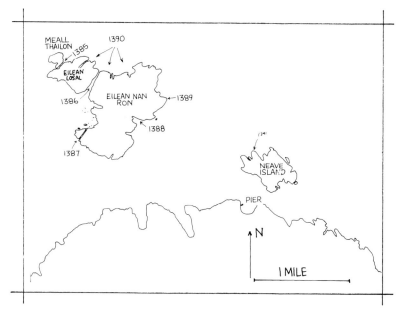

Sites near Eilean nan Ron

1385 Meall Thailm, Eilean losal. NC629661. There is a tunnel along the split in Meall Thailm (Meall Halm on 1-inch OS map) which is 24m deep and has vertical walls and house-sized boulders on the bottom. Outside the tunnel the water is 30m deep. An excellent dive, with boat access from Talmine (NC588632). Tidal streams are rather weak. LW slack +0300, HW slack −0310 Dover.

1386 Eilean losal channel. NC635660. This gives an excellent dive among rocks and clefts with seals abounding. Access as Site 1385.

1387 An Innis, Eilean nan Ron. NC633649. Just South of An Innis, there is a very deep cave. There is no life in it and it is quite dark, though the visibility can be 20m in calm conditions. Access as Site 1385.

1388 Port na h-Uaille, Eilean nan Ron. NC643653. This small port was abandoned in 1940; six empty houses remain. Depths reach 18m on a rocky bottom. Access as Site 1385.

1389 Eilean nan Ron, East point. NC646656. An excellent dive down vertical rocky walls to about 25m. The rock is a rather bizarre-looking conglomerate. Access as Site 1385.

1390 Eilean nan Ron, North side. NC635662 (approx). The North side of Eilean nan Ron does not look to have great diving potential, but the diving is, in fact, superb – with arches, caves, and geos, all round. Depths can reach 32m down the cliffs. Access as Site 1385.

1391 Neave Island. NC665648. The North point of Neave Island has a number of inter-connected underwater tunnels at a depth of about 15m. These provide an unusual dive, swimming from tunnel to tunnel. Access as Site 1385.

1392 Skerray Bay. NC660640. This is accessible from the shore, but depths are shallow.

1393 Farr Bay. NC710627. This fishing station has a sandy beach leading to a rock-and-boulder seabed. The diving is not too exciting.

1394 Farr Point. NC716648 (approx). This is said to be undived, but it has been identified by local divers as a potentially excellent site.

1395 Kirtomy Bay, West. NC742643. Initial access is the same as Site 1393. There is a Y-shaped gully 9m deep and 2m wide giving access to the West of the island. The sandy bottom has rock strata projecting vertically from it.

1396 Kirtomy Bay, East. NC744643. There is a track leading to the water. To the East of the grassy ridge there is a pull-out for the boats from the fishing station. Underwater, quite rough scenery gives pleasant diving, though the depth is less than 10m.

1397 Port a' Chinn. NC786654. Good diving in shallow water with underwater tunnels and natural arches. Lots of life, especially lobsters. Long swim out, or a long snorkel dive.

1398 Strathy Point. NC828700. The East side of Strathy Point gives diving down steep rocky slopes to about 25m, with excellent fish-life. The headland is steep-to, so there is no suitable shore access for divers. Care should be taken because of a northerly-running eddy that is nearly continuous, whatever the state of the tide. LW slack −0610 Dover, HW slack at HW Dover. Spring rates up to 2.5 knots. Boat access is from Portskerra (NC877664). There is an aerial ropeway to the jetty for the salmon station fishing equipment. The diving is not too interesting, however.

1399 Wreck of the Hearty, Strathy Point. This stream drifter ran aground in 1930 near Strathy Point in dense fog and was a total loss.

1400 Geo South-west of unnamed island South-west of Rubha Ghoiridh, Portskerra. NC872664. This is the wider, more westerly, geo with the island at its mouth. Underwater, there is a fantastic wall dropping to a boulder seabed. Both are totally covered in life. Visibility of over 30m has been reported for February!

1401 Geo South-west of Rubha Ghoiridh, Portskerra. NC873664. This is the long, thin, geo which is the more easterly of the two. The diving is the same as Site 1397. This area is a dogfish breeding ground. In March there are vast numbers of egg cases and small dogfish: in September there are hordes of mature dogfish.

1402 Sgeir a' Phuirt, Portskerra. NC878665. Follow the track to the East of the headland. This gives shore access to a natural arch through a little promontory. The water is 15m deep and the underwater scenery is

The headlands and inlets around Portskerra offer superb underwater scenery in visibility of up to 30m.

fantastic. The local divers consider the Portskerra dives to be the best shore sites on the eastern part of the North coast of Scotland.

1403 Sandside Bay. NC959661. This gives a good snorkel over a shallow, sandy seabed with big flatfish. Easy shore access.

1404 Crosskirk Bay. ND023702. A shallow dive over a flat bedrock seabed with rocks and gullies. Maximum depth: 12m. The life is rich, but after a long, hot spell late in summer there is too much weed for comfort. Shore access. Note that the river, Forss Water, can spoil the visibility when it is in spate after heavy rain.

1405 Brims Ness. ND042713. A shallow site best dived early in the season to avoid the excessive kelp. There is lots of small life under the kelp beds in the crevices. The visibility rapidly becomes very poor in heavy swell. Shore access.

1406 Wrecks on Brims Ness. Three vessels are known to have become total losses after running on to Brims Ness. In 1928, the Dutch motor ketch *Noord Brabant* and the Hamburg steamer *SS Asse* were stranded and lost. In 1931 the British ketch *Pet* ran aground and was wrecked.

1407 Port of Brims. ND044711. Very similar to Site 1404, but without the river!

1408 Spear Head. NC096717. Similar to Site 1409.

1409 Clett, Holborn Head. ND105717. A memorable dive site. The depth reaches 15m on a bedrock seabed that has been scoured clean. In the breeding season puffins will 'fly' around you underwater, making for an unforgetable experience. Boat access is from Scrabster. LW slack −0600 Dover, HW slack at HW Dover. Spring rates are about 2.5 knots.

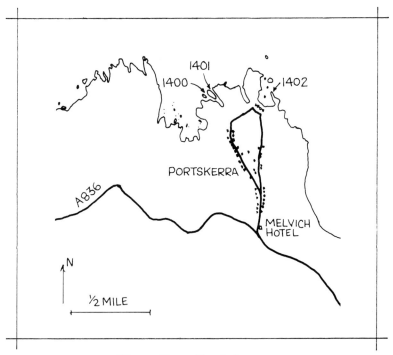

Dive sites: Portskerra

1410 Wreck of the Ben Rinneo. This steam trawler was lost in 1928 when she ran aground on Holborn Head and became a total wreck.

1411 Holborn Head lighthouse. ND107717. A wall to 15m with lots of life. At the bottom a boulder slope runs downwards. The life thins out towards Holborn Head. Shore access – but do not park at the lighthouse itself.

1412 Old Pier, Scrabster. ND103715. This has depths of 5-10m along it. Lots of life, including lobsters and congers. Ask the harbourmaster before diving there.

1413 Wreck of WW2 merchantman, Thurso Bay. ND107700 (approx). Straight out from the end of the old pier is the wreck of a WW2 merchantman. This lies at 20m and is covered and uncovered by sand in heavy seas. The wreck is very broken up and is being salved. The owner is S. Wishart.

1414 Aircraft wreck, Thurso Bay. NC111702 (approx). This lies about 700m East of the end of Scrabster harbour. It stands in 13m of water, about 3m proud of the sandy seabed.

1415 Clardon Haven. ND150700. A shallow site with the rocky seabed at 5m split by many gullies running out to sea and bottoming at 10m. These are full of big fish. It is best to dive here in early spring because there is much less weed then. Shore access, though a boat is easier.

1416 Murkle Bay. ND171694. This is flat, sandy, and weedy, with depths eventually reaching 5m! There are lots of big flatfish. Shore access.

1417 Wrecks in Murkle Bay: The Spur. In 1926 the SS *Jura* dragged her anchors from Dunnet Bay and was stranded near Murkle. Eventually she became a total loss. The *Spur* may also lie in Murkle Bay, but I have no further information.

1418 Pier East of Dwarwick Head, Dunnet Head. ND207713. A boulder-slope leads down to beyond 10m. Not too interesting a dive.

1419 Rowramps, Dunnet Head. ND183731. A steep, rocky bottom leads down in a series of kelp-covered steps and ledges to beyond 25m. Good life with many fish. Strong tides make boat cover absolutely essential. Launching at Dunnet Bay (ND218706) is very strenuous even at high tide!

1420 Easter Head, Dunnet Head. ND203769. This is the most northerly point on the mainland of Britain. It is very exposed, but gives a good dive, with rich marine life. There is a series of big bedrock steps which reach well beyond 36m. The 'big' scenery and excellent visibility makes this a memorable dive. LW slack +0500, HW slack −0100 Dover. Spring rates are about 3 knots.

1421 Wrecks off Dunnet Head. The *Camba* was lost West of Dunnet Head in 1925. In 1906, the SS *Petersburg* was wrecked with a cargo of coal on Dunnet Head itself. Finally, in 1944, a British submarine was being towed through the Pentland Firth into a North-west gale. She broke adrift off Dunnet Head in heavy seas and is presumed sunk in the vicinity.

1422 Little Clett. ND221743. This shallow dive is quite scenic at high tide! Shore access.

1423 Skarfskerry Point. ND251747. There is a small wreck of an old steamer lying 50m offshore in 10m of water. The engine-room shows above water at all states of the tide. Shore access.

1424 Wreck of the SS Linkmoor. This British steamer was wrecked at Scarfsferry in 1930 after becoming unmanageable in a strong gale and a heavy westerly sea.

1425 St. John's Point. NC312755. This is the point from which the fearsome tidal race called the "Merry Men of Mey" runs. Close to shore, the many rocks and shallows giving reasonable diving.

Notes on tides in the Pentland Firth area: The strongest tidal streams in British waters run in the Pentland Firth – they are recorded as reaching a maximum of 11 knots, though locals claim to have experienced up to 14 knots! The races, eddies, and overfalls, are the most dangerous off our coasts, and exceed those in the Gulf of Corryvreckan in extent, if not in ferocity. The Admiralty Pilot (NP52) devotes about five pages to their description, and this must be referred to before diving at sites other than the most sheltered. It is difficult to quote slack water times, though the streams should be quiet at about LW +0100, HW −0500 Dover.

1426 Scotland's Haven. ND316746. This curiously named coastal feature is a large tidal pool. It may be worth a snorkel.

1427 Wreck of the SS Malin Head. After salvage attempts in 1909, this vessel and part of her cargo of pig iron became a total wreck in Gills Bay (NC3373).

1428 Wrecks at the Ness of Duncansby. NC389738. Many vessels have been lost here over the years. The *SS Ardmore* with a cargo of wood was stranded and wrecked in 1899. In 1923, the Grimsby steam trawler *Aurelia* ran aground and was lost. Two years later, the Boston steam trawler *Salmonby* sank in deep water after slipping off the rocks here. In 1941, *HMS Salvage King* ran aground and could not be salvaged due to heavy surf. Finally, *HM Tug St Olaves* ran aground in 1942 while towing the *Golden Crown;* both vessels were lost, though much of the tug's gear was later salvaged.

1429 Wrecks on Duncansby Head. The *SV Isabella* was lost in 1916 when she struck rocks near Duncansby Head and sank with a cargo of coal. In 1927, the steam drift *Harry* was lost after grounding on the headland while under tow.

1430 Geo of Sclaites, Duncansby Head. ND406731. This 80m-long inlet is only a few metres wide. Depths reach 20m; visibility is up to 30m; and fish and crustaceans abound. The vertical geo walls are covered with sponges and other encrusting life. A memorable dive, out of the tidal streams. Boat access only: launch at Freswick Bay, 4 miles South of Duncansby Head (ND378677), or from the Bay of Sanwick (ND398735) which involves struggling down a very steep sandy beach.

1431 Headland South-west of the Knee, Duncansby Head. ND405727. A superb dive, with guillemots 'flitting' around at 20m. As well as the birds, there is lots of other life, including seals, to be seen. At low water the stack is connected to the mainland by a rib of rock, and a rock pool is formed. Access as Site 1430.

1432 Thirle Door, Duncansby Head. ND402724. This is a big sea stack. At its base the seabed of sandstone bedrock drops to 20m. Lots of life, especially in the shallows. Access as Site 1430.

1433 Stacks of Duncansby. ND401722. These are apparently undived, though they are expected to be similar to Site 1432. Depths just offshore drop quite rapidly to beyond 60m. Access as Site 1430.

1434 Wrecks on Duncansby Stacks. In 1911 the steam trawler *Mormon* became a total wreck after being grounded. Two years later the *SS Thyra* of Tonsberg ran aground and was wrecked, though the cargo and crew were saved.

1435 Wife Geo. ND392697. An incredible piece of rock architecture, this narrow geo connects to the sea by a 40m-long tunnel. Both the geo and the tunnel are boatable and diveable in calm conditions. The tunnel is pitch black in places and has 3m of water in it. Its walls are covered with red sea squirts. Access as Site 1430.

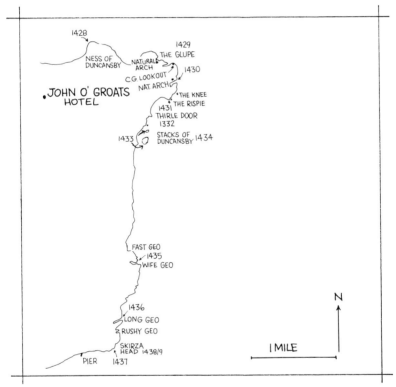

Dive sites: Duncansby Head

1436 Long Geo. ND395687. A long, thin, high-walled geo with interesting diving. Access as Site 1430.

1437 Skirza Head. ND394681. Sandstone bedrock at a depth of 20m. Lots of life, especially in the shallows. Access as Site 1430.

1438 Wreck of the SS Azalee. In the 1890s this vessel sank off Skirza head.

1439 Wreck of the Novar. This steam trawler was stranded at Skirza Head in 1939 and was totally wrecked.

Area information and services

Hydrographic charts: 1954 Cape Wrath to Pentland Firth 1:200,000; 2162 Pentland Firth & approaches 1:50,000.
Ordnance Survey 1:50,000 maps: 10 Strathnaver; 11 Thurso & Dunbeath; 12 Thurso & Wick.

Ordnance Survey 1:25,000 maps: NC66/76 Bettyhill; NC86/96 Strathy & Dounreay; ND06/16 Thurso; ND17/27 Dunnet Head; ND26/36 Freswick; ND37/47 Duncansby Head.
Local BS-AC branches: Thurso (119).
Local SS-AC branches: None.
Air supplies: Thurso BS-AC.
Boat charters: None known.
Local weather: Glasgow Weather Centre 041 248 3451; Wick Coastguard (0955) 2332.
Sea area: Fair Isle (close to Cromarty).
Tidal constants:

	DOVER	ULLAPOOL	ABERDEEN
Kyle of Tongue	−0330	+0050	—
Scrabster	−0227	—	−0455
Duncansby Head	−0052	—	−0320

Coastguard: Wick MRSC (0955) 2332.
Lifeboat: Scrabster.
Harbourmaster: Thurso (0847) 2779.
Police stations: Tongue (080 05) 270; Bettyhill (064 12) 222; Reay (084 781) 222; Thurso (0847) 63222; Castletown (084 782) 222; Wick (0955) 3551.
Hospitals: Dunbar Hospital, Thurso (0847) 63263; Raigmore Hospital, Inverness (0463) 34151.
Recompression chambers: Dunstaffnage Marine Laboratory, Oban (0631) 62244; Underwater Training Centre, Fort William (0397) 3786/3136; Glasgow Western Infirmary 041 339 8822; Aberdeen Royal Infirmary (0224) 681818.
Vehicle recovery: AA – Glasgow 041 812 0101; Inverness (0463) 33213 (office hours only).
Local tourist information: Bettyhill (064 12) 342; Thurso (0847) 2371; John O'Groats (095 581) 373.
Accommodation: There are numerous B & B and guest-house facilities (see Scottish Tourist Board guides).

Appendix 1: USEFUL ADDRESSES

Dive Centres:

Port Charlotte Hotel Diving Centre, Isle of Islay, Argyllshire;
Tarbert Dive Centre, Victoria Hotel, Tarbert;
Oban Divers Ltd, Laggan, Glenshallach, Oban, PA4 4QJ;
Mull Diving Centre, Salen Pier, Aros, Isle of Mull, Argyll;
Skye Diving Centre, 'Leyburn', Harlosh, Dunvegan, Isle of Skye;
Sail Mhor Croft, Camusnagaul, Dundonnel, by Garve, Ross-shire, IV23 2QT;
Jim Crooks, 6 Inver Park, Lochinver, Sutherland;
Scapa Flow Diving Centre, Burray, Orkney;
Dive Orkney, 1 Bridge Street, Kirkwall, Orkney;
Stromness Diving Centre, 108a Victoria Street, Stromness, Orkney, KW16 3BU;
Snipe Miller, 84 Meadowbank, Kirkwall, Orkney;
Ferry Inn, Stromness, Orkney;
East Coast Divers, West Pitkierie Farm, Anstruther, Fife;

Air Supplies:

All the above dive-centres have supplies of compressed air. All BS-AC and SS-AC branches in the area either have a compressor of their own, or know the whereabouts of one. Compressed air is additionally available as follows:

C Diving Services Ltd, Laigh Killoup, Girvan;
Clive Warren, Varenne, Tarbert, Argyllshire, PA29 6UG;
BHT Ltd, Rhu House, Tarbert, Argyllshire, PA29 6YF;
GMT Diving Co Ltd, 520 St Vincent Street, Glasgow, G3 8XZ;
Aquatron Marine Ltd, 3 Houston Place, Glasgow, G5 8SG;
Sub-C-Services Ltd, 16 Gardner Street, Glasgow, G11 5NG;
Johnstons' Marine Stores, Old Pier, Lamlash, Isle of Arran;
Kildonan Hotel, Kildonan, Isle of Arran, KA27 8SE;
Darroch Mhor Chalet & Watersports, Carrick Castle, Lochgoil, Argyllshire;
Seafare, Tobermory, Isle of Mull;
Tobermory Diving Centre, Main Street, Tobermory, Isle of Mull;
Portree Diving Services, 5 Achachork, Portree, Isle of Skye;
P Ebdon, 4 The Street, Edinbain, Isle of Skye;
Strollamus Boat Centre, Strollamus, nr Broadford, Isle of Skye;
Wester Ross Marine, South Erradale, Gairloch, Ross and Cromarty;
Taversoe Hotel, Rousay, Orkney, KW17 2PT;
Swift Diving Supplies (Scotland) Ltd, 11-12 Kittybrewster Centre, Aberdeen);
Edinburgh Diving Centre Ltd, 30 West Preston Street, Edinburgh;
Hunter Diving Equipment, 21 Constitution Place, inside Leith Docks, Edinburgh;
Scoutscroft Diving Centre, Coldingham, Eyemouth, Berwickshire;
Aquamart, Masons Wynd, Off Chapel Street, Eyemouth, Berwickshire.

Dive Boats

A number of the diving centres and suppliers of compressed air either have a boat of their own, or know where one can be arranged locally. The main dive boats operating in the waters of this area are:

Charna – Jim Kilcullen, 3 Dal-an-Aiseig, North Connel, Connel, Argyllshire;
Sweet Caroline – Ian Slade, Beadun, Eas Brae, Tobermory, Isle of Mull;
Hamnavoe – East Coast Divers, West Pitkierie Farm, Anstruther, Fife;
Jean de la Lune – Dave Burton, c/o The Harbourmaster, Colchester.
Snipe Miller of 84 Meadowbank, Kirkwall, Orkney, also hires out boats.
   The above boats all have good accommodation and a good track record. There are many other, smaller, dayboats operating in local areas. Where known, these are listed in the appropriate chapters. Details of any boats not mentioned will be welcomed for inclusion in a revised edition of this book.

Chart Agents:

Kelvin Hughes, 375 West George Street, Glasgow, G3 7DD;
Christie & Wilson, 44 York Street, Glasgow, G2 8JW;
W B Leitch & Son, Tarbert, Argyll;
Crinan Boats Ltd, Crinan, Argyll;
Nancy Black, 24/25 Argyll Square, Oban, Argyll;
Duncan MacIver Ltd, 7 Maritime Buildings, Stornoway, Isle of Lewis;
Bridgend Stores, Aultbea, Ross-shire;
Hay & Co (Lerwick) Ltd, 106a Commercial Street, Lerwick, Shetland;
Thomas Garden, Harbour Office, Commercial Road, Buckie, Banffshire;
Burghead Boat Centre, Burghead Harbour, Burghead, Elgin
Kelvin Hughes, 21 Regent Quay, Aberdeen;
Allison-Gray, 59-63 Dock Street, Dundee;
Chattan Shipping Services Ltd, 5 Canon Mills, Edinburgh.

Coastguard Stations:

(Marine Rescue Coordination Centres [MRCC], and Marine Rescue Sub-Centres [MRSC]).
MRCC Clyde – Greenock (0475) 29988;
MRSC Oban – Oban (0631) 63720;
MRSC Stornoway – Stornoway (0851) 2013;
MRSC Orkney – Kirkwall (0856) 3268;
MRSC Shetland – Lerwick (0595) 2976;
MRSC Wick – Wick (0856) 2332;
MRSC Moray – Peterhead (0779) 4278;
MRCC Aberdeen – Aberdeen (0224) 52334;
MRSC Forth – Crail (03335) 666.

Other Addresses:

Highlands and Islands Development Board, 27 Bridge House, Bank Street, Inverness;
Scottish Sports Council, 4 Queensferry Street, Edinburgh, EH2 4PB;
Scottish Tourist Board, 23 Ravelston Terrace, Edinburgh, EH4 3EU;
Scottish Tourist Board (London Office), 5/6 Pall Mall East, London, SW1;
Countryside Commission for Scotland, Battleby, Redgorton, Perth;
Nature Conservancy Council, 12 Hope Terrace, Edinburgh, EH9 2AS;
Forestry Commission (Scotland), 231 Corstorphine Road, Edinburgh, EH12 7AT;
National Trust for Scotland, 5 Charlotte Square, Edinburgh, EH2 4DU;
Scottish Wildlife Trust, 25 Johnston Terrace, Edinburgh, EH1 2NH;

Royal Society for the Protection of Birds (Scottish Office), 17 Regent Terrace, Edinburgh, EH7 5BN;
Scottish Rights of Way Society, 32 Rutland Square, Edinburgh, EH1 2BW;
Scottish Youth Hostels Association, 7 Glebe Crescent, Stirling, FK8 2JA;
British Sub-Aqua Club, 16 Upper Woburn Place, London, WC1H 0QW;
Scottish Sub-Aqua Club, 16 Royal Crescent, Glasgow, G3 7SL

Appendix 2: DECOMPRESSION TABLES

The decompression table used in Britain by amateur divers was specially computed at the request of the British Sub-Aqua Club by the then Royal Naval Physiological Laboratory at Alverstoke.

Before using this table it is imperative that you fully understand all its aspects.

You should particularly note that the repeat dive concession only applies to two divers, not three, per day (unless the third dive is only to 9m or shallower).

An extra degree of care is required when you are diving for a period of more than one day. If, on one day, you dive to 40m or beyond you must ensure that a morning dive on the following day does not encroach on the 16-hour decompression time of the previous day's second dive. You must also take care not to carry out three dives beyond 9m in any 24-hour period if you claim the two-dive repeat dive concession (it is quite immaterial if the period of 24 hours includes your overnight sleep).

One further note of caution. Many people like to combine a diving holiday in Scotland with some hill-walking and island exploration. The pressure reduction inherent in such activities should be considered if you plan to go to the mountains immediately after diving. There are no exact recommendations, though the diving at altitude restrictions may be considered.

Deep or Prolonged Dives: The RNPL/BS-AC table is based on the sound idea that virtually no amateur dives will require stage decompression longer than 30 minutes, or be deeper than 50m. However, experienced divers will occasionally exceed these limits, especially with regard to depth in Scottish waters. When this is planned, the full RNPL 1972 air diving table must be consulted.

The full table is reproduced in the BS-AC Diving Manual.

Appendix 3: RECOMPRESSION CHAMBERS IN SCOTLAND

As far as I am aware the list of chambers given below is complete.

It is prudent to know the whereabouts of the nearest recompression chamber relative to your chosen diving site. However, it would be unusual to go direct to the chamber (it might not be available).

The correct procedure to employ in Scottish waters if you suspect you have a case requiring recompression is open to some argument. The approved procedure in most of Britain is to phone *HMS Vernon* (0705 818888) and ask for the Duty Diving Medical Specialist or the Duty Lt-Cdr.

In Scotland, the best procedure is to phone Aberdeen Royal Infirmary (Aberdeen 871848), and ask for the Duty Diving Doctor if you are anywhere near the *GRAMPIAN REGION*. If you are in the *SOUTH-WEST* then the best plan is to contact Glasgow Western Infirmary (041 339 8822). In *ANY OTHER PART OF THE COUNTRY* it may be best to contact *HMS Vernon*. In any event, your first contact will be with the Coastguard, and it is they who will coordinate the rescue services and ask the Police to assist with transport to the nearest available chamber.

It is worth noting that if you are involved in an incident that may demand recompression after diving at an inland site then you should still contact the Coastguard in the first instance, as they are familiar with the procedures involved.

The chambers below are listed in a clockwise direction around Scotland, starting in the South-west.

Millport. Scottish Marine Biological Association, Millport Laboratory, Isle of Cumbrae. Tel: Millport (047 553) 581/2. (Out of hours Millport: 761/287/835).

Glasgow. Western Infirmary, Dumbarton Road, Glasgow. Tel: (041) 339 8822; ask for Intensive Care Unit.

Faslane. *HMS Neptune,* Clyde Submarine Base, Helensburgh. Tel: Helensburgh (0436) 4321; ask for Duty Lt-Cdr or Duty Diver.

Holy Loch. *USS Holland,* Holy Loch, nr Dunoon. Tel: Dunoon (0369) 4237.

Oban. Scottish Marine Biological Laboratory, Dunbeg, near Oban. Tel: Oban (0631) 62244; ask for Alan Gale.

Fort William. Underwater Training Centre, Inverlochy, Fort William. Tel: Fort William (0397) 3786. (Out of hours contact Dr Douglas at Fort William 3136, or Chris Robinson at Fort William 3773).

Orkney. Occidental of Britain Inc, Oil Terminal Dept, Flotta, Orkney. Tel: Longhope (085 670) 341.
NB: It has been made clear by the owners that this chamber is not available for sports divers, even in an emergency.

Aberdeen. Royal Infirmary, Forresterhill, Aberdeen. Tel: Aberdeen (0224) 681818. (Alternatively, contact 871848 and ask for the Duty Diving Doctor).

Institute of Offshore Medicine, 9 Rubislaw Terrace, Aberdeen. Tel: Aberdeen (0224) 55595/55596. (Out of hours, contact Aberdeen 671848 and ask for the Medical Officer in charge of recompression facilities).

MAFF Marine Laboratory, Victoria Road, Aberdeen. Tel: Aberdeen (0224) 876544.

There are also several professional diving contractors in the Aberdeen area, some of which have comprehensive recompression and medical facilities. Among these are:

Comex Houlder Diving Ltd, Bucksburn, Aberdeen (Tel: 714101).

Oceaneering, Pitmedden Road, Dyce, Aberdeen (Tel: 770444).

Wharton Williams Taylor, Farburn Industrial Estate, Dyce, Aberdeen (Tel: 722877).

Rosyth. Marine Services School and Salvage Unit, Dunfermline. Tel: Inverkeithing (0383) 42121 ext. 3127/3527.

Note: there are a number of other chambers in Scotland. Many oil rigs and all oil-rig support vessels have recompression chambers. Additionally, there may be naval vessels with recompression facilities operating in Scottish waters from time to time. These, however, are not generally available to sports divers.

Appendix 4: SCOTTISH PLACE NAMES

Most Scottish place names are of Gaelic origin, though there is a distinct Scandinavian influence in the far North-west, North, and especially in the Northern Isles. There is also the occasional word from English, Latin, and Welsh.

This appendix covers those words more commonly used in naming shore features. For fuller details, the books listed at the end of the appendix should be consulted.

Much can be learned about an area from a study of its place names. Those incomprehensible and unpronounceable Gaelic names usually hold a description of the feature to which they apply, so careful use of this appendix, and of a Gaelic dictionary, can be most informative.

A word of warning, however, concerning the superfluous 'h' or 't'. When names are hyphenated eg: *h-Iolaire*, the rule is to miss out the 'h' and look up *isolaire* – an eagle. This rule also applies to words prefixed by 't'. When the second letter of a word is 'h', this can usually be ignored too.

The definite article in Gaelic can also confuse. The following table may help:

NOMINATIVE: singular (masculine) – *an, am, an t-*
singular (feminine) – *a', an, an t-*
plural (masculine & feminine) – *na, na h-*

GENITIVE: singular (masculine) – *a', an, an t-*
singular (feminine) – *na, na h-*
plural (masculine & feminine) – *nan, nam*

Pronunciation of Gaelic names is tongue-twisting! A detailed explanation is given in the references, especially MacLennan.

abhainn, airbhne	river
acairseid, acarsaid	an anchorage
aidh, aigh	place of
aig	small bay or creek
ail, aileach	rock, a stony place
aird, airdean, airde, ard	height
aiseag	ferry
alban, albane, albyne	Scotland
allt, alt, ald, auld, ault	stream
am	their
amhain	river
amar, amair	channel

an	the
aoineadh	steep, rocky hill, rocks rising straight from the sea
aonach, aonaich	high, bleak place
arkaig	dark
aumhach	cave
ay	island
bagh, baigh	bay
ban, bain, bhan	white
barr bar, barran	top, summit
bata, batachean, bhata	boat
beag, beaga, bag, bheag, beg	little
bealach, bhealaich	pass
beinn, beinne, beann, ben	mountain usually by itself
beith, bheithe	birch tree
bidean, bidein	pinnacle
biorach	sharp-pointed
birlinn, birlinne	galley, yacht
blaven	blue
bodach, bodaich, bhodaich	old man
bodha	breaker, sunken rock in the sea
borro, borg	castle, fort
brig	jetty, landing place
broch	ancient circular stone tower
brough	bold peninsula
buidhe, buie, buy	yellow
cabar, cabair, cabhar	hawk
cadha	a steep place
cailleach, caillich	old woman
cairn, carn, carnan	heap of stones; round, rocky hill
cala, caladh	harbour
calbh	small island which has broken away from a larger island
call, coll	hazel
camas, cambus, camus	channel
caol, caolas, coalais	narrow strait, firth
caorunn, caorann	rowan tree
castle	isolated stack
ceann, cinn, chinn	headland
chladaich	shore, beach
choit	boat
chraisg, chroisg	crossing
chreag	crag, rock
clach	stone
cladach, cladaich	shore, beach
clamhan	buzzard
cleit, clett	rocky eminence, a cliff
cnap, cnaip, cnoc, cnocan	knob, lump, hillock
coachan	stream
coille	wood, forest
coingheal, choingheal	whirlpool
coire	corrie
coit, coite, choit	small boat
corrach, chorrach	rugged, broken
cos, cois, cosan, cosaig	cave, hole
cra	red
crann croin	tree, mast
creag, creige	crag, rock
critheann, chritheagain	aspen tree
crois, croise, chroisg	a cross, across
crosg	crossing place
cruaidh	hard, stony place
cuan	ocean
cuil, chuile	nook, recess

cumhang, cumhainn	narrow
darach, daraich, darroch	oak tree
dearg, derg	red (bright)
deas	south
dhomhain, domhain	deep
dobhar	water
doirlinn	isthmus, a neck of shore left dry at low tide
donn	brown
dorch, dorcha	dark
dorus	door, opening
dow	black
down	brown
dromanach	elder tree
dubh, dubhan, dhuibh	black
dun, duin	heap, fort
ear, earrair	east, eastern
eas, easa, easan	waterfall
eilean, eilein, eileanan	island
ey	island
fada	long
fadhail	ford in a sea channel
faoilinn	beach
fasach	wilderness
fearn, fearna, fern	alder tree
fionn	white, fair
fioreun	eagle
fitheach, fihithich	raven
fradharc, fradhairc	sight, a look-out
fuar, fuaire	cold
gailbheach	stormy, furious
gaillionn, gailinne	cold and violent storm
gaineamh, gaimheach	sand
gair, gerr	short
gaoth, gaoithe, gaothach	windy
garbh, garbha, gairbhe	rough, stony
geal, geala, gile	white (brilliant)
geo, geodha	chasm, creek
glais	stream
glas, glass, glais	grey
glassich	foam
gloup	sea tunnel, with blow hole
gob, guib	point, beak
gorm, gorma	blue (green if applied to foliage)
gris	grey
guibhais	fir trees
haven	river
holm	small island
hope	bay
iar	west, western
iasg	fish
iasgach, iasgaich	fishing
iasgair	fisher
inbhear, inbhir, inver	mouth of a river
inch	island
iola	fishing bank or rock
iolair, iolaire	eagle
iomall, iomallach	remote part
iubhar, iubhair	yew tree
knap	knob, lump, hillock
kneep	a peak

knock	hillock, round hill
kyle	a strait, firth
lacha	wild duck
laimhrige, laimhrig	landing place, harbour
leac	flat stone, slab
leamh, leamhan, leamhain	elm tree
leathann, leathain	broad
leith, leithe, liath	grey
lic, lice, lick	flat stone, slab
linn, linne	pool
lionadh, lionaidh	flood tide
loch, locha	lake, arm of sea
lochan, lochain	small lake
long	ship
longhphort	harbour
losg, loisgte	burnt ground
machair, machrach	plain, level country
mam, maim mhaim	large round hill
maorach, maoraich	shellfish
mara	the sea
meal, meall, meallan	large round hill
mol, mal, mul	shingly beach
mor, more, mhor, mhoir	great, large
muir	sea
muireach, mhuirich	shingle bank
mull	promontory
mullach, mullaich	top, summit
nes, ness	promontory, cape
nish	point, cape
noop, noup	peak
oitir, oitire	shoal, drying rock
ord	round hill
reidh, reilean	level, smooth
reothairt	spring tide
rhu	promontory
rinn	promontory
ron, roin	seal
ross	cape
ruadh, ruaidhe	red (brownish)
rubha, rudha, ru, rue	promontory
ruinn	sharp point, promontory
saile, sailean, sal	salt water, sea
seabhag, seabhaig	hawk
sgarbh, sgaibh	cormorant
sgeir, sgeire	rock in the sea
sgorr, sgurr	rocky peak
snamh, snaime	swim
stac, staic, stacain, staca	steep conical hill, precipice
stob	little point
strome	current, stream
stron, strone	nose, point
tairbeart, tarbet, tarbert	crossing, isthmus
teas	heat
tob	bay
tolm, tuilm, tolmach	island near shore
tom, toman, tomain, tuim	wave
tor, torr	round hill
traigh, traighe, tragha	beach (tidal)
traogh, traoghaidh	ebb
tuath, tuathe	north

tulm, tuilm	islet
uaine	green
uamh, uamha, uaimh	cave
uig	bay
uinn	green
uinnseann	ash tree
uisge	water
vic	bay
voe	sea inlet
wick	sea inlet

References:
Scottish Place-names, Nicolaisen, 1979, 210pp;
Gaelic Dictionary, MacLennan, 1979 (reprint of first edition, 1925), 613pp;
Place Names on Maps of Scotland and Wales, Ordnance Survey, undated, 23pp;
Place-names of Scotland, Johnston, 1970 (reprint of third edition, 1934), 335pp;
Understand Highland Place-names, Owen, undated, 44pp;
Scottish Place-names – Their Meanings Explained, Eyers, 1980. 95pp;
Gaelic Without Groans, MacKecknie, 1962, 124pp.

Appendix 5: BIBLIOGRAPHY

In addition to the publications mentioned in Volume I of this series, the following reference books may prove useful:
Shell book to the British Coast, Robinson & Millward, 1983;
AA illustrated guide to Britain's coast, 1984;
The Highlands and Islands, Thompson, 1974;
Scottish Highlands, Holiday Which;
Beyond the Great Glen, Nicolson, 1975 touring guide, 1984;
Touring guide to Scotland – thirteen volumes: *Wester Ross*, Findlay, 1971; *Gairloch*, Dixon, 1886 (1980 reprint); *Staffa*, MacCulloch, 1975; *Six Inner Hebrides*, Banks, 1977; *Skye*, Sillar & Meyler; *The Isle of Mull*, MacNab; *Skye*, Cooper; *The Hebrides*, Murray, 1966; *The Islands of Western Scotland*, Murray, 1973; *The Island of Skye*, Slesser, 1970; *The Western Highlands*, Johnstone, 1973; *The Central Highlands*, Steven, 1968; *The Northern Highlands*, Strang, 1970.

INDEX

This index consists essentially of the names of the dive-sites described in this volume. There are also entries covering areas, general points, and individuals. Other names (especially villages and launch sites) are not listed. Entries in inverted commas are names of wrecks.

You demand, we'll supply. The best

We at Namron are dedicated to giving you, the diver a quality range of products from our own specially manufactured equipment to our individually selected imports.

You can be sure that the Namron range of diving equipment offers both quality and value, plus the finest service possible.

Our comprehensive range gives you the choice to fit your specific requirements, including Wet Suits, Fins, Power Fins in both Ladies and Gents style and sizes, Snorkels, knives, Weight Belts, Back Packs, Cylinder Boots and demand valve accessories (including the famed dust ball). To light your way

below we have the Bug Diver 400 a superbright long duration heavy duty lantern.

We also carry an extensive range of Safety Equipment including a diver's surface marker buoy (with Alpha flag), and the day-glow hood.

Namron also supplies communications equipment for both the professional and sports diver who wishes to widen his underwater activities.

Because of our policy of continual research and development of our own products, and our keen eye for spotting any new technological developments or improvements in diving equipment it is never very long before these products

are available bearing The Namron Label.

As experienced divers ourselves, it is obvious that your needs are much the same as our own and our continuing policy of product development ensures you that Namron are one of the leaders in the diving equipment world.

Get to know more about Namron's Pro-Diving Equipment and prices at your local Dive shop, if in doubt as to your nearest Namron Agent, phone us on (0709) 71006 and speak to one of our specialist staff who will assist and advise you on all your diving needs.

All a diver needs is Namron

Regulators. Sherwood & Blizzard   Concord ® Jet Fin. Namron   Life Jackets. Sea Quest

Bug Diver 400

Wet Suits. Namron

Torches

ASK FOR

BY NAME AT YOUR LOCAL DIVE SHOP

Manufacturers of Wet Suits and Diving equipment

Canklow Meadow Industrial Estate West Bawtry Road, Rotherham S60 2XL. Phone: (STD 0709) 71006. Telex: 547676 CHAMCO G ATT NAMRON

Johnson's Marine Store,
Old Pier,
Lamlash,
Isle of Arran.
Tel: 07706-333

Oban Divers Ltd.,
Laggen,
Oban,
Argyll.
Tel: 0631-62755

Seafare,
Tobermory,
Isle of Mull,
Argyll.
Tel: 0688-2277

Eric G. Kemp Sports,
31-33 Bridge Street,
Kirkwall,
Orkney.
Tel: 0856-2137

Gerrard & Sommers
Ltd.,
49 Broad Street,
Fraserborough.

Otter Diving Services,
3 Trinity Quay,
Aberdeen.
Tel: 0224-581588

Kings Marine,
The Harbour,
Balintore,
Fearn,,
Easter-Ross.

Burghead Boat Centre,
The Harbour,
Burghead,
By Elgin,
Morayshire.
Tel: 0343-61-634

W.C. Henderson & Son,
80 Market Street,
St. Andrews,
Fife.